Barry L. Callen

Journeying Together

A Documentary History of the Corporate Life of the Church of God Movement (Anderson)

Compiled and Edited by
Barry L. Callen

The Leadership Council
of the Church of God
and
Church Ministries Division
Warner Press
Anderson, Indiana

ISBN #0-87162-684-5 Stock #D8891
UPC #730817 088914

Printed in the United States of America
Warner Press, Inc.

David C. Shultz, Editor in Chief
Dan Harman, Book Editor
Cover by Todd Tufts

Previous volumes in the series,
edited by Barry L. Callen and published by Warner Press:

The Assembly Speaks, 1985
Thinking and Acting Together, 1992

Table of Contents

Foreword

The Leadership Council of the Church of God offers counsel and direction on many fronts of the church's life and ministry. The scope is far-reaching, as the contents of this book make very clear. The Council brings together leaders to deliberate, envision, and strategize. Through the World Forums, World Conferences, and International Dialogues on Doctrine, we worship, plan, and study together with our counterparts around the world. In unity efforts we learn and teach with those of other Christian affiliations in settings of mutual goodwill. In the General Assembly that meets annually in Anderson, Indiana, we determine directions under God to guide the Church of God movement forward in North America.

In 1992 the Council joined Warner Press in publishing the book *Thinking and Acting Together*. It carried, in well-organized and edited fashion, the position statements and major actions of the General Assembly since its beginning in 1917. Now, at the 1996 International Convention of the Church of God, we are privileged again to join our publishing house in presenting a much expanded book about our historical efforts to plan and work in united witness. Both the previous volume and now this expanded edition, titled *Journeying Together*, were compiled and edited by Dr. Barry L. Callen. We all are indebted to him for his wide perspective, diligence, and discipline which have made this publication possible. It will serve us well as we consider our church heritage at the end of the twentieth century and into the twenty-first.

How do we determine and then accomplish mutual goals in the Church of God movement? How do we prioritize our paths of service? With our loosely knit organization, what is the "glue" that holds us together? How do we move forward unitedly, relating to each other and to Christians generally? Most of the answers are revealed in these important pages. A commitment to each other and to our Lord and Master makes possible an accountability that no legislation ever could achieve.

Newly documented in this book are our initiatives over the decades in moving outside North American borders and beyond the limits of our own cultures and fellowship. Our cooperative endeavors are written in our actions and are here recorded helpfully in their original historical contexts. Refer to them often. They will inspire you with a realization of the scope of our vision and ministry, all made possible by the gracious hand of God. It also will expand your horizons to see our work in cross-cultural, ecumenical, and global perspectives.

Edward L. Foggs, General Secretary
Leadership Council of the Church of God

Preface

Most bodies of Christians establish for themselves a pattern of formal church authority (their "polity") which defines accepted doctrines and regulates group life. Sometimes the power inherent in this pattern centers in a pope or council of bishops, sometimes in synods, conferences, or superintendents. Such centralizing typically is justified either by claiming that God established things that way in the church or by assuming that biblical principles and practical necessity joined in given circumstances to evolve a pattern that is transitional, always to be reviewed and subject to change in changing circumstances.

This usual pattern of formalized church authority, however, has led to many distortions in church life. It has been resisted for over a century by a reformation movement known simply as the "Church of God" (Anderson, Indiana). From its beginning in about 1880 this movement has longed to return to the truths, simplicities and Spirit-directedness of the apostolic church. This longing has resulted in an unwillingness to accept and perpetuate what has been judged the centuries of corruption and humanization that have burdened unnecessarily the life of the Christian community.

In the face of a maze of brittle and binding church creeds, and a bewildering variety of complex and often coercive church organizations, this movement has attempted to remain open to the fresh and freeing moves of the Spirit of God. Its polity, or way of being together, has sought a dynamic flexibility featuring the constant guidance of the Spirit. While much of traditional church life has tended to function in mechanical and manipulative ways more related to the non-church world than to what the New Testament teaches, there has been a persistent determination in this movement of the Church of God. Such is not to be so among us!

Once only a vision burning in the hearts of a few, this movement now has emerged as a worldwide phenomenon with organized programming of gospel proclamation, education, and service. Ministers, initially isolated from one another, soon found themselves desiring fellowship, inspiration, and a coordination of activity. So assemblies of leaders developed and came to assume business as well as strictly "spiritual" roles in the church's life. They wanted to strategize for effective church mission without laying controlling human hands on the essence of the church itself.

By 1917 the most prominent of these assemblies in North America was meeting annually in Anderson, Indiana. Since then this General Assembly has formalized its identity and functions, created the Leadership Council as its legal arm and, while remaining a voluntary body, has become influential in the oversight of most of the movement's cooperative ministries ,which are based in the United States. This oversight is accomplished through the allocation of funds raised nationally for cooperative ministries, the ratification of trustees who govern a series of church ministry corporations, and the ratification of the chief executive officers of these corporations. Oversight also is accomplished by the influence of the Assembly's united voice when a consensus can be reached on issues of common concern.

Through the years this Assembly has sought to avoid "exercising ecclesiastical authority" in the process of its work. After all, it is not the church sitting in control of local church congregations; nor is it the superboard with legislative power over the several boards that direct the work of the national corporations of this church movement. Being the most representative body of the Church of God movement in North America, however, on many occasions the General Assembly has spoken its corporate opinion and even expectation to Church of God congregations, the national agencies, and even the church and society at large. It has announced convictions and sounded warnings. It has attempted to encourage vision, influence opinion, gather resources, and mobilize effort. While abhorring the very idea of organizing and controlling the church itself, God's family, it certainly has sought to coordinate, direct, and energize the work of the church. The challenge has been to be active and effective in common ministry and mission without being guilty of manipulating and denominationalizing the life of the church.

This volume presents three sections of historical material, grouped by themes and then chronologically. Part One focuses on the General Assembly in North America, highlighting the fruit of its life together since its beginning in 1917. Part Two seeks to review a range of statements and actions related to the vision of Christian unity that lies at the heart of this Church of God movement. Part Three traces the increasing multi-culturalism and internationalization of the Church of God movement.

Together these three parts provide a good overview of the cooperative life of one church movement that is seeking to be prophetic at the national (US), ecumenical, and international levels. The intent here is not to further enhance the "organizational" side of church life, but to remember the milestones and celebrate what God has done as one body of Christians has sought to journey together for the sake of the divine mission in today's world.

Barry L. Callen
Anderson, Indiana
June, 1996

Part One: The General Assembly

(North America, 1917–1996)

Section I
General Assembly: Introduction

A. The Setting
B. The Nature
C. The Origin
D. The Role
E. The Constitution
F. The Leadership
G. Reflections

Part One: The General Assembly

Section I
General Assembly: Introduction

A. General Assembly: Setting
1. Functioning Above Sectarianism (Leslie W. Ratzlaff)

Editor's note: The following provides theological perspective on the nature of local Christian congregations as traditionally perceived among Church of God people. Congregations relate voluntarily to the reformation movement and to any agencies or assemblies formed to assist with the work of the church.

Excerpted from an article by Leslie W. Ratzlaff in VITAL CHRISTIANITY, June 1985, 22.

Sectarian chains bind God's people, mar their work, and keep the church from reflecting God's full glory. To forever throw off sectarian cords takes eternal vigilance. The following points suggest transcending and rising above all sectarian cords:

1. The Church of God transcends any human beginning! God gave it birth on the Day of Pentecost as attested to in Acts 2. The year 1881 may be a year when bold action based on discoveries about the Church of God was taken. It, however, was not the beginning but the affirmation of a reality in existence;

2. The Church of God belongs simply to the triune God! To be other than the Church of God "from whom every family in heaven and on earth is named" (Eph. 3:15) is sectarian and to be called other than that presents a confusing witness;

3. The Church of God transcends any human geographical center! God's headquarters are not in Jerusalem (John 4:20–24) and certainly not in Anderson, Indiana. Yet each local congregation is planted in a specific geographical area and should be so identified;

4. The Church of God transcends any reformation movement! Paul took a firm stand against the tendency to sectarian spirit (1 Cor. 1:10–13; 3:1–9). God uses human agents, but only God is to be exalted and glorified. The Church of God is greater than any reformation movement. Neither does it exist to serve the reformation movement. Rather the movement exists to serve the church;

5. The Church of God with its biblical base honors and incorporates into its lifestyle all truth. It is greater than any or all of them; therefore, to call it baptist, pentecostal, presbyterian, or any of a host of other names restricts the church, its witness, and its commitment to Christian unity;

6. The Church of God transcends any human alliance! Alliance separates from fellow Christians. Cooperation, yes; formal alliances, no. The Church of God is married to Christ alone and responds ultimately only to the Divine drumbeat.

In summary let it be understood that the Church of God reformation movement along with other reforming movements is an important servant of Christendom. Its task is to help the church awaken and constantly measure up to God's standard. It plays a John-the-Baptist role in helping the church come into God's own. The reformation movement serves to provide agencies that help the Church fulfill her Kingdom-building assignment.

The local Church of God congregation is under the sovereignty of God and is a divine-human organism answerable to God alone. Its relationship to the Church of God reformation movement is voluntary.

B. General Assembly: Nature

2. Parallel to a Local Church Business Meeting

(Russell R. Byrum)

Excerpted from the 1922 *Yearbook of the Church of God* (Anderson, Indiana), 6.

The General Ministerial Assembly of the Church of God is the ministers of the church at the International Camp Meeting assembled in business session. The General Ministerial Assembly is for the purpose of giving general direction to the business and to the various business agencies of the church in general. It sustains practically the same relation to the general church that a business session of a local congregation sustains to the local church. As the local church assembled in business session discusses and determines its business policies in a general way, and appoints financial officers, trustees, or other business agencies for the accomplishment of its work, so the General Ministerial Assembly discusses and determines in a general way what general business interests the church shall conduct and appoints certain men to be responsible for the carrying out of certain business policies. For example, it elects the twenty-four members of the Gospel Trumpet Company, the members of the Church Extension Board, and the registrar of the Clergy Bureau.

It is also parallel with the local church business meeting in that it has no power to determine standards of doctrine or practice, to confer ministerial authority upon any one, to appoint ministers to particular fields, or to do any other thing that is properly the work of the Holy Spirit in his church.

Its officers consist of a chairman and a secretary and it is organized under constitution and bylaws according to common parliamentary practice. Only ordained ministers have the franchise.

C. General Assembly: Origin

3. A Modest Beginning Motivated by Need

(Marvin J. Hartman)

Excerpted from a thesis submitted to the School of Religion of Butler University, Indianapolis, Indiana, 1958.

Much of the information concerning the background of the General Ministerial Assembly has been lost in the history of the movement. Because there was no organization, much of the discussion that took place in the early ministers' meetings was never written down. Indeed, there seems to have been an aversion to writing deliberations down. One wonders if this was not done because it may have been an indication that there was not full and strong unity. It must have been frustrating for those who believed so strongly in the unity of the saints to have to admit that the saints did not always agree.

Although it was not until 1917 that the General Ministerial Assembly officially organized, there were, prior to that time, what were called "general assemblies." These seemed to have a pattern across the church of taking place whenever a group of ministers got together to discuss their work. As early as 1902, at Yellow Lake, Indiana, this happened. Charles E. Brown reports:

> The first Assembly that I remember attending took place at the Yellow Lake Camp Meeting in 1902. The ministers present at the camp meeting assembled in the men's dormitory and sat around on the beds and talked. The only touch of a formal organization in this meeting was the appointment by this informal gathering of one man to represent the group in talking to the railroads concerning the availability of clergy rates.

Dr. Brown suggests that 1917 is only the formalizing date of an already existing organization. As early as 1906, there was always held—in connection with the Anderson Camp Meeting—a general assembly. This, indeed, was like the other general assemblies that took place whenever ministers got together. The main interest in these general assemblies was preaching. Influential ministers would exhort and encourage the brethren along the lines of the true doctrine. Sometimes in these early assemblies a discussion would take place. The discussion generally would go far enough along to start drawing various differences of opinion. Frequently, at this point "one of the more influential brethren would stand and say, 'Now, brethren, this is the way we believe the question.' "

Evidence of the significant role played by the Gospel Trumpet Company is seen in the very first meeting of the temporary organization of the assembly which was held on June 14, 1917. At this meeting, the Gospel Trumpet Company submitted a slate of nominees for company membership. This was significant because prior to this time the company membership was chosen in a self-perpetuating manner. This change was a wise move. It gave the ministry a feeling of participation, and set a precedent, both legal and moral, for future organizations tied legally with the assembly to have their membership likewise elected by the assembly [in 1995 such elections would be changed to ratifications of prior board elections]. Although the voting was done by yes and no votes on a slate of twenty-four candidates, there was remarkable unity at this first thrust of responsibility.

The other modest business taken care of in that first General

Ministerial Assembly meeting is shown in the following items listed from the minutes of that first meeting (June 14, 1917):

A motion was made that in the temporary organization only ordained ministers of the Church of God have the right to vote. Motion seconded. Motion carried.

Motion was made and seconded that all ordained ministers of the Church of God in the congregation be requested to rise and stand for purposes of identification. Motion carried.

A motion was made and seconded that a majority of votes of the Assembly shall be sufficient for election to any office for which the Assembly may hold election. Motion carried.

Motion that voting and elections be by ballot. Motion seconded. Motion carried.

Motion that members of the Gospel Trumpet Company who are ordained ministers have a right to vote in this Assembly. Motion seconded. Motion carried.

Motion moved and seconded that the chair appoint a committee of five to draft a constitution and a permanent set of by-laws to govern the Assembly. Motion carried. [J. W. Phelps, A. B. Frost, H. A. Sherwood, O. E. Line, R. R. Byrum. These names were written in pen, in long-hand in the minutes, with these two words after their names: "were appointed"].

Temporary organization was effected by nominating R. L. Berry, A. T. Rowe, and E. A. Reardon as chairmen pro tem. E. A. Reardon was elected.

Since the Anderson Camp Meeting in these early days was ten days long, the committee to draft the constitution and bylaws had time to work on that task. Evidently for this reason there were no other meetings of the Assembly for a week. Then on June 21 the report of the committee on the constitution was read and approved.

The *Gospel Trumpet* gave considerable space to comment on the 1917 General Ministerial Assembly. It, no doubt, was concerned with reaffirming in the minds of the ministers who were there the wisdom of this step, and also in communicating to those who were not there exactly what happened. There would always be a danger that some of those who were against organization might misrepresent or misquote to those who were not there. Therefore, the brethren were prompted to give considerable space to this historic 1917 meeting.

Indeed, while the meeting was going on, the *Trumpet* said in the June 28 issue (no doubt written a week prior to its publication), the following:

All things of the meeting have been marked by a sweet spirit of unity that is most convincing to those who visit these camp grounds that God is truly in our midst.

The business interests of the church are receiving more careful attention than ever before. The Lord has given the ministry a larger vision of our unparalleled opportunities for spreading the pure gospel to the end of the earth. A deep desire is manifested to see a great forward movement along lines of activity and gospel work—both in the homeland and in the foreign fields. Our vision is not localized, but worldwide in its scope and purpose. In order to insure a sound financial basis for these increased activities, better business methods are being considered for the future than we have been accustomed to in the past.

It has also been felt for some time that there should be a more direct legal relationship existing between the publishing work and the general body of the ministry. Steps have been taken to place this great work in more immediate touch with the ministry, and thereby increase their responsibility for and their interest in this important phase of gospel work. New members have been added to the Gospel Trumpet Company, increasing the number to twenty-four. These twenty-four names were ratified by a vote of the ministers in session at the present camp meeting.

The motivating drive and power which characterized all the development of the organizational machinery of the General Ministerial Assembly seemed to be one of "need." To do the work of God, the early leaders discovered they had to "render unto Caesar" in some areas. The government—local, state, and national—made certain requirements regarding corporations, holding real and personal property, and so forth. The railroad needed a sponsoring national agency to clear membership of clergy for discount in rail travel. The boards and agencies were forced to comply with certain restrictions, which in turn affected the assembly. In short, the General Ministerial Assembly found it could not do the work of the Lord unorganized in a highly organized society. Many times, as the organizational pattern was developing, the thread-worn (but nonetheless, answer of the hour) phrase, "We can organize the work of the church but not the church," was marshaled in defense of the developing organization at Anderson.

D. General Assembly: Role
4. Provision of Guidance to Boards and Agencies

Excerpted from the 1960 *Yearbook of the Church of God,* 12.

The Church of God is composed of many people in many congregations scattered all around the world. The GENERAL MINISTERIAL ASSEMBLY is the most representative body within the Church of God through which its world mission and concern can be expressed unitedly and its worldwide work can be approached cooperatively.

The cooperative worldwide work in the main is carried on by duly authorized boards and agencies serving to help all our churches do together what they could never accomplish separately. Through the GENERAL MINISTERIAL ASSEMBLY, our worldwide agencies are set up, and to them was delegated responsibility for particular areas of cooperative work.

The GENERAL MINISTERIAL ASSEMBLY gives direction and guidance to these boards and agencies in the following five ways:

1. Establishment of Policies. Through charters, articles of incorporation, constitutions, and bylaws, the GENERAL MINISTERIAL ASSEMBLY defines the areas of work of the particular agency, its scope of activities, its power, duties, and limitations.

2. Elections. The ASSEMBLY delegates authority for action in particular areas of its work through the election of responsible persons to serve on its boards and agencies. Through these elections to duly authorized boards, work in particular assigned areas of the church's concern can be carried on effectively.

3. Ratifications. Through periodic ratification of the chief executive of each board or agency, the ASSEMBLY approves the delegation of responsibility to that person. This is done at the beginning of each term of office of that chief executive.

4. The Right of Review. Through annual reports which are required from each board, the ASSEMBLY may review the work of that board periodically. Through its Executive Council the work of that board is

coordinated with that of other boards. The ASSEMBLY also on occasion has exercised the right to review the work of the particular board through the appointment of a special committee or commission. Thus the ASSEMBLY may satisfy itself that the work assigned is being carried on in accordance with the established policies of the ASSEMBLY.

5. Adoption of Annual Budget. Through its adoption of the annual budget, the ASSEMBLY continues to support and give guidance to the various areas of work assigned to particular boards and agencies.

E. General Assembly: Constitution
5. Constitutional Guidelines (June 1990)

ARTICLE I
Name
The name of this body is the General Assembly of the Church of God (hereinafter referred to in this Constitution and Bylaws as "Assembly") with general offices located in Anderson, Indiana.

ARTICLE II
Purpose
The purpose of this Assembly shall be to function as a temporary presbytery in the conduct of the general business of the Church of God and its annual International Convention. In the continuing fulfillment of this purpose it shall provide for and devise measures to create and maintain a legally incorporated coordinating council (hereinafter referred to as the Leadership Council) and such other legally incorporated general agencies and/or boards as shall be necessary to arrange for and promote the work of the Church in its national and international relations.

ARTICLE III
Limitations
This Assembly shall be regarded as a voluntary association. It shall not exercise ecclesiastical jurisdiction or authority over the Church in general or over individual congregations in particular. But it shall, however, retain the right of a voluntary association to define its own membership and to declare, on occasion, when individual ministers or congregations are not recognized by the Assembly as adhering to the general reformation principles to which the Assembly itself is committed.

ARTICLE IV

Membership

The members of this Assembly shall consist of the following persons who are present at any authorized and duly called meeting of the Assembly.

Section 1: Ordained ministers of the Church of God in good and regular standing.

Section 2: Unordained ministers who are pastors or full-time associate pastors of recognized congregations.

Section 3: Laity who are elected or appointed members of the Leadership Council, a subordinate board, committee, or commission of the Assembly or the Leadership Council.

Section 4: One layperson selected by each recognized state or provincial assembly; a representative selected by each recognized state or provincial organization of Women of the Church of God; and a representative selected by each recognized state or provincial organization of the Church of God Men, Churchmen.

Section 5: Beginning with the 1993 General Assembly: one layperson from each congregation with an average a.m. attendance to 100; two laypersons from each congregation with an average a.m. attendance of 101–500; three laypersons from each congregation with an average a.m. attendance of 501–1,000; and four laypersons from each congregation with an average a.m. attendance of 1,001 and above.

Editor's note: Articles V—VIII contain detailed guidelines for meetings, amendments to the Constitution, the definition of a quorum, and so on.

F. General Assembly: Leadership

6. Persons Chosen to Lead

Elected Chairs of the General Assembly, 1917 to Date:

E. A. Reardon	1917–1919
R. L. Berry	1919–1923
J. Grant Anderson	1923–1925
Charles E. Brown	1925–1927
Joseph T. Wilson	1927–1929
Charles E. Brown	1929–1931
Joseph T. Wilson	1931–1932
E. E. Perry	1932–1934
Albert F. Gray	1934–1936
Joseph T. Wilson	1936–1939
Albert F. Gray	1939–1954
Harold W. Boyer	1954–1968
Arlo F. Newell	1968–1974
Leonard Snyder	1974–1975
Arlo F. Newell	1975–1977
Paul L. Hart	1977–1983
Samuel G. Hines	1983–1989
Oral Withrow	1989–1990
G. David Cox	1990–

G. General Assembly: Reflections

7. Observations of a Longtime Assembly Member

(Robert H. Reardon)

Excerpts of the comments made by Robert H. Reardon, President Emeritus of Anderson University, made by request near the conclusion of the 1992 General Assembly.

I have attended this Assembly for forty-one years. There have been some years when we were so fearful of each other that we were afraid to talk. I thank God for the way we now are able to speak our minds and not be afraid of one another. That says to me something about the maturity of this Assembly—and that means a great deal to me.

My father, E. A. Reardon, was the first Chair of this Assembly. Once he came and made a speech to the Assembly in which he talked about a sectish spirit that was developing among us. We were building some high walls around ourselves, which never were intended to be. He was very blunt and it made a lot of the pastors in the Assembly very angry. They gathered in little knots, out under the trees on the campgrounds. They discussed what he said and they implied a lot of things in their discussions that he never said. At any rate, when they took the next vote, my father was voted off the Missionary Board, where he had been a charter member. He lost his office as a member of the Board of Anderson College and Bible School.

Arlo F. Newell, chair
General Assembly
1968–74, 1975–77

Samuel G. Hines, chair
General Assembly
1983–89

G. David Cox, chair
General Assembly
1990–

When the voting results were posted, it was the usual practice that all the ministers went by to see who got elected and who lost—and this time my father lost. So when the Assembly met the next day, everybody wondered what Dr. Reardon was going to say. He walked in, got recognized from the Chair, stood up in that Assembly and said, "Well, I've been over and looked at the Assembly vote. I see you voted me off both of these boards." There was dead silence. "I just have one thing to say to you," he continued. "The Assembly gave, the Assembly has taken away, blessed be the name of the Assembly." The next year they voted him back on!

There is a second event in this Assembly's history that I want us to recall. It always moves me very deeply. Brother F. G. Smith was the Editor of the Gospel Trumpet Company from 1917 to 1930. This man put a theological spine in the Church of God movement with his book, *What The Bible Teaches.* He surely used the power of the pen and effectively used his influence during his editorship. But as time went on there had begun to be in the Assembly a growing uneasiness about the centralizing of that much power.

So in 1930 the twenty-four members of the publishing company did not agree to re-elect Brother Smith as editor, the most powerful office in our movement at the time. They then asked themselves the question, "Who are we going to put forward?" Now Brother Rigel was the Billy Graham of the Church of God, a powerful evangelist. They asked him. Brother Rigel agreed to be their candidate. They sent his name across to the Assembly to be ratified. The Assembly said "no." So the twenty-four went back and asked Brother C. E. Brown. He said, "I will do it on the condition that Brother F. G. Smith walk across the street with me and openly support the election." Brother Smith rose in the Assembly and did the gentlemanly thing, the honorable thing, the thing which showed where his love and loyalty really were. He supported Brother Brown, who became a very successful editor.

That is what makes an assembly an effective Christian body. It is an evidence of the way the Holy Spirit works. It is a wonderful example of what charismatic church government is all about. Let us always proceed together in such a way.

Section II
Selected Position/Action Resolutions

A. Organizational Guidelines
B. Identification of Reformation Principles
C. Distribution of Resources
D. Christian Higher Education
E. Major Social Issues
F. Emphases, Studies, Celebrations

Section II
Selected Position/Action Resolutions

A. General Assembly: Organizational Guidelines

8. Only Ordained Ministers Can Vote (June 1917)

The General Ministerial Assembly passed its first motion in its initial year of formal existence. Because of the long pattern which it established, not to be altered for decades, it is significant to note a motion recorded in the Assembly minutes of June 14, 1917.

A motion was made that in the temporary organization only ordained ministers of the Church of God have the right to vote. Motion seconded. Motion carried.

9. Establishment of the Executive Council (June 1932)

The Golden Jubilee celebration in 1931 marked a time of historic review and future projections for the reformation movement. One result was the 1930 General Ministerial Assembly authorization of the appointment of a commission on Assembly reorganization. The commission's report, which included a plan to make the Assembly a delegated body, was rejected by the 1931 Assembly, but another action of the 1930 Assembly did become reality. It called for the consideration of a "business body" to manage the general interests of the church. In 1932 the Assembly altered its bylaws to provide for the creation and incorporation of the Executive Council of the Church of God. The June 20, 1932, minutes read:

The objects and purposes of the corporation are hereby declared to be to promote the religious and benevolent work of the Church of God, and for such purposes such corporation shall have power to receive, take and hold real and personal property, donations of money and property, legacies and bequests, and to sell, transfer and otherwise convey such property, on behalf of the Church of God, to sue and defend any and all actions in any court, and to have, hold and enjoy all the rights, privileges and powers of corporations at common law.

In 1947 the General Ministerial Assembly authorized a Commission on Revision and Planning to study ways for achieving better coordination of the general work of the church. As a result, the 1954 Assembly amended the Articles of Incorporation of the Executive Council and in 1956 took even further action by increasing both the membership and responsibilities of the Council. According to Article III, Section I of the constitution of the Assembly as revised in June 1980:

The Executive Council shall serve as coordinating council for the Assembly. It shall coordinate the work of the general agencies authorized by the Assembly in their interrelated and cooperative functions, in their promotional and fund-raising activities, and in the services they offer to the Church at large. It shall promote the general welfare and cooperative work of the Church of God.

Then in 1991 the Assembly approved a new set of expectations for the Council. Its name was changed to Leadership Council.

The following persons have provided significant leadership for the work of the Council (years listed are those of the respective yearbooks where these names appear):

Presidents, Board of Directors
Robert L. Berry, 1934–1937
Elver F. Adcock, 1937–1946
John A. Morrison, 1946–1948
William E. Reed, 1948–1955 W.
Steele C. Smith, 1955–1960 I.
Marvin J. Hartman, 1960–1965
Carl M. Poe, 1965–1970
Marcus H. Morgan, 1970–1981
R. Dale Whalen, 1981–1984
Betty Lewis, 1984–1990
David Lynch, 1990–1995
Merv Bennett, 1995

Secretary-Treasurers
W. Burgess McCreary, 1934–1936
Earl L. Martin, 1936–1937
Adam W. Miller, 1937–1938
Dale Oldham, 1938–1944
K. Dawson, 1944–1947
Lawrence E. Brooks, 1947–1955

General Secretaries
Clarence W. Hatch, 1955–1960
Charles V. Weber, 1960–1971
William E. Reed, 1971–1980
Paul A. Tanner, 1980–1988
Edward L. Foggs, 1988–

William E. Reed
General Secretary
Executive Council
1971–80

Paul A. Tanner
General Secretary
Executive Council
1980–88

Edward L. Foggs
General Secretary
Leadership Council
1988–

10. Join the Federal Council of Churches? (June 1944)

During the 1940s a wave of criticism rolled through the Church of God. Some pastors felt that all of the organizational and program growth had become dysfunctional, that a few "big boys" were trying to "run things" from Anderson "headquarters," that the national leadership was steering the movement away from its historic commitments.

One focus of this concern was an action of the 1944 General Ministerial Assembly establishing a committee to explore a possible relationship with the Federal Council of Churches. Critics saw the very idea of such exploration as a negation of the movement's understanding of Christian unity. The committee reported in 1946 that "due to the pressure of other duties" it had not yet accomplished its task. A motion to continue the committee was lost (149 yes, 158 no). The chairman stated his opinion that the Assembly could not commit the Church of God to membership in the Federal Council even if it so desired. E. F. Adcock, chairman of the committee, clarified that committing the church to regular membership in the Council had not been the intention of the committee. The case was closed.

11. Faith in the Integrity of the National Work (June 1947)

In a time of considerable tension and misunderstanding, with many ministers in the Church of God openly distrustful of the integrity of the Anderson-based agencies of the church, the General Ministerial Assembly decided it must speak. In June, 1947, it adopted the following:

WHEREAS sixty–seven years ago D. S. Warner and his associates in the faith brought into being a new religious movement conceived by the Holy Spirit and predicated upon the ideal of a pure and undivided church; and

WHEREAS to the promulgation of this ideal these hardy pioneers gave their time, talent, money and very lives, and died in the faith that through their humble instrumentality God was working a great work in the world; and

WHEREAS even in their brief day these pioneers hammered out the beginnings of effective organizational instruments for the publishing of this divine message; and

WHEREAS this Assembly has implemented and added to these instrumentalities as need dictated through the years; and

WHEREAS all through its history this work has been attacked both from without and within, but to no permanent avail, because of the strong foundation upon which our work rests; and

WHEREAS now for two and a half years a new attack has been waged against the work, an attack not upon one front of the work alone, but upon every front—a total attack upon the total program and leadership of the work—bitter and persistent, covering every part of our corporate program: evangelism, publication, home and foreign missions, education, Sunday school and youth; including charges specific and general against persons and groups, covering the grossest evils, such as ministerial apostasy, malfeasance in office, misuse of funds, falsification, fraudulent behavior, wholesale doctrinal defection, and extreme worldliness; and

WHEREAS if in the main these charges were true, our Christian conscience would demand that strong measures be taken to remedy such a situation, but since charges in the main are not true, then the same Christian conscience demands that such charges, false and deliberately made, and persistently circulated, be condemned as grossly unchristian, and that those responsible for such unbecoming conduct make proper amends; and

WHEREAS one year ago this Assembly appointed an Investigating Committee of seven competent and trustworthy brethren with the instruction that they investigate the truthfulness of these charges; and

WHEREAS this committee, at the expense of great labor on their part and at a considerable expenditure of money, have so investigated these charges; Now, therefore, be it

RESOLVED: First, that we hereby reaffirm our faith in and loyalty and dedication to the doctrines, ideals, and objectives which gave birth to the movement; and at the same time we express our confidence in the boards and general agencies which serve the Church at home and abroad under the authority of this General Ministerial Assembly; and

Second, that we emphatically disapprove of the spirit and methods employed in the attacks made upon the general work of the Church as unchristian, unbrotherly, and unfair; which attacks have resulted in division and discord among the ministry and the laity as well; and

Third, that this General Ministerial Assembly go on record as being opposed to this program, and to any program by an individual or group that is calculated to cause division among us and break the worldwide unity that has characterized our movement from the beginning; and

Fourth, that we call upon all those responsible for the program which has caused such confusion and division within the Church forthwith to discontinue all such activities; and this Assembly does hereby entreat with all Christian brotherliness of spirit Brother Earl Slacum and those associated with him in the present agitation to acknowledge their error and to make due amends, so that Christian fellowship may be restored and the unity of the Church be preserved; and

Fifth, that we strongly urge our ministers when faced with problems related to our general work, to handle all such matters through the proper channels in a definitely Christian spirit; and

Sixth, that we recommend to the Indiana Ministerial Assembly and to all other state ministerial assemblies where such a program of division may be carried on, if the decision of this General Ministerial Assembly as herein expressed is disregarded, that such disciplinary action be taken as will safe-guard and insure the unity of the Church; and

Seventh, that copies of this resolution be mailed to all ministers of the Church of God, and that this action be recorded as a part of the permanent minutes of this Assembly.

12. Anderson Camp Meeting to Be Continued and Housed
(June 1960)

Editor's Note: It was not possible to convene the 1960 Anderson camp meeting because of the collapse of the south end of the large tabernacle in which the meeting had been held annually for some forty years. A debate followed in the Assembly concerning the appropriate course of action. The final decision read:

WHEREAS this Assembly has spoken in clear and unmistakable terms favoring the continuance of the Camp Meeting and the Annual General Ministerial Assembly meeting at Anderson, Indiana, and

WHEREAS facilities for such meetings must be provided; be it therefore

RESOLVED, that the General Ministerial Assembly does hereby authorize and instruct the Executive Council of the Church of God, its legal entity, to proceed at once to provide the facilities for such Camp Meeting and General Ministerial Assembly by one of the following possibilities:

1. The repair of the present partially existing tabernacle at an engineer's estimated cost of $70,500 plus;
2. The erection of a colorable Stran-Steel building over the present tabernacle floor, meeting the state of Indiana building code;
3. Or, some other similar priced construction. Be it further

RESOLVED, that the Division of World Service and the Budget Committee of the Executive Council arrange the necessary financing plan for covering the approved construction costs in cooperation with the Executive Council; be it further

RESOLVED, that authorization for awarding the construction contract be made jointly by the Executive Committee of the Executive Council and the Board of Directors of the Gospel Trumpet Company; [and] be it further

RESOLVED, that this Assembly express its desire on these possibilities by ballot in this meeting today.

Editor's note: In 1961 the site for the present Warner Auditorium, an entirely new facility, was dedicated. The decision for the future had been made.

13. Establishment of a Commission on Social Concerns (June 1964)

WHEREAS there is manifest interest in a Commission on Social Concerns in the Church of God, and

WHEREAS the Executive Council has received from different sources requests for the establishment of such a Commission on Social Concerns, and

WHEREAS there is manifest urgency for the careful and prayerful study of ways in which articulate calls may be given to the congregations for them to carefully consider Christian responsibility in the fields of temperance and general welfare, particularly with alcohol problems, gambling, tobacco, pornographic literature; in areas of peace and world order, particularly with military policy and legislation for conscription, disarmament and nuclear weapon control; and in the area of human relations, particularly in race relations, civil liberties, church-state relationships, housing, and civic responsibility, and

WHEREAS the Executive Council through its Executive Committee and the National Association of the Church of God (West Middlesex, Pennsylvania) through its appointed standing committee on race relations, have concurred in the call for the establishment of a Commission on Social Concerns, and

WHEREAS in other years this Assembly has appointed committees and commissions with responsibility in the areas of social Christian concerns, therefore, be it

RESOLVED, that the General Ministerial Assembly authorize the establishment of a permanent Commission on Christian Social Concerns responsible to the Assembly through the Executive Council, and be it further

RESOLVED, that this Commission on Christian Social Concerns shall be established with the purpose, the general areas of concern, the grant of power and lines of responsibility, the determination of membership, and other similar factors within the limitations described in the recommendation from the Executive Council to the General Ministerial Assembly which is attached to this resolution, and which is dated June 15, 1964.

14. Establishment of a Committee on Christian Unity (June 1965)

WHEREAS for several years there has been manifest interest in a Committee on Christian Unity, and

WHEREAS resolutions have come from several state ministerial assemblies to the General Assembly or Executive Council calling for such a committee, and

WHEREAS the All-Board Congress and Planning Council expressed deep concern for and the need of such a committee, and

WHEREAS the General Assembly has instructed the Executive Council and its Division of General Service to study the need, structure, and responsibility of such a committee and bring a report to the General Assembly, and

WHEREAS representatives of the Church of God have already been in conversation with the representatives of certain other church groups who have sought to become acquainted with the Church of God, therefore, be it

RESOLVED, that a Committee on Christian Unity be authorized by the General Assembly and responsible to the Assembly through the Executive Council, making annual reports, with its concluding report in June 1969....

Editor's note: The life of this Committee was extended to 1975 when the General Assembly recast this body as a permanent Commission on Christian Unity because (a) "the need and responsibility for unity and cooperative work among Christians is so strategic to Christian witness and world evangelism" and (b) "the Church of God continues to need a representative group to make contacts, hold conversations, and develop lines of cooperation with other church bodies of similar spirit and concern."

15. Name Change to "General Assembly" (June 1965)

Editor's note: In 1958 the General Ministerial Assembly redefined its own membership to include "laymen who are elected or appointed members of the Executive Council, a subordinate board, committee, or commission of the Assembly." Although this was implemented immediately, the inconsistency of such action and the name of the Assembly was not addressed until 1965. The June, 1965, action read:

INASMUCH as we now have some seventy-five laymen who are duly elected and authorized members of this Assembly, which in fact, makes this a General Assembly rather than a General Ministerial Assembly, therefore, be it

RESOLVED, that the term "General Assembly" be hereinafter used to designate the title of this Assembly and such changes be reflected in the Constitution and Bylaws and other official papers. Article I—Name—to read: "The name of this body is the General Assembly of the Church of God (hereinafter referred to in this Constitution and Bylaws as 'Assembly') with general offices located in Anderson, Indiana." and, be it further

RESOLVED, That Article I, Section 2, of the Bylaws be amended by striking out the words, "Any ordained minister of the Church of God in good and regular standing," and inserting the words, "Any member of this General Assembly," making this part of Section 2 read, "Any member of this General Assembly shall be considered eligible for election or appointment to these offices."

16. Office of Associate Executive Secretary (June 1974)

The Executive Council recommends to the General Assembly that authorization be given for the employment of an Associate Secretary to serve with the Executive Secretary in the administration of the Council's work on behalf of the Assembly and the Church of God. The Executive Council further recommends:

1. That the office of an Associate Secretary be filled initially by a carefully selected black person who is to be nominated by the Board of Directors of the Executive Council, but with election by the members of the Executive Council and ratification by the General Assembly in the same manner as is the office of the Executive Secretary.
2. That the term of office for the proposed Associate Secretary shall be for five years, beginning January 1, 1975, subject to the Assembly's approval of this recommendation.
3. That the General Assembly grant the Executive Council the privilege of submitting the name of a person to fill this office for ratification prior to the adjournment of its June 18–20, 1974, meeting.
4. That the General Assembly approve the budget for the operation of this office recommended by the Budget Committee and by the Executive Council.
5. That the General Assembly will amend its Bylaws, Article V, Ratification of Officers, by adding sub-paragraph (14) to read: (14)

"Associate Secretary to the Executive Secretary of the Executive Council."

Editor's note: With the above action was a lengthy description of this new position. The following are two central portions of that description:

The Associate Secretary is to join with the Executive Secretary in interpreting the policies and decisions of the General Assembly and the Executive Council to other agencies of the Church of God and to any person or groups needing such information. In turn, he is to interpret to the Executive Council and the General Assembly his readings of what is happening on the field and recommend procedures for the strengthening of understanding and cooperation.

The Associate Secretary is to serve in a liaison relationship between the Executive Council and the black membership of the Church of God. His special assignment will be that of trying to bring about closer ties and relationships within the Church. He shall be responsible to keep the Executive Council, its Board of Directors, and the Executive Secretary fully aware of the needs, feelings, and developments in the black church.

17. Cooperation in Missionary Work (June 1975)

The 1974 General Assembly authorized the appointment of a twelve-member committee to:

1. Study the work and impact of the several "mission groups" at work in the Church of God;

2. Study their relationships with the duly constituted national agencies of the Church of God;

3. Study the implications of their promotional efforts on the total programming and fund raising for the agencies authorized by the General Assembly, state assemblies, and other national assemblies.

The report of this committee, presented to and adopted by the 1975 General Assembly, included these five recommendations:

1. We recommend that the Executive Council of the Church of God study the feasibility of inviting each of the following organizations now serving the interests of the Church of God to appoint an observer to attend and participate in the annual meeting of the Council when budgeting is done for the general work of the church:

- Project Partner with Christ
- Vacation Samaritans
- Men of the Church of God

The purpose of this recommendation is twofold:

(1) To provide opportunity for a paramission organization to receive current information on programmatic and budgetary decisions reached by the Executive Council;

(2) To provide opportunity for the Executive Council to receive current information on the operations and activities of paramission groups and to give counsel on how coordination can best be achieved.

2. We recommend that the following groups set up a regular schedule of meetings to review planning and coordination of programmatic concerns:

- The Missionary Board of the Church of God
- The Board of Church Extension and Home Missions
- Project Partner with Christ
- Vacation Samaritans
- Women of the Church of God
- Men of the Church of God

The Executive Secretary of the Executive Council will convene the initial meeting of this group.

3. We recommend that the paramission organizations which solicit their financial support from the general body of the Church of God congregations and members in the United States report on a yearly basis their financial operations. In implementing this recommendation, it is requested that a copy of the annual Statement of Financial Condition be filed with the office of the Executive Secretary of the Executive Council for placement in the files of the General Assembly and its Executive Council.

4. We recommend that paramission organizations, which receive their primary support from the Church of God as represented by the General Assembly and its Executive Council, always consider themselves to be morally and ethically related to the Church of God and follow the practice of selecting a majority of persons of Church of God membership to serve on their Boards of Directors and in their corporation memberships.

5. We recommend that each paramission organization, which receives its primary support from Church of God congregations and members, include in its Articles of Association and Bylaws a provision whereby in case of dissolution the assets of the corporation will be retained for the benefit of the Church of God and not inure to the benefit of any private persons.

18. Increasing the Participation of Laypersons (June 1979)

WHEREAS this Assembly has authorized its Committee on Bylaws and Organization to study ways of increasing lay participation in the General Assembly of the Church of God, and

WHEREAS said committee has spent three years in such a study and has developed a suggested "model" for reconstituting the membership of the Assembly to include more laypersons, therefore, be it

RESOLVED, that the committee be instructed to prepare copies of this "model," along with a packet of explanatory materials, to be sent no later than October 1979 to each congregation listed in the current *Yearbook of the Church of God,* and be it further

RESOLVED, that each congregation be asked to discuss this model and to respond to the Bylaws Committee no later than April 1, 1980, on a form provided, and be it further

RESOLVED, that the committee bring to the 1980 Assembly specific recommendations for changing the Assembly's bylaws along the lines suggested by a consensus of responses from the congregations.

Editor's note: The model referred to is that the membership of the General Assembly should be newly defined to include all members of all Church of God congregations who are present at designated meetings of the Assembly; from this group a selected number would be identified as voting members to provide a manageable and representative base for decision making; the voting members would include all ministers and laypersons who currently constitute the General Assembly and, in addition, at least one layperson designated by each local congregation.

The Bylaws Committee did bring to the 1980 Assembly the results of a congregational survey for the purposes of information and further clarification. No action was requested. The committee brought to the 1981 Assembly a review of the history of the question and proposed that "this same model for increasing lay representation in the General Assembly remain before us for continued refinement and discussion and that it be brought before the 1982 General Assembly for a vote." See entry 21.

19. Procedure for Grievances (June 1980)

Editor's note: The 1980 General Assembly sessions included criticism directed at a national agency of the church, Anderson College. The criticism had been focused publicly by an "open letter" mailed by a minister to all Assembly members just prior to the convening of the Assembly. Apart from the substance of the criticism, the attention of the Assembly was directed toward affirming more appropriate ways for future grievances to be handled. Thus, the Assembly adopted the following resolution as procedural guidance for the future. It should be noted that in the 1985 Assembly, in the midst of criticism being directed at another national agency of the church, Warner Press, the Assembly's Business Committee reaffirmed this 1980 action, redistributed it to Assembly members, and urged that it be honored. In 1989 the Executive Council and General Assembly reaffirmed a modest revision and annual reissuing of this procedure. The original resolution read:

The National Agencies of the Church of God are servants of the church and have been brought into being by action of the General Assembly. Each agency is incorporated and governed by a board of trustees duly elected by this Assembly, and answerable to this Assembly.

It is likely that some agency decisions will be unpopular. Members of this Assembly must know that they do have a voice and that their voice will be heard. Therefore, an accepted procedure for sharing differences, grievances, and suggestions is needed. The Business Committee recommends that the biblical basis found in Matthew 18:15–17 be the accepted norm and procedure. The following process shall then be our guide:

1. Agency

a. A letter to the chief executive officer of the agency in question shall be written seeking an answer or solution. If a solution is not easily resolved by mail, an official meeting with the chief executive officer shall be established at the convenience of both parties.

b. If such a meeting is unsatisfactory, it will then be appropriate to seek a meeting with the elected officers of the corporation, including the chief executive officer, to seek a solution.

c. If no solution to the problem is found, attempt shall be made to have the larger governing group of the corporation consider the matter.

2. Executive Council

a. If the above steps to solve the problem with the agency in question have been exhausted, consultation with the Board of Directors of the Executive Council may be sought to see if proper negotiation can be achieved. The Board of Directors may make the concern an agency item for the Executive Council.

3. General Assembly

a. If the concern is not satisfactorily resolved, the grievance may be presented to the General Assembly, through its Business Committee.

b. If the Business Committee does not agree to make the concern an agenda item, it may be brought to the floor of the Assembly. By a two-thirds vote of the members present it may then be dealt with directly by the Assembly.

Editor's note: The 1989 revised form of this 1980 grievance procedure laid stress on resolving differences with agency administrators and governing boards at the agency level. The General Assembly was referred to as "the body of last resort" only.

20. Maintaining a Responsible Business Committee (June 1981)

The established procedures for conducting the business of the General Assembly seemed to some members of the 1980 Assembly to be designed to obstruct their full participation. One minister stated with considerable frustration that, while Assembly members were urged to follow orderly procedures, some members often found it difficult to get through the proper channels. Therefore, a motion was adopted that called on the Bylaws Committee of the Assembly to take appropriate action in regard to this concern. The specific recommendation was that any item of business be permitted on the Assembly floor if a majority of voting members so desired (instead of the two-thirds vote traditionally required).

In conflict with this specific recommendation, however, was another action also taken by the 1980 General Assembly. Because of an "open letter" distributed nationally by an Assembly member just prior to the 1980 Assembly, and in the face of widespread questioning of the appropriateness of this means of bringing a concern to the attention of those in positions of responsibility, the Assembly approved a policy governing grievance procedures (see entry 19). The first step called for in this procedure was written contact with the chief executive officer of the agency related to the concern in question. The final step in this procedure, should all else fail to bring some resolution of the problem, was a bypassing of the action of the Business Committee of the Assembly by a two-thirds vote of Assembly members, thus allowing direct action on the floor of the Assembly. This grievance procedure also was forwarded to the Bylaws Committee for appropriate action.

The Bylaws Committee saw the conflict in these two actions of the 1980 General Assembly, one calling for movement from two-thirds to a majority and one specifically retaining the two-thirds vote necessary to bring an item of business to the floor when the Business Committee of the Assembly has not agreed to make that concern an agenda item. In light of this conflict, in view of the long-standing two-thirds bylaw of the Assembly, and with the knowledge that the two-thirds guideline is widely accepted as sound parlimentary procedure, the Bylaws Committee recommended to the 1981 Assembly that its standing bylaw not be changed. The Assembly accepted this recommendation.

21. Lay Representation in the General Assembly (June 1982)

Editor's note: The following was presented to and approved by the 1982 General Assembly.

Backgrounds

The Bylaws Committee, through its extensive studies, has noted widespread support for some increase of lay representation to the Assembly. The committee has decided to bring a proposal for adoption to the Assembly this year. The committee acknowledges its responsibility to listen carefully to the church and that its proposals should reflect procedures that enhance the unity we desire. Therefore, this proposal differs from the one given to the Assembly previously. This proposal comes as a result of the committee's desire to achieve Assembly-wide consensus on this question.

Proposal

Therefore, the Bylaws Committee proposes that the Constitution of the General Assembly, Article IV, Membership, Section 4, which now reads:

> One layperson may be selected by each state (district), or provincial assembly, to attend the General Assembly as an observer.

be changed to read:

> One layperson selected by each recognized state or provincial assembly; a representative selected by each recognized state or provincial organization of Women Of The Church Of God; and a representative selected by each recognized state or provincial organization of the Church of God Men, International.

Explanation and Effect

"Recognized" is understood to mean:

(1) State or provincial assemblies which are recognized by the General Assembly of the Church of God through its Division of Church Service;

(2) State or provincial organizations of the Women of the Church of God which are recognized by the national organization of the Women of the Church of God;

(3) State or provincial organizations of the Church of God Men, International, which are recognized by the national organization of Church of God Men, International.

The effect of this change is to bring those persons now designated as observers in the Assembly into full membership in the Assembly. In addition this change brings into the life of the Assembly key proven leaders of two of the church's vital national organizations. Both organizations endorse heartily the possibility of their participation in the Assembly. The likelihood of faithful participation by these persons is good because of their demonstrated concern for the work of the church and the high percentage of their attendance already in the convention. The potential addition to the Assembly is approximately one hundred and thirty-five persons.

Editor's note: See entry 124 for another action approving a significant further expansion of lay Assembly members beginning in 1993.

22. Ratification Procedures for New Executives (June 1984)

WHEREAS the General Assembly prescribes in its bylaws that certain agency executives shall be presented to it for ratification; and

WHEREAS it is appropriate that the General Assembly know the qualifications and central convictions of persons they are asked to ratify; and

WHEREAS the size and setting of the General Assembly do not make it feasible to engage in a lengthy cross-examination style of questioning; and

WHEREAS a board duly elected by the General Assembly has already reviewed the qualifications of, and elected, the person to be ratified; and

WHEREAS the Assembly requires pre-Assembly mailing of information about nominees; therefore be it

RESOLVED, that the corporate agency presenting the name for ratification state the qualifications, home church, and credentials of its nominee; and be it further

RESOLVED, that the candidate to be ratified share in writing his/her own experiential testimony and spiritual pilgrimage, including a personal statement of doctrinal convictions; and be it further

RESOLVED, that the Executive Council mailing to General Assembly members in May include both of these documents for their advance study and reflection; and be it further

RESOLVED, that should any agency fail to have such materials ready for advance mailing, such information shall be given to the General Assembly, in session, at least one day prior to the ratification vote; and be it finally

RESOLVED, that no person shall be ratified by the General Assembly on the same day that his/her name is presented to the Assembly for ratification.

23. Warner Press: Concerns and Changes (June 1983–1986)

Editor's note: During 1981–82 criticism was heard from several sources about various structures and practices of Warner Press. In response, the Publication Board of Warner Press named a Consultation Committee which brought to the 1983 General Assembly a progress report of the early stages of its work. The committee reported that it was studying:

1. The function and purpose of Warner Press in relation to the Church of God;
2. The propriety and sufficiency of the organizational structure of Warner Press regarding the relationship of the president and editor in chief;
3. The latitude and freedom of the editor in chief to pursue and fulfill this defined function;
4. The editorial policy and its manner of determination; and
5. The sufficiency of the present organizational structure for oversight or review of Warner Press (from the General Assembly through the lowest echelon).

The committee promised to report again to the 1984 General

Assembly. In that Assembly the chair of the Publication Board spoke for the committee, which had already mailed its final report to Assembly members. With the support of the officers and Consultation Committee of Warner Press, there was introduced and adopted a resolution from the Winchester, Kentucky, and Pryor, Oklahoma, Pastors' Fellowships. This resolution noted reception of the report of the Consultation Committee, expressed concern that "spiritual considerations be given preeminence over the financial and operational policies of Warner Press," and called on the Publication Board to bring to the 1985 and 1986 General Assemblies a full report on the implementation of the changes outlined in the final report of the Consultation Committee.

Prior to the 1985 Assembly, in which the president of Warner Press was scheduled for ratification for a new term, renewed criticism was directed toward Warner Press. In its annual meeting in May, 1985, the Executive Council heard the grievances and appointed a Special Committee on Warner Press Grievances, comprising persons outside Warner Press, and charged it to report to the 1985 General Assembly prior to the ratification vote on the company's president.

In the 1985 Assembly the Publication Board of Warner Press brought its scheduled implementation report, which was followed by the report of the Special Grievances Committee. This latter report spoke specifically to the issues of bonuses, salaries, and the tenure of board members and called for the ratification of the president of Warner Press for an abbreviated two-year term. It was reported that the Publication Board had agreed to implement all of the recommendations made. Consequently, the president's special two-year term was voted.

The Special Grievances Committee made an additional and extensive report to the 1986 Assembly. It included a review of the committee's assignment and work, a summary of expressed concerns about the publishing work, and a series of recommendations grouped in four areas. They were: the mission and operational philosophy of Warner Press; the renewal and expansion of the publishing ministries; the utilization of income; and restructuring for effective leadership.

24. Limitation of Terms for Board Members (June 1985)

Editor's note: For some years it had been the conviction of some members of the General Assembly that the church would be better served if a limitation were placed on the number of consecutive years that any one person could serve on a governing board of a national agency. In the Assembly of 1985 the Bylaws Committee presented a recommended bylaws change which, as amended on the floor to be even more restrictive, was adopted as stated below.

No person shall be nominated for membership on any subordinate Board who has already served as a member of that Board for two consecutive five (5) year terms or ten consecutive years until after a lapse of two years.

In 1986 this limitation was broadened to three consecutive five-year terms for those governing the institutions of higher education. Then in 1990 the maximum of three terms (fifteen years) was applied to all persons affected by the original 1985 action.

25. Inter-Church Cooperation (June 1985)

The following resolution was developed and adopted by the Committee on Long Range Planning (April 1985) and approved by the Executive Council of the Church of God (May 1985). It then was presented to members of the 1985 General Assembly for information and guidance.

WHEREAS the Church of God Reformation Movement has historically affirmed the unity of the Body of Christ as expressed in its many forms, yet one; and

WHEREAS the Church of God Reformation Movement for over eighty years has participated in mutually supportive relationships with other communions through its national and state agencies in missionary education, missions education, and ministerial continuing education; and

WHEREAS ministers and laypersons of the Church of God Reformation Movement have been involved in significant ways in local cooperative ministries such as community concerns, leadership training, and evangelism; and

WHEREAS the Commission on Christian Unity of the Church of God in its 1983 Statement of Concern and Guidance on Christian Unity urged the church "to work toward an intentional togetherness to exercise a willed movement toward each other"; and

WHEREAS the 1984 Consultation on Mission and Ministry established as one of its five priority areas of concern that of being the body of Christ, with one of its stated goals "to expand ministries through voluntary relationships with Christian groups outside the Church of God Reformation Movement and seek to live out the vision of unity through broader interdependent relationships that serve mutual needs for training, fellowship, and witness"; therefore, be it

RESOLVED, that the Committee on Long Range Planning supports the historical stance of the Church of God Reformation Movement to seek intentional inter-church relationships through which its own ministries are strengthened and enriched and which provide opportunity for the Church of God Reformation Movement to live out its message of Christian unity through enriching the entire Body of Christ; and be it further

RESOLVED, that all Church of God Reformation Movement national, state, and local structures be encouraged to participate in inter-church relationships as a means of expressing our belief in Christian unity and our desire to effect cooperative ministries.

Editor's note: The 1987 General Assembly heard criticism of the National (USA) and World Councils of Churches and the suggestion that national agencies of the Church of God might be involved with them inappropriately. It adopted a resolution calling for the establishment of a special committee to study, document, and evaluate the current involvements of general agencies of the Church of God with the National Council of Churches (USA) and the World Council of Churches. This committee's report was presented and received with appreciation by the 1988 Assembly. It excluded discussion of the World Council since no involvement was found except an occasional "observer status." Portions of this report follow.

Summary Perspectives

The study committee is united in its strong conviction that the Church of God must find increasingly effective ways to express its commitment to Christian unity and to fulfill the mission of the church in the world. We are called to make a difference, but we cannot do it alone.

Diversity and interdependence are both facts of contemporary church life. There is considerable and increasing diversity of backgrounds, beliefs church traditions and priority agendas now seen in Church of God congregations and among Church of God leaders at all levels of church life. Church of God colleges increasingly are being populated by students from other than Church of God congregations. Many Church of God pastors participate actively with local and area inter-church bodies that provide fellowship and/or cooperative ministry opportunities. Often these bodies include a wide spectrum of church traditions, commitments, and agendas. Pastors have the freedom to participate as they judge appropriate and sometimes they do in very visible, formal, and influential ways. Interdependence among Christian communities appears necessary for the effective accomplishment of some ministry goals. It also appears to be a natural implementation of the burden for Christian unity carried by the Church of God reformation movement.

Church of God general agencies, with major ministry mandates and limited resources in a complex world, also have evidenced need for "outside" ministry relationships and resources. In a very few instances they have developed limited relationships with working units of the National Council of Churches in Christ as a partial means of fulfilling this need. In such instances the agencies have been especially sensitive to public allegations made against the Council and they have walked carefully the narrow path of restricted involvement designed only to enrich their own work and witness without formal membership or direct involvement in the larger life of the Council itself.

Admittedly there are risks in all sharing relationships; but the isolationist alternative would be a denominationalizing of the Church of God reformation movement, an alternative which inevitably would bring its own high price. Given the risks associated with all alternatives, then, the study committee seemed to face a choice between (a) calling for a blanket prohibition of all such participation with working units of the NCCC or similar inter-church bodies and (b) calling for no action, thus leaving the general agencies free to relate to whom and as they see fit. The committee judged neither of these choices acceptable. Rather, the committee saw wisdom in developing a set of Relationship Guidelines which the General Assembly would be asked to adopt for the guidance of general agencies accountable to the Assembly. These guidelines are viewed by the committee as reasonable expectations, ones open where ministry needs justify and limiting where limitation clearly appears necessary.

Proposed Relationship Guidelines

Any general agency, commission, division or committee, accountable to the General Assembly of the Church of God in the United States, which chooses to relate in any manner to any working unit associated with the National Council of Churches in Christ or other inter-church body should do so only within the assumptions, affirmations and limitations contained in the following guidelines:

1. Any inter-church relationship should be guided by the clear understanding that the Church of God, as represented by the Executive Council and the General Assembly, has not and should not become formal institutional members of the National Council of Churches in Christ. Such organizational identity is not the best way to express Christian unity!

2. Any inter-church body involved in a relationship should be committed publicly to the divinity and lordship of Jesus Christ. He is central to the meaning and the mission of the church!

3. Inter-church relationships should be seen as opportunities to serve and witness in light of the distinctive heritage of the Church of God reformation movement. We have something important to share as well as receive in any such relationship!

4. An inter-church relationship should not be maintained if that relationship gives support to beliefs or actions which clearly violate beliefs or actions generally held to be true and proper by the Church of God reformation movement. We in the Church of God must be accountable to each other and maintain the integrity of our doctrinal heritage!

5. Any Church of God participants in an inter-church relationship should not attempt to speak in the inter-church setting for the Church of God reformation movement as a whole. Participants always should make clear that they function by individual or agency choice and do not necessarily represent their brothers and sisters at large!

6. Church of God general agency staff or dollar resources invested in an inter-church relationship should be limited to the ministry function justifying that relationship. The Church of God does not control and sometimes does not condone all that large inter-church bodies say and do!

Postscript

The study committee wishes to affirm an important call issued to the Church of God by the Consultation on Mission and Ministry of the

Church of God in 1984. It was a call "to expand ministries through voluntary relationships with church groups outside the Church of God reformation movement" so that we can "achieve our mission more effectively and expand our ministries." This present committee report and the relationship guidelines proposed above are intended to support, not impede this call. It is the committee's hope that such guidelines will enrich appropriate inter-church relationships and, at the same time, avoid inappropriate ones. It also is our hope that the Church of God will give continuing attention to the opportunities associated with working relationships among Christians for the sake of the church's mission in the world.

26. Recommendations: Task Force on Governance and Polity (June 1992)

Editor's note: In 1987 the General Assembly established a "Task Force on Governance and Polity" to "undertake a wide-ranging analysis of present governance and polity traditions, assumptions, structures, and relationships; to develop recommendations for enhancing the effectiveness of governance and polity—congregational, state and national—to the end that mission and ministry are strengthened." The Task Force brought to the 1992 Assembly a series of affirmations and nine recommendations. All recommendations except #4 were approved. They were:

1. Resolved, that the General Assembly encourage each congregation of the Church of God to have in place current mission, vision and covenant statements as its ministry moves into the 21st century.

2. Resolved, that the Division of Church Service convene representatives from the groups presently conducting in-service training and programs, to extend dialogue and joint planning, and report annually to the Executive Council.

3. Resolved, that the Executive Council be authorized to undertake a study of the possibility of holding one International Convention and General Assembly elsewhere; that the study when completed will be brought to the Council for action and to the General Assembly for decision no later than 1994.

4. Resolved, that the General Assembly approve the establishment of the "Mission and Ministry Triennial" as described here and in Exhibit A.)

5. Resolved, that the General Assembly concur with the Executive Council in changing its name to "Leadership Council of the Church of

God" and its chief executive officer's title to "General Secretary": that it authorize steps to amend its bylaws accordingly.

6. Resolved, that the General Assembly favor the direction proposed in the above recommendation regarding services to the ministry of the Church; that it support a study group with members from the Council and Division, to propose means by which these recommendations may be implemented.

7. Resolved, that the General Assembly commend and encourage the Commission on Christian Higher Education and the member institutions in their efforts described above to enhance interdependence and accountability.

8. Resolved, that the General Assembly accept the above recommendation of the Task Force regarding church-wide discussion, coordination by the Executive Council, and reporting to the General Assembly in 1994 [about possible restructuring at the national level].

9. Resolved, that the General Assembly approve the above recommendation that "fresh efforts, styles, and initiatives in program coordination and collaboration begin immediately": that it support the process described above.

27. Conflict of Interest (May 1993)

Religious institutions are under scrutiny more than ever with respect to the ethics of how they conduct business. This scrutiny is coming from self-monitoring by the church, governmental bodies, and the general public. One of the most sensitive arenas of concern lies in the matter of conflict of interest.

The Leadership Council proposes that those general agencies answerable to the General Assembly and those para-church or other groups which draw their primary financial support from the constituency of the Church of God have in place a written conflict of interest policy which addresses at least the areas identified in this document.

A conflict of interest may be defined or described as follows:

1. When a person has a duty to promote one interest but chooses to promote a competing interest instead;

2. When an institutional insider (board member, officer, or staff person) chooses to promote an interest in competition with that institution's ministry;

3. When an institutional insider (board member, officer, or staff person) stands to profit personally by promoting his/her own interests or the interests of friends, relatives, or business associates.

Examples of potential conflicts of interest are:

1. When institutional insiders have an interest in a vendor to the institution;

2. When employees of one institution are loaned to other organiza-tions;

3. When institutional fund raisers give financial advice to donors;

4. When an attorney represents two clients with conflicting interests;

5. When institutional employees accept gifts from vendors;

6. When institutional insiders are also insiders of a related organi-zation.

Conflicts of interest are not always avoidable and may not necessarily be unethical. Certain actions, however, are essential to avoid questionable and unethical conduct.

1. Conflicts of interest must be disclosed to the institution as soon as any conflict is discovered.

2. After disclosure is made, the insider with a conflicting interest must not participate in judging the merits of that interest. This, at a minimum, would require one to abstain from voting and to refrain from otherwise promoting the outside interest. It could, under some circumstances and at the discretion of the body, call for one to absent him/herself during the period of the discussion and/or action on the matter of interest.

Many institutions, religious and secular, require their board members to complete an initial conflict-of-interest questionnaire when they become board members and to make periodic (often annual) declarations regarding personal conflict of interests. The Leadership Council has not attempted to formulate a uniform conflict of interest policy. It does, however, urge the General Assembly to adopt this statement as a reference document for guidance to general agencies and others in formulating their own conflict of interest policy.

Approved, Leadership Council, May 6, 1993

28. Governing Boards Now To Elect, Assembly To Ratify
(June 1995)

Editor's note: During 1994–95 an Election Study Committee worked in relation to a series of General Assembly election/ratification issues of concern to some members of the Assembly. In response to its report to the 1995 Assembly, the Bylaws Committee of the Assembly brought proposed bylaws changes. They were approved. The main one was the change from the Assembly electing members of the agency governing boards (from a pair of names nominatd by the boards) to the Assembly ratifying those members elected previously by the boards.

B. Identification of Reformation Principles

29. Principles of the Reformation Movement (Andrew L. Byers)

Excerpt of an address to Church of God ministers, Eugene, Oregon, 1929.

The reformation principles, upon which our movement of the Church of God may be defined, may be expressed as follows:

1. Divine spiritual life received in regeneration and witnessed to by the Holy Spirit, and more than this, a true consecration to God, constantly maintained, which permits of no interpositon of selfish ambition in the progress of the movement;
2. A disposition to obey the truth and the truth only and to let the Holy Spirit have his way and rule;
3. An attitude entirely receptive to, and which really welcomes, any further light and truth, one which assumes no infallibility and which is not satisfied with interpreting Christianity and the Scriptures in the light of traditions and old ideas;
4. Acknowledgment of good wherever found; regarding no door into the church other than salvation, and no test of fellowship other than true Christianity possessed in the heart. The placing of no barrier that would exclude any who might be Christians. A regard for souls, whether believers or not, as far-reaching and inclusive as that of Christ's.

No person can truthfully say he is of this reformation who is not of its principles, even though he may take the *Gospel Trumpet*, worship in the Church of God, and testify that he is saved and sanctified. These principles characterize the true church in her unity and integrity. They are as narrow as the New Testament on the one hand and as broad as the New Testament on the other. It is by lacking in one or more of these essentials that a sect is a sect. We have assumed these principles; therefore, we have much at stake. It is easy to fail or come short by reason of such a high standard. All that a sect assumes is their creed, or system, or belief. We have assumed the whole and must not permit ourselves to be carrying out only a part.

A minister whose activities are along this line is truly a reformer. We must not think only of the pioneers in this movement as reformers; the reform spirit must continue, and characterize the whole movement. If it does, great results will follow, for we indeed have the greatest message ever preached since the apostles' days, and I sometimes think it is even greater than theirs. Billy Sunday said, not so long since in a sermon at Niagara Falls, when referring to the line of reformers, that the principles advocated by D. S. Warner (mentioning him by name) would one day sweep the world. The fact is, these principles are the bedrock of truth, and nothing can get under it to upset it. But the question is, Are we keeping to these principles? To the degree that we do we shall see the fruits of true evangelism.

30. General Assembly Reserves a Right

Editor's note: For many years the General Assembly has reserved for itself the right to define its own membership, partly by the potential process of passing judgment on adherence to "general reformation principles." Article III of the 1992 revision of the Constitution of the General Assembly, for example, reads:

This Assembly shall be regarded as a voluntary association. It shall not exercise ecclesiastical jurisdiction or authority over the Church in general nor over individual congregations in particular. But it shall, however, retain the right of a voluntary association to define its own membership and to declare, on occasion, when individual ministers or congregations are not recognized by the Assembly as adhering to the general reformation principles to which the Assembly itself is committed.

Editor's note: Two other related matters are crucial to note. One was a positive Assembly action in 1990. It regarded the status of persons whose names were appearing on Assembly ballots (nominated by various national bodies) but who were not attending or supporting local congregations of the Church of God. That action follows.

WHEREAS some members of this General Assembly of the Church of God are very much concerned about the appearing in the ballots of names of persons who are not attending or supporting local congregations of the Church of God; and

WHEREAS these persons are being placed into positions of vital importance to this reformation, i.e., college boards of trustees and agencies; and

WHEREAS many of us in this Assembly recognize the latent danger to the biblical and historical message of this reformation movement by such continuing practices; be it

RESOLVED, that all future "Who's Who" for General Assembly balloting include in parentheses the home congregation of said candidates, that we of this Assembly may be better informed and thus enabled to vote more intelligently.

Editor's note: The other related matter involved a negative Assembly action. In 1991 the Assembly addressed an issue related to religious affiliation and Assembly elections or ratifications. In 1990 a motion had been introduced calling for the Assembly to "go on record as requesting that all agencies, committees or commissions not place on ballots to be presented to this Assembly for election or ratification the names of persons who do not attend or support local congregations of the Church of God." This motion was referred for study by the Commission on Christian Higher Education. In the Assembly of 1991, then, the Commission recommended that the 1990 motion not be adopted. The Assembly concurred. The Commission's report included an extended rationale, summarized by these concluding paragraphs:

Careful review by the Commission on Christian Higher Education has revealed that adequate criteria are in place for membership on all our boards and that sensitivity to and compatibility with the message and tradition of the Church of God have been considered in nomination processes. The colleges in particular have missions which, in part, involve their positioning themselves for service in the larger arena of the Christian community and sometimes beyond to the general public. These missions call for creative and courageous flexibility and they need increased attention and understanding both by the church and the other constituencies being served.

An absolute restriction against any inclusion in collegiate governance structures of committed Christians with unusual understanding and influence who may not be actively affiliated with the Church of God would seriously hinder the accomplishment of institutional missions. Thus the Commission recommends that no additional restrictions be placed on the nomination processes of the several boards.

Editor's note: In summary, there is the Assembly expectation that persons, to be associated with the Assembly, will be "in fellowship and doctrinal unity," and it is preferred that typically they will be living out their lives of discipleship in relation to Church of God congregations. Doctrinal unity is to be defined by the direct teaching of the Bible (see entry 32).

31. Executive Council Can Decide Adherence to Reformation Principles (June 1977)

WHEREAS Article II of the Constitution vests in this General Assembly of the Church of God the authority "to declare on occasion when individual ministers or congregations are not recognized by the Assembly as adhering to the general reformation principles to which the Assembly itself is committed"; and

WHEREAS this body only meets regularly one time annually; and

WHEREAS this General Assembly has heretofore caused to be created an Executive Council of the Church of God, Inc., with specific purposes, including the following:

Section 3b: "To coordinate the work of the general agencies of the Church of God in their inter-related and cooperative aspects as authorized by the General Assembly"; and

WHEREAS the General Assembly finds it necessary and expedient to delegate to the said Executive Council of the Church of God, Inc., between the annual meetings of the General Assembly, its authority to declare on occasion when individual ministers or congregations are not recognized as adhering to the general reformation principles and practices to which the Assembly itself is committed; and

WHEREAS this General Assembly finds the above-quoted language of Article III of its Constitution to include authority to find that a minister or congregation is no longer in fellowship and doctrinal unity with the Church of God; now, therefore, be it

RESOLVED, that its above-quoted authority under Article III of its Constitution be hereby delegated to the Executive Council of the Church of God, Inc., to exercise in its sole discretion between annual meetings of this General Assembly.

Editor's note: Until the 1981 General Assembly none of these "general reformation principles" had been identified formally by the Assembly. In 1981, however, one such principle was identified. It was the principle of the central authority of the Bible in the life of the Church. The statement of this principle follows (see entry 32).

32. One Principle: Biblical Authority in the Life of the Church
(June 1981)

During 1980–81 concern was expressed across the church that the authority of the Bible in the life of the church needed to be reaffirmed pointedly and publicly. Resolutions seeking to accomplish this purpose were passed in at least two area fellowships of ministers. These resolutions, however, contained "inerrancy" and "binding" language. Such language aroused wide-spread opposition, including arguments that inerrancy, as popularly understood, is a controversial theory of the Bible's inspiration not clearly taught by the Bible itself and not accepted by millions of evangelical Christians and scholars. Further, the call to "bind" was said to be contrary to the constitution of the General Assembly and alien to the heritage of the reformation movement of the Church of God.

A new resolution finally was drafted by a group of concerned ministers in an attempt to accomplish the central intent of the area fellowships without including the controversial concepts of "inerrancy" and "binding." This resolution eventually was presented to the General Assembly, but with the word "requirement" added in the final paragraph at the last minute by the Business Committee of the Assembly. The Assembly, however, acted to reinstate the word "expectation," thereby maintaining integrity with its understanding of its own Constitution and clearly affirming its opposition to the very idea of binding creedal statements being established in the church.

The following, then, is the resolution as finally approved. It is a clear statement of a "reformation principle" to which the Assembly is committed, namely, the genuine inspiration and central authority of the Bible in the life of the church.

PREFACE

For a century the reformation movement of the Church of God has proclaimed a vision of the church which transcends the artificial and divisive barriers of rigid denominational structure and restrictive creedal statement. In this context, the General Assembly of the Church sf God has limited itself as follows:

This Assembly shall be regarded as a voluntary association. It shall not exercise ecclesiastical jurisdiction or authority over the Church in general nor over individual congregations in particular. But it shall, however, retain the right of a voluntary association to define its own membership and to declare, on occasion, when individual ministers or congregations are not recognized by the Assembly as adhering to the general reformation principles to which the Assembly itself is committed.

The continuing rightness of this self-limitation of the General Assembly is recognized and reaffirmed.

Without intending to exercise ecclesiastical authority, this General Assembly nonetheless desires to record its conviction and expectation in regard to the authority of the Bible in the life of today's church. The following, then, states a general reformation principle to which this Assembly is committed.

WHEREAS the intent of this resolution is to be understood in the light of the self-limitation of the General Assembly as stated in its Constitution (as quoted above) and is meant in no way to violate the reformation principle that "the spirit of the movement is to acknowledge good wherever found and to regard no door into the church other than salvation and no test of fellowship other than true Christianity possessed within the heart" (A. L. Byers, *Birth of a Reformation*, Anderson, Indiana: Gospel Trumpet Company, 1921); and

WHEREAS from its beginning the reformation movement of the Church of God has been committed to the general theological stance that the Bible is our only creed and Christ alone is Lord, so that the Bible, supported by the interpretative ministry of the Holy Spirit, has had a central significance among us; and

WHEREAS a public restatement of this historic commitment to the authority of the Bible in the life of the Church appears timely in light of the secular humanism and doctrinal confusions of our day; therefore, be it

RESOLVED, that this Assembly declare its convictions that the Bible truly is the divinely inspired and infallible Word of God. The Bible is without error in all that it affirms, in accordance with its own purpose, namely that it is "profitable for teaching, for reproof, for correction, for training in righteousness, that the man of God may be adequate, equipped for every good work" (2 Tim. 3:16–17, NASB), and it therefore is fully trustworthy and authoritative as the infallible guide for understanding the Christian faith and living the Christian life; and be it further

RESOLVED, that this Assembly call the reformation movement of the Church of God to a new dedication to faithful biblical scholarship and proclamation, based both upon a commitment to its authority as described above and upon a fresh quest for studied insight and divine guidance in the crucial tasks of responsible biblical interpretation, teaching and preaching; and be it further

RESOLVED, that this Assembly state its expectation that all programs within this reformation movement of the Church of God reflect a genuine commitment to the Bible as the inspired and authoritative Word of God; and be it finally

RESOLVED, that this Assembly state its expectation that governing boards and elected officials, charged with oversight of the operational policies of agencies and the credentials of ministers related to this Assembly, will act responsibly and forthrightly in establishing the central significance of the authority of the Bible and in interpreting and implementing the teachings and directives of the Bible in their respective areas of the work of the Church.

Editor's note: As one way of fulfilling this concern, in the 1991 Assembly a resolution was passed endorsing the "Discover Life In Daily Bible Reading" program and urging every congregation to enlist persons in reading through the Bible during 1992.

C. Distribution of Resources

33. Establishment of a Coordinated Budget Plan (June 1927)

The 1927 General Ministerial Assembly received favorably the report of its Coordinated Budget Plan Committee. Robert L. Berry presented the plan, which previously had been agreed upon by the various national boards. It called for "boards or agencies having work that calls for general church support" to prepare annual budgets which would be examined by a "General Budget Committee." This committee would then "determine the sum to be set as the goal for each individual cause." It further called for "the program coordination of all promotional plans, whether of advertising or of special field representatives" and it designated guidelines for the distribution of designated and undesignated gifts. Finally, the Assembly, prepared to activate this plan immediately, authorized its chair, Charles E. Brown, to appoint five members to this General Budget Committee.

The concept of "Associated Budgets" was implemented in the years to follow. By 1941 the unified effort was known as "The World Service Commission." After reorganization of the Executive Council in 1955, the name was changed to the "Division of World Service."

34. Allocation of World Service Budgets

The following are percentages of the annual World Service budgets as approved by the General Assembly for national solicitation and formula distribution to the several agencies and causes listed. The total budget figures used for determining these percentages include all basic, nonleveled, and restricted categories for each year in question, except for anticipated relay, budget promotion, and treasury/stewardship transactions and expenditures.

	1970–71	1980–81	1990–91	1995–96
Missions				
Missionary Board	35.05	36.47	39.84	39.69
Mission Latin America	3.41	0	0	0
Church Extensio and/ Home Missions	14.79	8.63	10.36	8.81
Hope Hill Children's H.	0	3.22	3.15	5.47
Mass Communications	4.10	3.78	4.26	4.07
Literature Evangelism	0.95	0.46	0	0

Disaster Fund	0	0.08	0	0
World Hunger	0	1.54	2.10	2.97
Million for Missions	0	3.45	0	0
TV Special	0	3.84	0	0
Church Planting	0	0	0	0
Vision 2 Grow	0	0	0	1.37
Contingency Reserve	0	0	0	0.18
(Sub Total)	58.30%	61.47%	59.94%	62.56%
Education				
School of Theology	0	3.96	4.16	3.15
Seminary Tuition Fund	0	1.84	1.52	1.09
Anderson University	11.65	6.98	6.72	8.46
GBC/Mid-America Bible College	4.42	3.85	7.26	7.04
Warner Pacific College	7.56	7.21	6.03	6.71
Board of Christian Ed.	5.51	4.82	5.46	4.33
Black Ministerial Ed.	0	1.15	0	0
(Sub Total)	29.14%	29.81%	31.15%	30.78%
Service				
Leadership Council/ General Service	3.87	3.62	6.98	5.32
Special Committee/ Properties	0	0	0.06	0
General Assembly	4.42	2.86	0	0
Board of Pensions	1.91	1.05	0.49	0.35
Division of Church Ser.	1.68	0.85	0.96	0.76
Ministers Aid	0.68	0.34	0.42	0.23
(Sub Total)	12.56	8.72	8.91	6.66
Total %	100.00%	100.00%	100.00%	100.00%

35. Giving Response of the Church

The following total giving figures include all gifts that received credit from the Division of World Service, including any relay funds handled.

Year	Members	Per Capita	Increase (Decrease)	Total Giving	Increase (Decrease)
1970	147,752	16.36	8.4%	$ 2,416,513	9.1%
1971	150,198	17.20	5.1%	$ 2,582,497	6.9%
1972	152,787	17.04	-0.9%	$ 2,603,428	0.8%
1973	158,264	18.51	8.6%	$ 2,930,226	12.6%
1974	159,733	20.05	8.3%	$ 3,202,307	9.3%
1975	165,928	22.96	14.5%	$ 3,809,844	19.0%
1976	169,372	26.12	13.8%	$ 4,423,982	16.1%
1977	172,756	27.57	5.6%	$ 4,762,919	7.7%
1978	173,940	30.98	12.4%	$ 5,388,512	13.1%
1979	175,405	34.93	12.8%	$ 6,126,234	13.7%
1980	177,407	37.20	6.5%	$ 6,599,349	7.7%
1981	180,772	38.99	4.8%	$ 7,047,486	6.8%
1982	187,485	38.69	-0.8%	$ 7,254,160	2.9%
1983	191,508	38.82	0.3%	$ 7,433,992	2.5%
1984	195,105	38.14	-1.8%	$ 7,440,912	0.1%
1985	197,713	40.04	5.0%	$ 7,916,592	6.4%
1986	197,625	43.60	8.9%	$ 8,216,543	3.8%
1987	203,226	42.71	-2.0%	$ 8,679,527	5.6%
1988	203,552	42.30	-1.0%	$ 8,610,006	-0.8%
1989	200,062	45.64	7.9%	$ 9,131,141	6.1%
1990	202,215	44.75	-2.0%	$ 9,049,443	-0.9%
1991	206,445	45.47	1.6%	$ 9,387,502	3.7%
1992	213,872	45.35	-0.3%	$ 9,698,167	3.3%
1993	217,614	46.04	1.5%	$10,468,594	7.9%
1994	217,681	49.94	8.5%	$10,870,948	3.8%
1995	224,061	52.13	4.4%	$11,679,417	7.4%

D. Christian Higher Education

36. Proper Restrictions for a Church College (June 1918)

Editor's Note: The establishment of Anderson Bible Training School in 1917 was seen by many in the church as a questionable or even dangerous event. In the 1918 General Ministerial Assembly the following report from an appointed committee was read and accepted.

Your committee appointed for the purpose of considering restrictions for the Anderson Bible Training School submits the following report:

1. We believe that such a school can be conducted to the glory of God and the welfare of the ministry and church if kept within certain bounds.
2. We believe that no effort should be made to create a sentiment to the effect that young ministers must attend this school in order to secure recognition.
3. It is our opinion that in many cases the education of ministers can best be obtained in those sections of the country where their ministerial work is to be done so that the practical can be more definitely combined with the theoretical. In other words, we do not believe that the Anderson Bible School should supersede or replace other training schools of the church.
4. Students should be left free to choose their own course of study from among such branches as the school provides.
5. No recommendation or diploma should be given any student. Satisfactory gradings in school constitutes no proof that an individual is called of God to preach the gospel. Hence every student must be left on his own responsibility so that he will not possess in this respect any authority proceeding from this school which will give him an advantage over those ministers who have not attended school. In the Church of God every minister must stand on his own merits and earn his place of responsibility whether educated or uneducated.
6. We believe that the training of ministers in this school should include more than their intellectual development along educational lines. The most prominent feature must be their personal development in spirituality, faith, and the gifts of the Spirit of God.

37. Anderson Bible Training School Separated from the Gospel Trumpet Company (June 1925)

WHEREAS the Anderson Bible Training School has heretofore been a part of the Gospel Trumpet Company's sphere of responsibility, but has outgrown the meager organization provided for it in the company's byLaws; and

WHEREAS it represents one of the general phases of the work of the church and requires that it be constituted a legal entity; and

WHEREAS it desires to be separated from the Gospel Trumpet Company and organized in accordance with the same general principles upon which the other general boards of the church are organized; and

WHEREAS the Gospel Trumpet Company has thoroughly considered and approved the separation, as well as the school's proposed Articles of Association as now modified; therefore, be it

RESOLVED, that this Assembly approves the proposal to have the school separated from said company, and organized in the manner desired.

38. Pacific Bible College Becomes a National Agency (June 1956)

The 1956 Assembly voted the necessary changes in its own bylaws to establish Pacific Bible College as a subordinate board of the Assembly. In 1959 the Assembly concurred with the action of the college's board of trustees changing the school's name to Warner Pacific College. In 1970 the Assembly took major action in assisting the college in a time of the school's financial crisis.

39. Establishment of the Commission on Christian Higher Education (June 1958)

WHEREAS the study Commission on Higher Education, authorized by this General Ministerial Assembly in June, 1952, after five years of study and research is convinced of the need of a permanent Commission on Higher Education, a conviction shared by those connected with our educational institutions as well as by ministers and laymen; be it therefore

RESOLVED, that this General Ministerial Assembly hereby authorizes the creation of a permanent Commission on Higher Education as outlined in the By-Laws herewith submitted, whose general purpose shall be to promote the cause of Christian higher education within the Church of God Movement, said Commission to function within the framework of the Executive Council, and be it further

RESOLVED, that immediately upon adoption of this resolution and its accompanying By-Laws, the educational institutions named in these By-Laws, the Board of Christian Education, and the Executive Council be hereby instructed to appoint those persons who shall constitute the Commission.

40. Policy on Starting New Colleges (June 1964)

In this time of growth in higher education in America many church colleges are finding it increasingly difficult to remain in operation or to uncover the resources necessary for an adequate program. Within the Church of God it appears evident that: (1) at present there are enough colleges to serve the Church of God student population able and willing to attend those colleges; (2) adequate support is not being provided for existing colleges, most of which are struggling financially for their very lives; and (3) new colleges in the Church continually enter the talking/planning stage, are presumably designed to meet the needs of a particular geographic area, but generally are without adequate student and financial support necessary for existence and growth.

The Commission on Christian Higher Education of the Church of God believes it is imperative that great caution be exercised in the establishment of new Church of God colleges, acknowledging that considerable hurt may derive to the Church and its young people through a college not built on an adequate foundation. Specifically:

We urge that a new college be contemplated only within the framework of careful consultation with the Commission on Christian Higher Education, recognizing that through this means we are most likely to achieve the coordination so necessary to the total advancement of higher education in the Church;

We urge that in the establishment of any new college, careful plans be developed for financial support and underwriting, recognizing that the costs of maintaining an adequate program at the college level are enormous;

We insist that, if a prospective college would ever expect or hope to seek the support and assistance of the total Church, it should seek that support and assistance in the crucial stages of planning and establishment.

The Commission on Christian Higher Education continues to make itself available to the Church and its educational institutions as a resource, a stimulus, and a guide in these days of unusual problems and opportunities in the Church and in higher education.

41. Gulf-Coast Bible College Becomes a National Agency
(June 1968)

WHEREAS Gulf-Coast Bible College, Houston, Texas, has served the Church of God since September, 1953, as an institution of higher education, and during these years has trained an increasing number of young people for Christian service; and

WHEREAS the Texas State Assembly of the Church of God, to which Gulf-Coast Bible College is responsible organizationally, adopted a resolution in 1963, with the knowledge and concurrence of the trustees of Gulf-Coast Bible College that requested the Executive Council of the Church of God that the college be permitted to share in the budget for higher education through World Service; and

WHEREAS at that time, in the judgment of the Executive Council, Gulf-Coast Bible College had not attained the status of a general agency of the Church of God and therefore the request was referred to the Commission on Christian Higher Education for study in depth and to recommend guidelines to the college in obtaining additional strength and to make recommendations to the Executive Council for further consideration of the request from the Texas State Assembly; and

WHEREAS during the past five years Gulf-Coast Bible College has cooperated closely with the Commission on Christian Higher Education in making a self-study and in the implementation of recommended guidelines whereby the college might obtain accreditation by the American Association of Bible Colleges (Gulf-Coast Bible College now holds an associate membership in the American Association of Bible Colleges and is working toward possible full accreditation in 1968); and

WHEREAS the Board of Trustees of Gulf-Coast Bible College and the members of the Texas State Assembly of the Church of God, in keeping with their indicated desire for the college to have the status of a general agency of the Church of God, have approved provisional changes in the charter, articles of association, and bylaws of the college in order to comply with the requirements of the bylaws of the General Assembly of the Church of God as pertains to a general agency and, by so doing, have indicated their willingness to abide by the regulations, privileges, and limitations of a general agency, and as a member within the family of agencies, organized by and responsible to the General Assembly of the Church of God; and

WHEREAS the Executive Council of the Church of God, in session February 21, 1968, voted (23-3) to recommend to the General Assembly of the Church of God that recognition be given to Gulf-Coast Bible College as a general agency of the Church of God; therefore be it

RESOLVED, that the members of the General Assembly of the Church of God, in session on June 18, 1968, recognize Gulf-Coast Bible College as a general agency of the Church of God, with understanding that such recognition will entitle Gulf-Coast Bible College to have representation in the membership of the Executive Council, and participation in the World Service Budget; and be it further

RESOLVED, that the Executive Council be authorized by the General Assembly to work with the Texas State Assembly and the Board of Trustees of Gulf-Coast Bible College in the implementation of this action.

42. Action Concerning the "Foundation for Religious Studies"
(June 1972)

Editor's note: During 1971–1972, in the face of low enrollments, rising costs, and an apparent need for revitalizing the curriculum, the seminary's administration and board of trustees set in motion a series of changes in the School of Theology. Included was the establishment of the Center for Pastoral Studies and an affiliation with the Foundation for Religious Studies (an evolving ecumenical consortium of theological schools in Indianapolis, Indiana). The following resolution was offered:

WHEREAS we, members of the Board of Trustees of Anderson College, are assured that the effective education of pastors, evangelists, missionaries, and other Christian teachers and workers is one of the most urgent needs of the Church; and

WHEREAS this Board of Trustees, in its search to determine what set of relationships and circumstances will provide the best training and preparation for the ministry in the Church of God, initiated a major study of theological education during the past year through the appointment of a special committee composed of the chairman of the General Assembly, the executive secretary of the Executive Council, College and School of Theology administrators, and members appointed from the Board of Trustees; and

WHEREAS the committee, through its year-long study took testimony from pastors, faculty members, School of Theology alumni, and present students; and

WHEREAS the recommendations of the committee included the development of new and expanded programs in the School of Theology, including a Center for Pastoral Studies and certain cooperative relationships with the Foundation for Religious Studies and Asbury Theological Seminary; and

WHEREAS the expanded programming makes available new resources for theological education in the Church of God and lays greater emphasis on preaching, evangelism, and field work experiences; and

WHEREAS this board feels that the expanded program will result in well-prepared ministers who are able to preach the Word effectively, teach, counsel, evangelize, and build up the Church; and

WHEREAS certain questions have been raised relating to the scope and involvements of the expanded School of Theology program, be it, therefore,

RESOLVED, that the General Assembly of the Church of God, meeting in annual session in Anderson, Indiana, on the 20th day of June, 1972, call for the establishment of a special committee, composed of three (3) pastors appointed by the chairman of the General Assembly, two (2) members of the Anderson College Board of Trustees, and two (2) members appointed by the Commission on Christian Higher Education of the Church of God, to make a study of the School of Theology's expanded program during its third year, to assess the effectiveness of the program for the preparation of ministers for the Church of God, and to present a report to the Board of Trustees and the General Assembly.

Editor's note: The above resolution was defeated. It was replaced by the following resolution, which was adopted by a 499-422 ballot vote.

In view of the defeat of the resolution establishing a special committee to study theological education, we the following ministers whose names appear below, hereby move that the association with the Foundation for Religious Studies be dissolved within the next three months or at the end of the first semester of the academic year.

43. Recommendations of the Study Committee on the Seminary (June 1973)

Editor's note: The 1972 General Assembly, following considerable discussion and a negative action on the School of Theology's new relationship with the Foundation for Religious Studies (see entry 42), authorized a one-year seminary study committee. It was commissioned to bring to the 1973 Assembly a report containing "recommendations for the continuation of a Church of God seminary, responsible to the General Assembly." A major report was so brought. It included a series of observations and suggestions and twelve specific recommendations. The total report was received and approved by the Assembly. The following is a brief summary of the recommendations, with page references to the fuller statement of each within the report itself.

1. Commission on Christian Higher Education consider broadening the program of the Center for Pastoral Studies (page 7).
2. World Service Budget show askings of both graduate School of Theology and Anderson College undergraduate program (page 8).
3. Move toward increased World Service support to the School of Theology (page 8).
4. Move toward per-student base in Anderson College support (page 8).
5. Budget Committee bring viable plan to achieve these goals, for Assembly review in June, 1974 (page 8).
6. Promote for seminary student scholarship funds (page 8).
7. Executive Council establish Special Trust Fund (page 9).
8. Commission on Christian Higher Education give high priority to seminary needs and problems (page 9).
9. Provide for additional meetings of the Commission on Christian Higher Education (page 9).
10. Establish a "blue ribbon" committee to give particular and continuing attention to the School of Theology (page 9).

11. Assembly ratification of the seminary dean (page 9).
12. In June, 1977, General Assembly again test the thesis of a free-standing seminary—separate from Anderson College (page 10).

44. Seminary Budget in World Service (June 1974)

The Assembly chair recognized F. Eugene Fauntleroy, who called attention to a report titled "Budget Committee Recommendations" regarding a recommended increase of $40,000 in the basic budget allocation to Anderson College for its School of Theology in the 1974–75 World Service Budget and that the Division of World Service concur with the Budget Committee in recommending to the 1974 General Assembly that this plan of additional support to Anderson College be extended over the following four years, or through the 1978–79 World Service year. A copy of these recommendations and the assumptions upon which the Budget Committee based them is attached to the original minutes. Fauntleroy moved the adoption of these recommendations, seconded by Dan Harman. Fauntleroy clarified that the five-year proposal would amount to $200,000 by 1978–79. Motion carried.

45. Seminary Tuition Aid Fund (June 1974)

Editor's note: The Assembly chair recognized G. David Cox, chair of the Seminary Advisory Committee. Cox moved and the Assembly concurred in the adoption of this resolution from the Committee:

The General Assembly instruct the Division of World Service to establish strategy for raising a goal of $50,000 for the year 1974–75 to be retained as a separate account established by the School of Theology, to be activated in the 1975–76 year, for the purpose of defraying tuitional costs now required from the students. These funds are to be expended for tuition costs for Church of God students in the School of Theology and, if available, also for extraordinary moving expenses and then also for student aid in exceptional situations. This dollar goal should be reviewed annually by the Budget Committee and made a part of the World Service Budget.

46. Relationship of Seminary to Anderson College (June 1976)

WHEREAS the General Assembly of the Church of God, in its June 21, 1971 meeting, charged the Commission on Christian Higher Education to make a thorough and extensive study of theological education and ministerial training in the Church of God; and

WHEREAS the General Assembly, on June 19, 1972, approved the appointment of a Special Advisory Committee to advise with the board of trustees and administrative staff of Anderson College regarding the program of the School of Theology, with the stipulation that this committee was to function "until the completion of the study which the Assembly in its June 1972 session requested the Commission on Christian Higher Education to make, but not beyond June 1977"; and

WHEREAS the Commission on Christian Higher Education has now completed its study and submitted its report to the General Assembly; and

WHEREAS the Seminary Advisory Committee, in a communication under date of March 15, 1976, has communicated the following information to the Commission on Christian Higher Education, to wit:

We, the Seminary Advisory Committee of the General Assembly, unanimously and strongly reaffirm and wish to further encourage the concept set forth by the General Assembly's Special Study Committee in its major report to the Assembly in 1973 that there must be "a willingness and commitment in the Church of God to concentrate its graduate and ministerial education in the seminary."

In the light of our work over the past three years and in the light of the very encouraging developments in the School of Theology during that period, we, the Seminary Advisory Committee of the General Assembly, see no reason to consider further the question of a free-standing seminary, and we hereby encourage the Commission on Christian Higher Education to concur in this judgment and to so recommend to the General Assembly in its 1976 report.

WHEREAS the Commission on Christian Higher Education, in its meeting on May 1, 1976, did consider the recommendation from the Seminary Advisory Committee, and did wholeheartedly concur in it; therefore, be it

RESOLVED, that the General Assembly of the Church of God affirm this recommendation mutually agreed upon by the Seminary Advisory Committee and the Commission on Christian Higher Education; and grant its approval, for the present time, for the seminary, the graduate School of Theology, to remain in coordinate relationship to, and under the administrative guidance of the Anderson College Board of Trustees and its administrative officers; and be it further

RESOLVED, that special commendation be given to the board of trustees and administrative officers of Anderson College for the attention they have given to the School of Theology over the past four years; to the Seminary Advisory Committee for the excellent work they have done in keeping the needs of the School of Theology before the General Assembly; and to the pastors and congregations that have shown concern in the seminary by becoming convenant churches in the seminary internship program and in helping to underwrite the tuition costs of eligible ministerial students; and be it further

RESOLVED, that the General Assembly, by its adoption of this resolution, consider the work of the Seminary Advisory Committee terminated and that the assignment of the Commission on Christian Higher Education in regard to theological education and ministerial training is now complete.

47. Recommendations for Ministerial Education (June 1976)

Editor's note: The 1972 General Assembly was the scene of extended debate over matters related to the training of ministers (see entry 42). One result of that debate was a charge to the Commission on Christian Higher Education "to make a thorough and extensive study of theological and ministerial training in the Church of God." The 1976 General Assembly received and approved the final result of this commission study which was presented in the form of a lengthy written report. Included was a set of affirmations and proposals. These are to be found on pages 536–541 of *The First Century,* volume 2, edited by Barry L. Callen (Anderson, Indiana: Warner Press, 1979).

48. Black Ministerial Education Fund (June 1977)

Editor's note: As part of its 1976 study (see entry 47), the Commission on Christian Higher Education reviewed the statement in the Bylaws of the General Assembly pertaining to general agencies and the document adopted by the Executive Council in 1965 titled "What Is a General

Agency?" In the light of the provisions in the Bylaws of the Assembly and the findings of its study, the Commission and consultants unanimously agreed not to recommend general agency status for Bay Ridge Christian College (a status the college had been seeking actively). It was agreed that an alternative to general agency status would be in the best interest of training black leaders to serve the Church of God at the present time. The following resolution was presented and approved to accomplish this purpose:

WHEREAS in June, 1975, the General Assembly of the Church of God referred a request from the Southern Association of the Church of God to the Commission on Christian Higher Education concerning potential general agency status for Bay Ridge Christian College; and

WHEREAS the General Assembly recommended to the Commission a thorough study of the best way to train leaders to serve the black church in the South, to include an in-depth study of Bay Ridge Christian College if needed, and with the assistance of a team of black consultants and with the full cooperation of the administration of Bay Ridge Christian College and representatives of the Southern Association of the Church of God; and

WHEREAS the Commission on Christian Higher Education and its eight black consultants have unanimously agreed as a result of these studies that the need is urgent, complex in nature, and national in scope, necessitating an approach other than the recommendation of general agency status for Bay Ridge Christian College; therefore, be it

RESOLVED, that the General Assembly of the Church of God establish within the annual budget of the Commission on Christian Higher Education, beginning with the 1977–78 budget, a Fund for Black Ministerial Education; and be it further

RESOLVED, that the administration of the fund be done in consultation with representative black leaders of the Church of God; and be it further

RESOLVED, that the commission in the administration of this fund give priority consideration to the following areas of need: (a) the urgent need for the development of the academic program of Bay Ridge Christian College, (b) the underwriting of scholarships for eligible black ministerial students to attend Church of God colleges, and (c) the development, in cooperation with the Center for Pastoral Studies, of an in-service training program designed primarily for black church leaders with limited formal training; and be it further

RESOLVED, that in the World Service Budget for 1977–78, the Fund for Black Ministerial Education be $55,000, with the understanding that gifts for this purpose would receive World Service credit; and be it further

RESOLVED, that the Boards of Trustees of Bay Ridge Christian College and Gulf-Coast Bible College be encouraged to explore the possibilities of joint programming and other mutual uses of the available human and material resources and that each of these institutions give annual progress reports in this regard to the Commission on Christian Higher Education; and be it finally

RESOLVED, that the Commission be instructed to make an intensive evaluation of the fund and the above programming during 1979–80 and that the commission make a report to the General Assembly.

Editor's note: Based on the research and recommendation of the Commission on Christian Higher Education, the 1981 General Assembly acted to discontinue this fund. This action included the future granting of World Service credit for funds channeled through World Service for Bay Ridge Christian College and a continuing assignment for the commission to identify and address "the gaps or shortcomings" of the several national programs of black ministerial education.

49. Anderson College Board Speaks to the Church (June 1981)

Editor's note: On June 16, 1981, the Board of Trustees of Anderson College made a major report to the General Assembly. This report spoke directly to concerns of the Assembly as these had been focused in the 1980 Assembly and then by a select committee that worked with high national visibility between the 1980 and 1981 Assemblies. The concerns centered on certain of the existing policies and personnel of the college, including questions of clarification regarding the nature of the school's mission, particularly as that mission related to the church and its stated convictions. Following lengthy discussion, the Assembly voted overwhelmingly that:

The General Assembly register its appreciation for the thorough manner in which the Board of Trustees of Anderson College addressed the recommendations of the Select Committee, and that the General Assembly accept the report and commit itself to work with the college in the realization of these objectives.

50. Church and Colleges: A Call for Clarification (June 1981)

Editor's note: The 1981 General Assembly accepted with appreciation a major report from the Board of Trustees of Anderson College (see entry 49). In a section of that report identified as "Critical Issues Ahead," there was a call for clarification of the relationship between the church and its colleges. It read:

Historically, the relationship of the Church of God to its colleges has been largely informal and undefined. There has been the relationship created by the election of trustees, the ratification of chief executive officers, budgetary support, and general reporting. However, there is little clarity regarding the Church's expectations of its colleges and there has not been a widespread understanding of what constitutes a responsible relationship between a church body and its institutions of higher learning. We urge an exploration of this subject.

51. Gardner Bible College: 50th Anniversary (June 1983)

WHEREAS Gardner Bible College, this year of 1983–84, will be celebrating its 50th year of service to the Church of God; and

WHEREAS Gardner Bible College is the second oldest Church of God institution of higher education in North America [Anderson College the oldest]; and

WHEREAS the Gardner Board, its faculty and staff, and the General Assemblies of both Western Canada and Ontario have reviewed the original purpose of the school and have affirmed its viability for the present and future and have recommitted themselves to that purpose (original purpose stated below); and

WHEREAS Gardner Bible College is filling a significant role in the brotherhood of Church of God institutions of higher education, be it, therefore

RESOLVED, that this Assembly commend Gardner Bible College on this milestone in its life and ministry, and be it further

RESOLVED, that this Assembly call upon the church to enter into celebration with the Canadian church wherever and whenever possible in this year it has set aside as Gardner Bible College's Year of Jubilee.

Editor's note: Following is the original purpose of this school as stated in THE ACT OF INCORPORATION by the Province of Alberta, March 31, 1947:

THE PURPOSE of Gardner Bible College is the providing of intellectual and spiritual training for prospective ministers, missionaries, and gospel workers and of promoting the true principles and teachings of the Bible as taught and exemplified by Jesus Christ.

52. Support for Move of Gulf-Coast Bible College to Oklahoma City (June 1984)

Editor's note: President John Conley of Gulf-Coast Bible College reported to the 1984 General Assembly on the finalized plans of the college to move its operations to Oklahoma City, Oklahoma, in the summer of 1985. Concern was raised from the Assembly floor that the Assembly should approve such moving plans since such a move would require a change in the college's articles of incorporation (such a change requires Assembly approval). A motion emerged from the floor calling for the Assembly to approve the moving plan already underway. This motion carried unanimously. Soon the school's unexpected inability to sell its former property in Houston, Texas, brought about a major financial crisis that had to be addressed by the national church.

53. New Name for Gulf-Coast Bible College (June 1985)

Editor's note: The 1985 General Assembly approved the third restated articles of incorporation of Gulf-Coast Bible College. This restatement assumed the school's relocation to Oklahoma City, Oklahoma, and its intent to do business in Oklahoma under the name "Mid-America Bible College."

54. New Process for Electing Warner Pacific College Trustees (June 1985)

Editor's note: For years there was concern that many members of the General Assembly were not acquainted with any of the candidates from whom the Assembly elected members to the Board of Trustees of Warner Pacific College. That Board and the West Coast Ministerial Assembly now recommended and the General Assembly approved the following:

1. That nominations for lay members be voted on at the West Coast Ministerial Assembly, with the name of the final candidate brought to the General Assembly for ratification.
2. That the college continue to take nominations for each ministerial position on the Board of Trustees to the West Coast Ministerial Assembly and place the names of two candidates on the ballot of the General Assembly.

Editor's note: In 1995 (see entry 28) ratification became the typical Assembly procedure in relation to all governing boards related to the Assembly.

55. Reconstituting the Membership of the Commission on Christian Higher Education (June 1985)

Editor's note: Following a 1984 meeting of the presidents, deans, and board chairs of the Church of God colleges in the United States and the annual meeting of the Commission on Christian Higher Education in January 1985, the following proposal was presented to the Executive Council and then to the General Assembly. It received approval from both bodies. A central assumption was that the proposed new composition of the Commission's membership would enhance the Commission's functioning by assuring that key decision makers in higher education would participate fully in the work of the Commission. This action increased the size of the Commission and eliminated the category of associate non-voting members. Effective July, 1985, the commission's membership was established as:

Anderson College president, dean, and board chair	3
Warner Pacific College president, dean, and board chair	3

Mid-America Bible College president, dean, and board chair	3
Bay Ridge Christian College president, dean, and board chair	3
Warner Southern College president, dean, and board chair	3
Anderson School of Theology dean	1
Azusa Pacific University president	1
Executive Council representative (staff director)	1
Elected representatives (General Assembly)	6
Board of Christian Education executive secretary	1
Gardner Bible College president, dean, and board chair	3
Total	**28**

56. Fiftieth Anniversary of Warner Pacific College (June 1986)

WHEREAS Warner Pacific College will be celebrating in 1986–87 its fiftieth (50th) year of service to the people and mission of the Church of God, having been founded as Pacific Bible College in Spokane, Washington, in 1937; and

WHEREAS the college moved to Portland, Oregon, in 1940, changed its name to Warner Pacific College in 1959, and received full accreditation in 1961; and

WHEREAS the college has shared the time of many of its distinguished leaders with the general work of the Church, including Albert F. Gray who served as Chair of this Assembly for fifteen years and Milo L. Chapman who was a long-term member and officer of the Commission on Christian Higher Education; and

WHEREAS these fifty years of the college's existence and service have been characterized by sacrifice and dedication in the quest for excellence, informed by the central convictions of both the Christian faith and higher learning; therefore, be it

RESOLVED, that the General Assembly of the Church of God, in session June 17–18, 1986, join with the Commission on Christian Higher Education in recognizing, commending, and thanking Warner Pacific College on this fiftieth anniversary occasion; and be it further

RESOLVED, that this General Assembly of the Church of God call upon the church to enter into the various events of the anniversary celebration and, by so doing, dedicate herself anew to the importance of Christian higher education in these troubled times.

57. Limitation of Terms: An Exemption (June 1986)

Editor's note: In June, 1985, the General Assembly placed a limitation of terms on any person serving on the governing board of a national agency. The following year the Commission on Christian Higher Education initiated a request that this limitation be less restrictive for the board memberships of the colleges. The Commission argued that "the functions and procedures of members of the college boards are distinctive...." The Assembly agreed, extending to a maximum of fifteen consecutive years the allowable tenure of service of any one person (although after a lapse of two years that person could be renominated). In 1990 this broadened limitation of terms was extended to all persons affected by the original 1985 action. (See entry 24).

58. New Name for Anderson College (June 1987)

Editor's note: In 1986–87 the administration and board of trustees of Anderson College studied the possible wisdom of adopting for itself the name "university" (in part to reflect better the breadth of its academic programming, including the graduate School of Theology). Having made the decision to change its name, the Assembly then acted as follows:

RESOLVED, that this General Assembly of the Church of God, in its annual meeting assembled at Anderson, Indiana, this 17th day of June, 1987, hereby approves the recommendation of the Board of Trustees of Anderson College, Inc., that Article I of the restated Articles of Incorporation of said Anderson College, Inc., be amended, and does hereby adopt the following proposed amended Article I:

"NAME. The name of this Corporation is Anderson University, Inc."

59. The Year of Christian Higher Education (June 1988)

WHEREAS the Church of God (Anderson, Indiana) has a long and rich heritage of Christian Higher Education; and

WHEREAS the church supports the following predominantly Church of God colleges and university (Anderson University, Anderson University School of Theology, Bay Ridge Christian College, Gardner

Bible College, Mid-America Bible College, Warner Pacific College, and Warner Southern College); and

WHEREAS the Commission on Christian Higher Education is celebrating thirty years of service to the Church of God; and

WHEREAS well equipped lay and clergy leadership will enhance greatly the church's concern for revival; be it

RESOLVED, that this Assembly go on record as affirming the ministry of Christian Higher Education; and be it

RESOLVED, that July 1, 1988, to June 30, 1989, be declared jointly as a year of Christian Higher Education and revival; and be it further

RESOLVED, that local congregations, state and regional agencies, and national agencies find ways to promote Christian higher education, to sensitize the church to the values of Christian higher education, and to lift up the importance of attending a Church of God college/university.

60. Covenant Relationship: Anderson University and the Church of God (June 1992)

Editor's note: Anderson University, the oldest and largest of the institutions of higher education related to the Church of God movement, decided to reaffirm and state more formally its "covenant" relationship with the Church of God. The resulting ten-page booklet, presented to the 1992 General Assembly, was received with appreciation. Following are excerpts from this document.

Since the [Anderson] school's founding in 1917, there have been times of tension and debate with the church. There have also been times of affirmation and celebration. Throughout the school's history, however, there has been an unwavering commitment from both the university and the church to be vital partners in the larger mission of the church. Specifically, the university covenants with the Church of God:

- to maintain in an excellent manner its undergraduate, graduate, and seminary programs of Christian higher education;
- to respect and treasure the authority of the Bible and the distinctive heritage of the Church of God;
- to provide preparation for Christian ministry both in the undergraduate schools and in the graduate School of Theology; to offer meaningful

in-service training opportunities to current ministers;

• to work diligently to attract and provide assistance to Church of God students who enroll in its programs; to be open, attractive, and hospitable to other students to whom it can minister effectively;

• to reflect in its community life a commitment to diversity as found in the life and mission of the Church of God;

• to represent the Church of God well in the world of higher education;

• to exercise good stewardship of its human, physical, and financial resources;

• to be accountable, through its board of trustees, to the Church of God which founded it and helps sustain it;

• to work with other ministries of the Church of God—international, national, state, regional and local—in a supportive and interdependent manner.

Editor's note: The responding Assembly action to the University's covenant presentation was:

BE IT RESOLVED that on the occasion beginning the celebration of the 75th anniversary of Anderson University, we the General Assembly, in session June 16–18, 1992, receive the covenant statement and confirm the relationship between the University and the Church of God, and pledge to continue the activity to discuss, modify, and expand the covenant document through dialogue between the representatives of Anderson University and the Church of God.

E. Major Social Issues

61. Support for Prohibition (June 1928)

Editor's note: The prohibition of the sale and use of alcoholic beverages was written into the United States Constitution as the Eighteenth Amendment, effective 1920. By 1928, however, Prohibition was being challenged vigorously by some prominent politicians. Attempts were being made to repeal this law. The 1928 General Ministerial Assembly spoke clearly.

WHEREAS we regard this propaganda as a challenge to the morality and public welfare, therefore be it

RESOLVED, that we urge a strict enforcement of the present prohibition laws, and be it further

RESOLVED, that we put ourselves upon record as favoring no candidate or political party that favors modification of the present prohibition law.

62. Objection to Peacetime Conscription of Youth
(June 1928, 1932, 1947)

Editor's note: The General Ministerial Assembly of 1928 spoke sharply against "war as a method of settling international disputes" and declared itself "in favor of every effort being put forward ... to propagate the principles of peace." Again in 1932 the Assembly addressed this subject by stating bluntly that "war is unchristian, futile and suicidal.... We will never again sanction or participate in any war." By 1947, with the tragedy of World War II still fresh on all minds, the Assembly spoke once again.

WHEREAS this suffering and battered world even yet staggers under the shock of wars past, present, and future; and

WHEREAS the only bright rays of hope appear in the valiant efforts of relief of hunger and suffering abroad and in the aid given toward achieving material and spiritual reconstruction; and

WHEREAS we as a religious body have participated in such efforts and expect to continue to do so to the extent of our abilities; but

WHEREAS there is a vigorous campaign for conscripting the youth of our churches and nation for compulsory peacetime military training; and

WHEREAS the alleged benefits of such training are nullified by exposure to immoral influences coincident with the military life; and

WHEREAS the use of atomic warfare techniques would nullify the use of traditional armed forces; and

WHEREAS such preparation for war is no guarantee of peace, but, rather, creates an atmosphere which crystallizes the threat of war into the actuality; and

WHEREAS education for peacetime pursuits for uplifting mankind would be replaced by education for death and destruction; and

WHEREAS the need of our day is the erasure of malice, suspicion, and misunderstanding; and for the promotion of brotherhood, mutual trust, and the ministry of healing; and

WHEREAS the democratic processes of our government would be threatened by further growth of the military establishment; therefore, be it

RESOLVED, that the General Ministerial Assembly of the Church of God, assembled at Anderson, Indiana, June 18, 1947, commend the leaders of our nation for the splendid work of relief and rehabilitation which they have directed; but be it further

RESOLVED, that we register vigorous objection to any plan for peacetime conscription of youth for military training; and be it further

RESOLVED, that the secretary of this Assembly be instructed to send a copy of this resolution to the President of the United States, to the presiding officers of both houses of Congress, and to their respective military affairs committees, and to the Secretary of War.

63. Supreme Court on Segregation (June 1954)

WHEREAS the United States Supreme Court has rendered a decision to end race segregation in the public schools, and

WHEREAS this decision brings to focus certain tensions in the areas of employment, housing, transportation, dining, and other public facilities, and

WHEREAS the principles of brotherhood and unity of God's children without regard to distinctive racial groups have been commonly taught in our movement, therefore, be it

RESOLVED, that this Assembly go on record as being in accord with the spirit and intent of the Supreme Court ruling, and be it further

RESOLVED, that this Assembly recommend to our people:

(1) Restraint, patience, and humility in meeting this problem of segregation;

(2) That they take an active part in study and efforts in their respective communities to find wise means of solving the problems of segregation; and be it further

RESOLVED, that there be a continuous demonstration of Christian brotherhood and unity on these campgrounds [Anderson, Ind.], and that there be fair and equitable treatment of all peoples regardless of race or economic status, and

WE FURTHER RECOMMEND that we enter into a covenant of prayer and personal rededication to the end that the will of God be accomplished in the relationships of all people.

64. Federal Tax Funds for Education (June 1961)

WHEREAS there has been wide discussion in the public press and in the current session of the Congress of the United States concerning the issue of granting federal funds to education, and

WHEREAS there are many facets of this issue which are of particular concern to the churches of America, therefore, be it

RESOLVED, that we, the General Ministerial Assembly of the Church of God, met in annual session in Anderson, Indiana, this 22nd day of June, 1961, do hereby express the following convictions regarding the use of federal tax funds for education:

1. We reaffirm our confidence in and our support of the public school system as an indispensable means of providing educational opportunity for all children; we recognize the great problems now being faced by the public schools and urge provision for increased resources for the operation and improvement of these public schools within a framework of proper safeguards.
2. We oppose any grants from federal, state, or local tax funds for the operation and support of non-public elementary and secondary schools.
3. We are concerned that the historic principle of separation of church and state be maintained and promoted and urge all branches of the government to avoid any infringement of the ideal of religious liberty which would inevitably arise when taxes paid under compulsion by all people are used to aid non-public schools.

Be it further RESOLVED, that a copy of this resolution be sent to the President of the United States, and that additional copies be made available to the public press and such other media of communication as may desire them.

65. Separation of Church and State (June 1962)

In view of the tremendous pressure now being brought to bear on our federal government for subsidies and handouts by the Roman Catholic Church for its parochial school system, it is now apparent that a definite stand needs to be taken by those of us who favor and believe fervently in the separation of church and state. We believe in the basic principle of the sacred nature of man's relationship to God. We do not believe that this can be legislated nor that it should become a part of political jurisdiction which is a direct possibility if we were to accept government aid for parochial systems.

Be it, therefore, RESOLVED, that a special committee be appointed by the Executive Council of the General Ministerial Assembly to study the field of church-state relationships as it relates to our colleges, agencies, and local church problems and to return to this Assembly with a report as to our stand regarding the above-mentioned relationships.

Editor's note: A major report of this special committee, dated June 17, 1964, was made available to the Assembly and was included with its 1965 minutes. A portion of that report reads as follows:

1. We believe in the public school system as an indispensable means of providing educational opportunity for all children.

2. While supporting the right of religious groups to establish and maintain schools that meet prescribed educational standards at their own expense, and the right of parents to decide whether their children should attend public or non-public schools, we have serious questions concerning:

a. Grants being made from federal, state, or local tax funds for parochial elementary and secondary schools;

b. Payments being made from public funds for tuition or scholarships for children to attend private or church related elementary or secondary schools, and grants being made to parents for that purpose;

c. Tax credits, tax forgiveness, and exemption from school taxes for parents whose children attend non-public elementary or secondary schools.

3. There seems to be community value in supplying dental or medical and welfare services ... to all children in any school ... when assurance is given that such services are known to recipients as public services and expenditures are administered by public authorities who are responsible to the electorate.

4. In any provision of federal funds for tax-supported elementary and secondary public schools:

a. There be no discrimination among children on the basis of race, religion, class, or national origin;

b. There be adequate safeguards against federal control of educational policy.

66. Major Statement on Race (June 1964)

Editor's note: See entry 75 for a later attempt to implement the "open door" aspect of this present action.

In order clearly to define our stand as members of the General Ministerial Assembly of the Church of God, and to encourage Christian action, we affirm that:

We base our stand toward basic human rights on the teaching of the Scriptures. God has "made of one blood all nations of men" (Acts 17:26). "For we are all the children of God by faith in Jesus Christ ... for we are all one in Jesus Christ" (Gal. 3:26, 28). The first of these speaks as to origin, the second as to relationship. We believe that in the Church of God there should be no racial barriers because we are all brethren in Christ. We believe that man was made in the image of God, that every person is of intrinsic worth before God, and that every individual has a right to the fullest possible opportunities for the development of life abundant and eternal. We believe that these rights are given by God and that the church has a responsibility to defend them and work for their guarantee.

Firmly believing that the New Testament teaching sets forth a brotherhood without racial discrimination, we will work to achieve an experience of fairness and honest love toward all our brethren, free from discrimination based on race. This calls for patience, understanding, forgiveness, and unselfish service from every member regardless of race. The law of love should be the rule by which we live under all circumstances. The General Ministerial Assembly defines its membership in this manner:

Ordained ministers of the Church of God in good and regular standing who are present at any authorized and duly called meeting of the Assembly. Unordained ministers who are pastors or full-time associate pastors of recognized congregations. Laymen who are elected or appointed members of the Executive Council, a subordinate board, committee, or commission of the Assembly.

All members of all races who qualify are urged to participate fully in the Assembly business and to exercise the common privileges granted to all members. Membership on national boards, committees, and the programs of the International Convention are open on the basis of qualifications.

Brethren of all races are urged to seek and develop those qualities which will make their ministries beneficial to the whole church and to remember that the ministry of prayer to undergird those in general responsibilities makes one a partner and co-worker in carrying them out, even though he may not hold an office or be on the program. We urge ministers of state assemblies to:

1. Make special efforts to get ministers of all races to work toward a united expression of brotherhood and oneness;

2. Attempt to see that persons, regardless of race, arc nominated for committees and offices in the state work according to qualifications;

3. Where there are segregated assemblies, begin the steps which will eventually bring all the brethren into one working fellowship.

We commend the hundreds of our congregations whose life and doors are open to people of all races and urge that they make this fact known by appropriate announcement. We urge that local congregations make special efforts to integrate those of other races who come into their midst. Because strangers may be timid and fearful, special care and concern should be exercised for them.

We urge each individual member to examine his life patterns in the light of the nature of the gospel and to fully welcome into congregational life fellow members and all persons without regard to race, color, or nationality.

We urge all our congregations which have not practiced an open door policy to honestly appraise their position in the light of New Testament teaching and the commitment of the Church of God to its teaching.

We recognize the difficult situation of our brethren where the social pattern is fixed and hostile to the brotherhood of all people. In love we extend confidence to them in their difficult situation. We trust that through prayer they can find ways of applying the principles of brotherhood and human rights even though the environment might be unfriendly.

We urge that we will always be guided by sound biblical principles rather than the highly emotional pitch so prevalent in our world. Ours is a call to prayer and study and deliberate Christian action. We are not called to conform to the demands of the world or society. We are called to follow the Lord and obey Him. This call is to every one of us, regardless of race or culture.

We, the members of the General Ministerial Assembly, pledge our prayers, concerns, and moral support to those pastors, congregations, and members who are faithful to their Lord.

67. Civil Rights Legislation (June 1964)

WHEREAS our nation is currently confronted with a grave social revolution, and

WHEREAS the nation's conscience has become increasingly aware and sensitive regarding racial discrimination and injustice to minority groups in our nation, and

WHEREAS the United States Constitution gives a clear status in law to a fundamental Christian and American principle, namely, the Constitutional guarantee of equal freedom and equal justice to all citizens, and

WHEREAS there is currently before the United States Senate, civil rights legislation designed to protect the Constitutional rights of all citizens of our nation, and

WHEREAS the Church of God Reformation Movement believes that the principle of segregation based on color, race, caste, or ethnic origin is a denial of the Christian faith and ethic, which stems from the basic premise taught by our Lord that all men are the children of God, be it, therefore,

RESOLVED, that the General Ministerial Assembly of the Church of God, in session at Anderson, Indiana, go on record as favoring the passage of that type of civil rights legislation which will guarantee justice and equality to all our citizens regardless of race, nationality, or religion.

68. Constitutional Guarantee of Voting Rights (June 1965)

WHEREAS the General Assembly of the Church of God in its 1964 meeting adopted a "Statement on Race Relations" which contains this statement: "The right to choose a place of residence, to enter school, to secure employment, to vote or attend church should in no way be limited by a person's race or culture," and

WHEREAS the 1965 General Assembly continues to bear witness to the stand it has taken in the area of race relations, be it, therefore,

RESOLVED, that the General Assembly of the Church of God, in session at Anderson, Indiana, supports legislation in support of Amendment XV of the Constitution of the United States which guarantees equal voting rights for all citizens in all fifty states of the Union without any discrimination based upon racial, religious, or economic differences as early as possible. Be it further

RESOLVED, that a copy of this resolution be mailed to the President of the United States and to the appropriate legislative committees.

69. General Agency Initiatives for Equal Rights (June 1965)

WHEREAS the time for making ringing declarations against racial discrimination has passed, having moved from saying to doing, be it, therefore,

RESOLVED, that the General Assembly of the Church of God in session at Anderson, Indiana, encourage and support the general agencies of the Church to take the steps and risks they deem wise and necessary to involve the church more deliberately in the struggle for equal rights.

70. Involvement in Racial Justice (June 1965)

WHEREAS the General Assembly in its 1964 June meeting affirmed that we should boldly stand on the principles of basic human rights because they are Christian; and that the right to choose a place of residence, to enter school, to secure employment, to vote, or attend church should in no way be limited by a person's race or culture, and

WHEREAS the essence of integrity is to demonstrate ideals and not merely talk about them, be it, therefore,

RESOLVED, that the General Assembly of the Church of God in session at Anderson, Indiana, urge its members to take direct action as a religious duty to do their part in their local communities to see that voting, jobs, housing, education, and public worship facilities are available to all citizens, and be it further

RESOLVED, that the Assembly urge each pastor to encourage greater personal involvement on the part of individual Christians in the struggle for racial justice.

71. Stand Against Tobacco (June 1965)

WHEREAS we in the Church of God movement have traditionally stood solidly against the use of tobacco in any form and have observed the general undesirability of the habit; and

WHEREAS we observe the vast amounts of money spent for tobacco, which expenditure could not be considered a constructive part of life or a contribution to human welfare; and

WHEREAS we have actively taught that the human body and mind is the temple of God, to be kept clean, pure, and fit for the Master's use; and

WHEREAS we consider it of great importance to protect our youth from the insidious advertising which seems to make the use of tobacco desirable by glamorizing the stars of the entertainment and athletic worlds; and

WHEREAS the report of the Surgeon General of the United States has injected a decisive, authoritative, and scientifically based analysis showing the harmful effects of tobacco, substantiating what we have long believed to be true; therefore, be it

RESOLVED, that in this General Assembly we reaffirm our convictions and teaching regarding the use of tobacco; be it further

RESOLVED, that this Assembly urge every minister to take a positive stand in discouraging the use of tobacco, to teach constructively, to help safeguard our youth, to help church leaders realize the importance of setting a good example, to lead the church in a redemptive attitude and effort toward those who are victims of the habit; and be it further

RESOLVED, that this General Assembly urge ministers and responsible church laymen to write their Congressmen, calling for stricter regulations on the advertising of tobacco in the mass media and on items for sale.

72. Military Conscription: The Right of Conscience (June 1966)

Editor's note: See entry 62 for reference to other Assembly actions (1928, 1932, and 1947) in relation to military conscription.

Like all true Americans, we as members of the General Assembly of the Church of God meeting in regular session in Anderson, Indiana, this sixteenth day of June, 1966, view with deep concern the escalating military involvement and the conscription of our youth for military service. We believe that war represents our moral failures. We abhor the causes that lead to war. We stand by the teaching and example of our Lord, who taught us and showed us the way of radical, sacrificial love.

We are thankful to God that we live in a land of basic freedoms whose law makes provision for alternative service by those "who, by reason of religious training and belief, are conscientiously opposed to participation in war in any form." We encourage our young men who conscientiously object to war to engage in such civilian work which contributes "to the maintenance of the national health, safety or interest."

We respect the right of each person to arrive at his own convictions. We believe in the principle of freedom of worship and freedom of conscience. We respect the rights of the individual conscience within our fellowship. We have never set up an authoritative creed. Instead, we accept the entire New Testament as our rule of faith and practice, and we seek to lead every member of our fellowship to full comprehension and full acceptance of the Spirit of Christ as the guide for all conduct. What we seek for ourselves we seek for every citizen of our land—the right of individual conscience which no governmental authority can abrogate or violate. We do not condemn or reject that person who differs with our position or participates in war. We shall seek to follow such persons with a ministry of help and guidance, but this is never to be construed as approval of war.

We fervently pray for the leaders of our nation and of other nations, many of whom we believe to be sincerely striving for peace. We pray that efforts by negotiation among countries, through the United Nations and every possible channel, may succeed in bringing peace to our troubled world. Let this statement of conviction be construed by any and all to mean that we fully support young men of the Church of God who sincerely and conscientiously are opposed to participation in military service. We encourage them to seek the constructive alternatives intended to bring health, healing, and understanding, and which serve the highest interests of our beloved country and of the whole world.

73. World Hunger (June 1966)

WHEREAS government and relief organizations have been making special studies of world hunger, giving special attention to India and other countries of the Eastern Hemisphere; and

WHEREAS churches and voluntary agencies have been expressing during recent months a mounting concern for the hungry of the world, the two-thirds of the world's population who suffer daily of recurrent hunger; and

WHEREAS the United States government and other world governments have made substantial contributions in recent years and months to supply emergency food commodities to prevent famine and to aid the governments of countries where hunger prevails to use technical skills to produce more and distribute more effectively all available supplies of food; and

WHEREAS for the first time in history the capabilities and techniques exist to prevent the warping of lives and the deaths caused by hunger; and

WHEREAS it should be recognized with regret that the food situation and its distribution around the world are not totally removed from world and local economics and world and local politics; and

WHEREAS united steps are being taken through world relief organizations to attack the long-range problem by caring for emergency feeding operations followed by a mounting aid program to enhance agricultural production, more adequate distribution of processed food, land reclamation, water provision, planned parenthood, and all related issues designed to get at the root causes of world hunger; and

WHEREAS all Christians, particularly those living in affluent societies, are faced with the moral and spiritual responsibility for compassionate action by acknowledging our common humanity and by giving food to the hungry in the name of Christ; be it, therefore,

RESOLVED, that this specter of world hunger be brought to the attention of the Church of God constituency through the medium of this resolution, as well as through current articles appearing in church and secular magazines and in the press; to awaken the conscience of each and every Christian to exert all his energies and to cooperate with efforts to help alleviate world hunger; and be it further

RESOLVED, that in view of the prevailing need in India today caused by the worst drought in seventy years with a resulting 80% of total crop failure in areas hard hit due to lack of monsoon rain, and in view of the possibility that large numbers now suffering from hunger may starve to death unless immediate assistance reaches India quickly; all who wish to respond to this great need and the prompting of their conscience do so by sending their contributions for world relief to the Missionary Board of the Church of God, all monies to be distributed immediately to direct need through Church of God missionaries involved in relief or through Church World Service, the most capable church-related organization to understand and meet the emergency needs found in India and other countries of the world.

74. Racial Justice a Spiritual Priority (June 1968)

WHEREAS our Assembly has received various resolutions across recent years concerned about race relations in the Church of God; and

WHEREAS the abundant supply of resolutions on the matter of race relations continues to call attention to our need to correct evident deficiencies and solve evident problems; and

WHEREAS the 1964 report from this Assembly's Commission on Race Relations stated our deficiencies and recommended appropriate steps for correcting our needs; and

WHEREAS it is the work of this Assembly to authorize, mobilize, and direct the interests common to our life and work as a church—and has effectively done so more recently by solving problems of finance (appropriations for college needs, building of Warner Auditorium); and

WHEREAS the church looks to the Assembly to advise and give direction on the particularly spiritual concerns of church life and work; therefore be it

RESOLVED, that this Assembly declare that its previous resolutions on the matter of race relations remain as issues of spiritual priority; and be it further

RESOLVED, that our national boards and agencies be directed to make deliberate moves to secure Negro leaders for executive and/or administrative roles wherever and whenever possible, this being a way to show a more truly inclusive pattern for ourselves on the national level; and be it further

RESOLVED, that this Assembly direct the Commission on Social Concerns to serve the Assembly by preparing such aids and guides for congregational use in resolving differences that keep some of our churches racially separate; and be it finally

RESOLVED, that this Assembly call upon the Church to repent for the deficiencies and failures as a people on the point of race relations, turning to God for renewal and grace during this International Convention.

75. Resolution on Race (June 1968)

Editor's note: In 1957 the Executive Council of the Church of God and the General Ministerial Assembly named a study commission on race relations to serve for a period of five years. In 1961, this study commission reported to the Executive Council and recommended elements of a positive strategy for reaching desirable goals in better race relations. These proposed action steps were:

1. Proceed with all deliberate speed to integrate ratification procedures in all states immediately.

2. Let ministers in all states arrange for fellowship meetings together and pave the way for integrated assemblies, beginning, also, to synchronize meetings, and procedures, adopt similar standards, and so on. Breakfast meetings or one-day prayer retreats might be employed.

3. National leaders should enter into serious discussions toward the integration of national agencies, it being understood that leadership opportunity, representation, and expression would be on the basis of qualification regardless of race.

4. That recognition and support be given to certain experiences and developments which our national boards are carrying out. That encouragement be given to local churches that are able to move ahead with courage in this field, and that these churches on the frontier of exploration be supported with prayer and the concern of the church, and to the churches of the community, whatever the racial situation may be.

5. Let the Executive Council and the General Ministerial Assembly pass resolutions directed to our own churches, urging inter-racial fellowship within the local church and among local churches, asking our people to press forward toward integration on a truly Christian basis.

6. To take a positive stance, by resolution and through publications, on the matter of integration and the employing of our rich traditions and spiritual resources toward the demonstrations of Christian principles at this point of need.

7. That our ministers and churches be encouraged to cooperate in interchurch and community endeavors toward overcoming the racial cleavages.

Editor's note: This 1968 presentation to the Assembly went on to make the following historical observations and resolution—which was accepted.

In 1964, the Executive Council offered and this Assembly adopted a further major statement on race, declaring that the urgency for action was growing in society and the need for the church to begin within its own fellowship to make corrections was imperative. Action was called for on the local, the state, and the national levels of our work.

Much progress has been made since these recommendations were adopted. On the local level, a large number of our congregations are now, to some degree, integrated with families of other races. The call for an open-door policy for all races was made, but has never been followed up.

On the state level, several assemblies have been merged and others are in the process of merging.

On the national level, there has been a ninety-percent increase in the number of black representatives serving on national boards and agencies. The Missionary Committee of the National Association of the Church of God has been merged with the Missionary Board of this Assembly. The program of the International Convention has become much more representative of all races.

While these gains are encouraging, they have not kept up with the changes in society, the progress is much too slow and the urgency is increasing. There are eleven states which still have two racial ministerial assemblies. Therefore, be it

RESOLVED, that this Assembly urge all state organizations to bring about full involvement and fair representation of Negro persons according to ability in the offices and boards and committees of the state organizations; and be it further

RESOLVED, that where there are Negro and white assemblies still existing, steps be taken in accordance with the recommendations adopted in 1964 to "integrate all ratification procedures in all states immediately"; and be it also further

RESOLVED, that state assemblies report the degree of progress now existing toward integration of assemblies as adopted by this Assembly in 1964, and that the Executive Council, through its Division of Church Service, be instructed to bring to this Assembly in 1969 a summary of the progress that has been made.

76. Open-Door Policy (June 1968)

Editor's note: Assembly chair Harold Boyer recognized Robert Reardon, president of Anderson College. Dr. Reardon referred to Charles Naylor's hymn, "The Church's Jubilee," and quoted the verse which includes the words "Reaching our hands in fellowship to every bloodwashed one." He stated that the Assembly had in the past expressed an "open-door policy for all races" [see entry 66], but that there was a need for more positive action. He presented the following resolution, which the Assembly then approved.

In view of the open-door resolution passed by this Assembly in 1964, be it

RESOLVED, that this Assembly call upon local congregations of the Church of God in the United States and Canada to ratify the following declaration and to make it known publicly through whatever means possible:

In accordance with the teaching of the Scriptures, this congregation of the Church of God welcomes fellow Christians without regard to race, color, or national origin, to participate fully and without any reservation in its fellowship and work. And be it further

RESOLVED, that the executive secretary of the Executive Council of the Church of God is instructed to place the above declaration before each local congregation of the Church of God, and to make public those congregations ratifying this declaration.

77. Refugees (June 1973)

RESOLVED, that the General Assembly of the Church of God urge local congregations to search out and discover refugees and devise ways and means of meeting their needs by participating with other like-minded groups in discharging a basic biblical imperative; and be it

RESOLVED, that this resolution and its accompanying document of information be disseminated to state boards of evangelism and to the pastors and official boards of local congregations in the areas where these refugee problems might appear, with an urgent request for serious implementation; and be it

RESOLVED, that the General Assembly of the Church of God urge individuals in congregations to keep currently informed regarding any major refugee situation in the world and how immediate relief and ultimate rehabilitation can be accomplished as the political situation will allow, and that the above information be secured through the Committee on Refugees of the United Nations, Church World Service of the Division of Overseas Ministries of the National Council of Churches, the Missionary Board of the Church of God, or the Executive Council of the

Church of God, as well as through the media of the press and news magazines; and be it further

RESOLVED, that the above resolution with the document "Refugee Settlement: Persons Outside the United Statess" be sent to all pastors of the Church of God, with the earnest request that the church be encouraged to study it and other available information to the end that it might bring Christian principles governing such matters to the attention of proper governmental authorities, both state and federal, in such a manner that the government and people of the United States might better serve their proper role in the settlement of refugee situations wherever and whenever they might occur.

78. Role of Women (June 1974)

The Church of God in its beginning and through its early history included both men and women in its ministry. Little or no thought was given as to whether one who went forth to serve in the name of the Lord Jesus Christ was masculine or feminine. The emphasis was on spreading the gospel of truth as proclaimed by the reformation movement. Women served in many capacities, as evangelists, teachers, musicians, and pastors. They have served well along with men down through the years.

A recent survey by the Division of Church Service, through a questionnaire, revealed that, while women make up around 55 percent of the membership of the congregations of the Church of God, the percentage of women in leadership roles has steadily declined.

Therefore, in light of the statistics which document the diminishing use of women's abilities in the life and work of the church, comes the following resolution:

WHEREAS women are equipped by their Creator to serve in a variety of roles, including that of homemaker, employment in jobs and professions, volunteer work, and full- or part-time Christian service, and

WHEREAS women have demonstrated their ability and their commitment to the church, and

WHEREAS God calls women to use their gifts and skills to their fullest potential, therefore be it

RESOLVED that more women be given opportunity and consideration for positions of leadership in the total program of the Church of God, locally, statewide, and nationally.

79. World Hunger (June 1975)

WHEREAS Christian people in the wealthy nations, especially Christian people in the United States, should be influential in bringing resources to help alleviate the current world hunger crisis; and

WHEREAS there has been a concern expressed in Church of God periodicals and in mailings from national agencies that feeding starving people should be a top priority of the Church; therefore, be it

RESOLVED that the church actively seek to raise $100,000 for World Hunger and Disaster Relief during the year of 1975–76. This effort would include the $25,000 that the Women of the Church of God are seeking to raise, the $7,500 listed in the budgets of the Missionary Board and the $20,000 Disaster Fund, leaving $50,000 to be raised by World Service. All money sent to World Service for World Hunger Relief will receive World Service credit.

80. Violence on Television (June 1977)

WHEREAS in recent years we have witnessed on television an alarming increase in the use of profanity and violence and the portrayal of lifestyles inconsistent with Christian values; and

WHEREAS the television networks and program sponsors have permitted profanity, violence, and the portrayal of lifestyles inconsistent with Christian values to be included in an increasing number of telecasts; and

WHEREAS we believe this trend to be detrimental to the well-being of our families—especially our children and youth; therefore, be it

RESOLVED that the General Assembly of the Church of God, Anderson, Indiana, adopt the following write-in plan to combat the use of profanity and violence and the portrayal of lifestyles inconsistent with Christian values on television:

The plan: Each congregation be asked to appoint a social action chairman (or the pastor may initiate this plan). The chairman (or pastor) enlist the entire membership locally to write a brief letter to the three network presidents and program sponsors stating their opposition to the use of profanity and violence and the portrayal of lifestyles inconsistent with Christian values on television. This could be done over a period of two or three months. The size of the local congregation would determine how many letters could be assigned for each week.

For example: A church of 100 members would enlist 8 persons each week so that in approximately three months all members would take their turn in writing to the television networks and program sponsors; be it further

RESOLVED that, if this plan is adopted, the General Assembly, through the Commission on Social Concerns, convey this plan with appropriate publicity to all local congregations, urging that every congregation of the Church of God be enlisted in this action.

81. Stand Against Homosexuality (June 1979)

Since the world is invaded by sex perversion in the form of homosexuality, we, the Church of God Reformation Movement, do hereby express our conviction concerning the issue:

WHEREAS we in the Church of God, being an evangelical people, committed to biblical holiness, give high regard to scriptural injunctions against homosexuality, we are also a redemptive body and seek to express love, compassion, and a chaste relationship in Christ for everyone; be it

RESOLVED, that the General Assembly of the Church of God go on record as affirming our conviction that biblically we believe homosexuality is sin. We hereby stand firmly opposed to the licensing, ordination, or approving of persons in leadership actively involved in this lifestyle; be it further

RESOLVED, that we stand opposed to any instruction in our church-sponsored institutions or the use of curriculum material which accepts homosexuality as either normal, desirable, or Christian.

Editor's note: See entry 95 for a later action on this same subject.

82. Stand Against Abortion on Demand (June 1981)

Editor's note: After years of activity in the United States directed at passage of an equal rights amendment (ERA) to the national Constitution and related decisions of the Supreme Court, the General Assembly decided to speak on the major social concern of the legal availability of abortion to almost anyone for almost any reason. The Assembly action read:

WHEREAS the United States Supreme Court has declared unconstitutional all state laws regulating abortion, and has opened the way for abortion on demand for any reason; and

WHEREAS the rights of the unborn child are being stripped away by reinterpretation of the Constitution by the Supreme Court; and

WHEREAS this opens the door to possible elimination of other unwanted or undesirable human beings, and

WHEREAS the Bible contains reference to God's personal acquaintance with children prior to birth, inferring the fetus has life, such as:

1. In Jeremiah 1:4, 5 "... the Word of the Lord came unto me saying, 'Before I formed you in the womb I knew you, and before you were born I consecrated you; I have appointed you a prophet to the nations.' " (NASB);
2. And in Psalm 139:13, King David, inspired by God, wrote: "Thou didst form my inward parts; thou didst weave me in my mother's womb. I will give thanks to thee, for I am fearfully and wonderfully made" (NASB); and

WHEREAS abortion on demand, we believe, greatly diminishes the moral values, not only of the one seeking the abortion, but of this whole nation; and

WHEREAS the unborn child cannot plead in its own defense; be it, therefore,

RESOLVED, that the General Assembly of the Church of God go on record as opposing abortion on demand, recognizing that the unborn fetus is a living human being and thus should be protected by the laws and Constitution of the United States of America; and be it further

RESOLVED, that the General Assembly of the Church of God urges all congregations to express compassion and concern not only to protect life before birth but to work to assure that the lives that are preserved may receive the care, attention, and help that God wants for all persons; to provide family life and marriage education that will foster such a reverence for God-given life that both the causes and consequences of unwanted pregnancies may be diminished; and that this resolution be publicized.

83. Nuclear Arms Reduction (June 1982)

The incineration of our planet may be imminent! Why? Because of the threat posed by the nuclear arms race in which our country and the Soviet

Union are principal participants. Planning the future of our global community is begging the question about a future for this nuclear age. The nuclear arms race itself could end with its destruction of the human race. We believe that the proliferation of nuclear weapons is a sin against the Creator and against His creation.

Because it may be the most urgent moral issue confronting our generation, we call Church of God people everywhere to fast and pray for world peace, and for global leaders as they make decisions which affect the destiny of the human family. We welcome the decision of the United Nations to hold a Second Special Session on Disarmament, and we invite concerned persons and groups to join in fervent prayer during those crucial days. We urge that families, pastors, Sunday school classes, youth, and other groups in local churches give serious study to the question of nuclear disarmament.

We commend the growing number of concerned persons in the Church of God who are expressing opposition to the nuclear arms race in letters to congressmen, senators, elected government leaders, and to local newspaper editors. The positive results of personal letters have been confirmed by both supporters and opponents of nuclear disarmament. We urge that these efforts in sending handwritten letters be continued and accelerated.

The nuclear arms race is not our fate but our choice. There is an alternative. No sinister external force or internal political system is imposing nuclear weapons upon us. Today we are playing brinkmanship with a nuclear shootout because of the accumulation of decisions made by our policy-makers elected and supported by voters and taxpayers. The decision about whether or not we go over the brink into a nuclear holocaust will be made by us, not by persons now in kindergarten, elementary or high school.

The alternative is the way of negotiation and agreement. Just as Mr. Nixon made creative efforts to normalize our relationship with China, and as Mr. Sadat won the admiration of the world when he carried the olive branch to Israel, we call upon Mr. Reagan and Mr. Brezhnev to say to each other and to the people of the world: "Enough of this; let us live in peace."

Our deliberate choice is to be faithful to Jesus Christ and to his gospel of reconciliation. His purpose for all people is life that is abundant and eternal. To place our trust in weapons of mass murder and destruction is irresponsible and idolatrous. We encourage Church of God people to accept our historical imperative to choose life and to find and support alternatives to the nuclear arms race.

Editor's note: The above statement was *received* rather than formally *adopted* by the Assembly so that members of the Assembly could feel free to act upon such convictions as they saw fit.

84. Turning the US Back to God (June 1983)

WHEREAS it appears that our nation is being confronted with the destruction of the principles upon which it was founded; and

WHEREAS the Declaration of Independence clearly cites "our reliance on the protection of Divine Providence"; and

WHEREAS in many ways the nation's conscience has become insensitive to our reliance on Divine Providence and to the destruction of the moral principles upon which this nation was founded; and

WHEREAS the President of the United States is currently urging the government authorities in this country to permit Bible reading and prayer in the schools and to cease the approval and financing of abortion; and

WHEREAS the Church of God Reformation Movement does not believe in the forbidding of the reading of God's Word or prayer to God in public schools and has gone on record as opposing "Abortion on Demand" (June 1981); be it, therefore,

RESOLVED that the General Assembly of the Reformation Movement of the Church of God, in session at Anderson, Indiana (June 1983), go on record, and so notify the President and the Congress of the United States, that this church body does strongly support the President of the United States, and all concerned members of Congress, in their efforts to turn this country back to God.

85. Pornography and Obscenity (June 1984)

WHEREAS the 8-billion-dollar pornography industry in America has grown to epidemic proportions and invaded every segment of society; and

WHEREAS the lifestyle propagated by the pornographic industry is contrary to the New Testament teachings; and

WHEREAS family, church, and community values are being seriously threatened by the pornography industry; and

WHEREAS the Supreme Court in 1973 reaffirmed the right of the community to protect its standards; and

WHEREAS the erosion of values has contributed to the increase in teenage pregnancies, child prostitution, and sexual assaults upon women; therefore be it

RESOLVED, that this General Assembly support the Executive Council and the Commission on Social Concerns in their effort to inform our congregations about the seriousness of the problem; and bc it further

RESOLVED, that this Assembly designate October 28—November 4 as Pornography Awareness Week, issuing a call to decency; and be it further

RESOLVED, that this Assembly request resource packets for our congregations so that they will be equipped to take positive action; and be it further

RESOLVED, that this Assembly urge our congregations to become involved in a plan of action in their own communities as well as using their voice as a positive influence in the media and law; and finally be it

RESOLVED, that this Assembly direct its executive officer to write the President of the United States:

a. Asking him to make a public declaration that enforcement of the Federal obscenity laws is a matter of importance to him;

b. Requesting him to order the Justice Department to enforce the obscenity laws which are now on the books;

c. Pledging him our prayers and support in this effort.

86. Apartheid (June 1986)

Jesus demonstrated and taught that we are to love God with all our hearts, souls, minds and strength and to love our neighbor as ourselves. The Good News is that God has reached out to all people with the offer of Salvation and Reconciliation and that we, having become beneficiaries of His grace, become ministers of Reconciliation.

Apartheid, the policy of racial separation in South Africa, obviously violates both the witness and the spirit of God for all people of that nation. Oppression and violence are instruments aligned with Apartheid and are further manifestations of the philosophy of racial superiority. Both in thought and in action, this policy is diametrically opposed to the witness of Christ.

Brothers and sisters of the National Association Ministerial Assembly of the Church of God have eloquently expressed their condemnation of Apartheid. They hold out for us an example of concerned, constructive involvement.

With them, we, the General Assembly of the Church of God, oppose Apartheid in South Africa and all that it implies.

We call upon individuals within the Church to become properly informed so that they might speak, write, and act to express their personal disapproval of Apartheid.

Finally, we encourage the Church of God to pledge her support to efforts at reconciliation and peace-making in South Africa.

Editor's note: A subsequent motion was passed calling for the above to be sent to the President of the United States and other appropriate government officials. Rev. Samuel G. Hines, chair of the General Assembly from 1983 to 1989, personally became internationally influential in this reconciliation effort in South Africa.

87. Domestic Violence (June 1986)

WHEREAS we recognize that domestic violence is a major problem in the United States today, affecting thousands of families in every economic, social, and ethnic group; and

WHEREAS we believe that awareness of the severity of the problem is the first step in combating this evil; and

WHEREAS we recognize that misinterpretation of Scripture has permitted some persons to justify domestic violence as being consistent with Christian doctrine; and

WHEREAS we also recognize that breaking the chain of violence is imperative to resolving the problem so that future generations do not perpetuate the evil; therefore, be it

RESOLVED that we call upon the Church of God Reformation Movement to break the silence barrier on domestic violence by recognizing and addressing the problem within our communities and within our own communion; and be it, also,

RESOLVED that we urge careful interpretation of Scripture, realizing that correct understanding of the Bible affirms the value and dignity of each individual; and be it also

RESOLVED that we regard violence to be inappropriate as a means of conflict resolution between adult family members; and be it also

RESOLVED that we recognize as unacceptable any behavior that goes beyond normal chastisement measures to use any form of violence in the family that grievously injures, maims, or causes psychological impairment (i.e., severe beatings, kicks, punches, or verbal abuse and depersonalization); and be it also

RESOLVED that we in the church assist persons in our communion to find alternative means of resolving conflict within the family, rejecting completely the practice of violence as defined above; and be it also

RESOLVED that we in the church work to find specific ways to provide protection and healing for the victims of domestic violence; and be it further

RESOLVED that we also commit ourselves to working for healing for the perpetrators of domestic violence.

88. Nuclear Weaponry (June 1986)

We are a biblical people …

"The earth is the Lord's and the fullness thereof" (Ps. 24:1).

We are called to stewardship of the earth, and life.

We therefore oppose the use of nuclear weaponry by any nation because it has the capacity to destroy God's creation.

Editor's note: A subsequent motion was passed calling for the above to be sent to the President of the United States and other appropriate government officials. See entry 83 on nuclear arms reduction.

89. Pornographic Materials (June 1986)

Editor's note: This 1986 action was preceeded by the above action of 1984 and then supplemented in 1990 by a vigorous action calling for specific steps against illegal pornography, "a dangerous and harmful evil in American society which must be eradicated."

WHEREAS there has been a rising tide of pornographic materials made ever increasingly available in the family marketplace of America; and

WHEREAS our movement, through the effective leadership of our

Executive Secretary, has taken a leadership role in joining with other concerned persons and groups to raise the standard of decency; and

WHEREAS as a Movement we have historically believed in and attempted to call our world to righteousness; and

WHEREAS we note with thanksgiving that through these united efforts in this battle, we have seen some victories, in that more than 15,000 stores have removed pornographic magazines in the last four months, including such chains as Seven-Eleven Stores, Eckerds Drug Stores, Stop and Go Markets, and Super-X Drug stores; and

WHEREAS we are aware that there is still much to be done in the battle to rid our society of this degrading influence; therefore, be it

RESOLVED, that we salute the past efforts of our pastors and leaders who have been involved in this fight against the pornographic tide; and be it further

RESOLVED, that we call upon the Church of God to redouble its efforts to lift up a standard of righteousness and to continue working in cooperation with other like-minded persons and groups until total victory is achieved.

90. Ministry with Older Adults (June 1988)

WHEREAS the current United States population of persons 65 and over is now approaching twelve percent (12%) of the total population, with future estimates projected to be approximately 20 percent by the year 2030 AD; and

WHEREAS the Bible affirms old age as a time when persons are able to reflect earnestly on their lives, share wise counsel with others, and develop the deep spiritual resources of their experiences; and

WHEREAS the Church of God (Anderson, Indiana) has an abundant number of older persons who are able to make significant contributions to their church, community and society; and

WHEREAS the local church is the center of life for a significant number of older persons who look to the church for spiritual nurture, inspiration, and direction; and

WHEREAS the National Board of Christian Education has launched the National Fellowship of Older Adults and has printed an Older Adult Ministry and Program Manual to assist local church leaders and state/regional organizations to plan and implement effective ministries and programs for older adults; and

WHEREAS Anderson University (School of Theology) has received a grant to train pastors, ministers and other key lay persons in developing their skills to minister more effectively with and to older adults; and

WHEREAS some local congregations, state/provincial/regional organizations, and national Church of God agencies have begun to initiate programs for the aged; and

WHEREAS we believe that older persons are an integral part in the life of the Church of God on whom we have been able to build strong and viable congregations; be it, therefore,

RESOLVED, that the General Assembly of the Church of God (Anderson, Indiana) proclaims 1989 as the "Year of Ministry to and with Older Adults"; and be it further

RESOLVED, that pastors, local congregations, state and regional/provincial organizations be encouraged to join with the National Fellowship of Older Adults, Commission on Social Concerns, and national agencies of the Church of God in promoting ministries and programs for and with older persons.

91. Responsible Sexual Behavior (June 1988)

WHEREAS forces in society encourage sexual intercourse before marriage; and studies indicate that in society in general, by age nineteen, 80 percent of today's males and 67 percent of today's females are sexually active; and in the United States alone more than 1,000,000 unmarried teenagers become pregnant every year; and

WHEREAS there is an epidemic of sexually transmitted diseases; and premarital sexual intercourse can damage physical, mental, emotional, and spiritual health; and

WHEREAS the home has come under attack on many fronts and the family is struggling against forces greater than those faced by previous generations, and as a result parents are seeking additional knowledge and skills for teaching scriptural principles concerning sexuality, sexual activity, marriage, and proper self-image; and

WHEREAS parents and teenagers desire better communication with one another but may lack the basic skills to accomplish this; and the church, as a basic support group for the family, is called to address and minister to these needs, be it, therefore,

RESOLVED, that the Church of God reaffirm its commitment to the sanctity of marriage and the reserving of sex for marriage; and be it further

RESOLVED, that the Church of God seek to train parents and other significant adults for effectively communicating biblical principles, especially those related to sexuality, sexual activity, marriage, and healthy self-image to young people, and that the Church of God seek to develop among parents, other significant adults, and teenagers improved relational skills in an atmosphere of love and acceptance; and be it further

RESOLVED, that the above-stated goals be addressed at every level and through every avenue of the church's ministry; through national agencies, through provincial, state, and regional ministries, through such major gatherings as provincial, state and regional youth conventions and camp meetings, through the Inspirational and International Youth Conventions, and through the local church; and be it further

RESOLVED, that the church avail itself of various excellent resources such as the "WHY WAIT?" materials supplied by Josh McDowell Ministry which have been adopted for use by other evangelical church groups. These materials, having been reviewed by a select group comprised of representatives from the national agencies of the Church, youth ministers and other special interest groups, are considered sound in their content, effective in their usefulness, accurate in their Biblical application, and are recommended for use across the church.

92. Thanksgiving and Responsibility (June 1988)

WHEREAS the celebration of a Thanksgiving season has been a national tradition observed by the people of the United States from the days of the early settlers to the present time; and

WHEREAS many of the great leaders of the nation, including Presidents George Washington and Abraham Lincoln, recognized the importance of setting aside a time of Thanksgiving, and presidential proclamations have established the last Thursday of November as a day of Thanksgiving; and

WHEREAS in 1941, the United States Congress established Thanksgiving as a permanent national holiday; and

WHEREAS we as a nation have been blessed above all other nations; and

WHEREAS the United States Constitution has adapted to changing times and is the oldest written constitution in the world; and

WHEREAS the people of the United States should better understand the history of this great nation; and

WHEREAS it is appropriate to give thanks to God for the everyday freedoms guaranteed by the Constitution that the people of the United States so often take for granted; and

WHEREAS the people of the United States should take time to appreciate a land of plenty, a nation of vast human and natural resources, while not forgetting the plight of the needy; and

WHEREAS the National Thanksgiving Foundation, which has as its purposes: "To promote grassroots and private-sector involvement to help in the elimination of hunger and homelessness and to encourage nationwide expressions of thanksgiving for the blessings of life and liberty in America" is sponsoring simultaneous "National Thanksgiving Dinners" on November 17, 1988, to assist the hungry and homeless; and

WHEREAS the Church of God of Anderson, Indiana, supports the objectives of feeding the hungry and housing the homeless as well as being thankful for the blessings of life and liberty in America; therefore be it

RESOLVED, that the Church of God of Anderson, Indiana, encourages its members and other groups and organizations to work together on this national celebration by holding National Thanksgiving Dinners or other such activities on November 17, 1988, to give thanks for our blessings and to raise funds to help the less fortunate.

93. Urban Mission of the Church of God (June 1989)

WHEREAS the Census Bureau reports that the U.S.A. is steadily growing more urban and that presently 75 percent of the population now live in metropolitan areas, and that in 1963 it was 63 percent; and

WHEREAS the world is rapidly becoming urban, with projections ranging from one-half to 80 percent of the world's population living in urban places by the year 2000 (83% for the U.S.A. and Canada), depending on how people are counted and how cities are defined; and

WHEREAS the original charter establishing the Board of Church Extension and Home Missions of the Church of God, Inc. (1921) assigns the Board the responsibility, among others, of engaging in urban mission, mentioning specifically encouraging "home missionary work among...city slums" and seeking "to establish churches in large cities and strategic centers or other places where work has not yet opened"; and

WHEREAS at the turn of the twentieth century the Church of God was intentional in its urban outreach ministry, establishing Missionary Homes as centers of urban evangelism and compassionate ministries in some 42 cities over three decades; and

WHEREAS many Church of God congregations today have moved away from the core city, largely leaving the urban mission of the church to ethnic minority congregations that often face overwhelming needs with impoverished resources; therefore, be it

RESOLVED, that the General Assembly affirm metropolitan/urban areas of the nation, in all their pluralism and problems, to be proper and fitting places for the Church of God to be on mission...; and be it, also,

RESOLVED, that the General Assembly go on record as urging:

(1) pastors of local churches to aggressively pursue a course of consciousness raising regarding our Lord's urban mission mandate;

(2) national agencies to target urban mission and city churches in developing resources for ministry within their assignments;

(3) Church of God colleges and the School of Theology to develop core curriculum that will assist students in understanding the city biblically, theologically, and missionally; and be it, also,

RESOLVED, that the General Assembly go on record as urging metro area churches to move beyond occasional fellowship and unity meetings to develop active ministry networks (within existing organizational structures) and be it further

RESOLVED, that the Board of Church Extension and Home Missions recommends that the General Assembly enthusiastically accept and endorse this resolution on the Urban Mission of the Church of God as in keeping with the "National Strategy of Church Planting for the Church of God for the Next Two Decades," approved by the General Assembly in June, 1984.

94. Sexual, Emotional and Physical Abuse (June 1992)

WHEREAS abuse, whether sexual, emotional, or physical, is a growing problem in society; and

WHEREAS the effects of abuse create lifelong problems for the abused, attacking their very self-understanding and their relationship to God and the Church; and

WHEREAS we increasingly recognize that the church community

includes both the abused and abusers in significant numbers; and

WHEREAS abuse is often a cycle where those who have been abused are more likely to become abusers; and

WHEREAS both persons who abuse and persons who suffer the abuse are in need of the redeeming power of the gospel and support from the Church; and

WHEREAS we acknowledge that healing from abuse comes only as a gift from God; therefore be it

RESOLVED that the General Assembly designate the month of October to focus on the need for healing of the abused and the abuser; and be it further

RESOLVED that the General Assembly urge churches to set aside one Sunday in October to pray for healing for both those who are abused and those who abuse; and be it further

RESOLVED that the General Assembly urge churches to initiate programs to bring justice, healing, and restoration for the abused and the abuser; and be it further

RESOLVED, that the General Assembly urge all persons to support programs and efforts to end abuse and aid in healing from abuse in their communities and throughout their nations.

95. Homosexuality (June 1993)

The General Assembly has, from time to time, deemed it appropriate to speak to the church regarding matters of spiritual, social, and ethical importance. In 1979 the Assembly passed a resolution titled "Statement Against Homosexuality" [see entry 81]. Since then the subject has emerged with spirited discussion in the public arena. It seems timely, therefore, that the Assembly once again address the subject with biblical conviction, compassion, and caring:

WHEREAS, there is a current national focus on homosexuality, frequently viewing it as an acceptable alternative lifestyle; and

WHEREAS, there is long-standing biblical evidence that a homosexual lifestyle is perverse and destructive to individuals and to society; and

WHEREAS, we in the Church of God are committed to biblical holiness and hold in high regard scriptural injunctions related to homosexuality and, therefore, cannot accept, endorse, or condone homosexual behavior; and

WHEREAS, we believe that the sexual relationship between man and woman within the bonds of marriage is viewed as something natural and beautiful—ordained of God; and

WHEREAS, we are a redemptive body and seek to express love, compassion, and concern for those who struggle with sexual identity or homosexual orientation to assist them in a chaste relationship in Christ; therefore be it

RESOLVED, that the General Assembly call on congregational and institutional leaders of the Church of God to demonstrate love and provide counsel and materials to assist families and persons confused or distressed by homosexual behavior and to bring redemption and wholeness to those persons; be it further

RESOLVED, that we respectfully urge all persons inclined toward homosexual behavior to seek the grace of God and such other aid and counsel as may be conducive to their relief; be it further

RESOLVED, however, that the General Assembly of the Church of God go on record affirming our conviction that, biblically, we believe homosexual behavior is sin; be it further

RESOLVED, that the General Assembly stands firmly opposed to the licensing, ordination, or approving for leadership those who are involved in this lifestyle; be it finally

RESOLVED, that the General Assembly supports instruction which brings understanding to issues related to homosexuality, but opposes instruction which endorses or promotes homosexual behavior as an acceptable alternate or Christian lifestyle.

96. Mental Illness (June 1993)

WHEREAS, approximately thirty million adult Americans suffer from one or more mental disorders, and of these as many as ten million are afflicted with chronic or prolonged mental illness; and

WHEREAS, approximately one percent of this country's population (about 2.5 million) have or will have the disease of schizophrenia, and about six percent have or will have a major affective disorder (major depression or manic depression); and as many as twelve million children suffer from some form of mental disorder, three million of whom have a serious mental illness; and

WHEREAS, persons with severe mental illness are estimated to account for as many as one-third or more of the nation's homeless, and occupy twenty-five percent of all hospital beds in the country; and

WHEREAS, the economic cost to society of mental illness is above $70 billion annually, of which $14.4 billion is for direct treatment and support costs; and

WHEREAS, because of ignorance, fear, and prejudice, mentally ill persons are not only stigmatized and discriminated against in housing, medical insurance, and employment opportunities, and are denied adequately funded treatment and support services, but are also often denied supportive fellowship in the church; and

WHEREAS, the families of mentally ill persons are frequently burdened by these illnesses and often serve as the primary caretakers of their loved ones, needing the support and love of friends and church, and yet often feel abandoned and shunned; and

WHEREAS, the church is called to engage in Christ's ministry of healing and advocacy on behalf of those who are ill in body, mind, and spirit and those who are discriminated against, lonely, unaccepted, and neglected; therefore be it

RESOLVED, that the General Assembly call upon the clergy and laity of the Church of God to avail themselves of knowledge of the plight of the mentally ill and their families and of the latest medical and scientific research into mental illness so as to dispel fear and prejudice; and be it further

RESOLVED, that the congregations of the Church of God be asked to evaluate their ministry among the mentally ill and seek a fuller, more imaginative, and compassionate ministry among this sizable segment of our society; and be it further

RESOLVED, that agencies of the General Assembly of the Church of God that are responsible for education and congregational nurture and ministry, including but not limited to the colleges, the university, the School of Theology, the Board of Christian Education, and Warner Press, be specifically encouraged to seek ways to assist the Church in fulfilling the intent of this resolution.

97. Ministry With the Disabled (June 1994)

WHEREAS, there is a national and worldwide focus on the needs of disabled persons; and

WHEREAS, in the United States alone, seventeen percent of the population suffers some disability (43 million persons); and

WHEREAS, there is long-standing biblical evidence of God's love and compassion being repeatedly extended to the disabled; and

WHEREAS, we in the Church of God are committed to biblical holiness and hold in high regard scriptural references and instruction in reference to the disabled; and

WHEREAS, we are a redemptive body and seek to express love, compassion, and concern for those who struggle daily with disability; therefore be it

RESOLVED, that the General Assembly call on the membership of the Church of God to demonstrate love, compassion, and counsel to assist disabled persons and their families in their struggle with disability; be it further

RESOLVED, that the Church of God seek to avoid any implication, by act of omission or commission, that the disabled person is a second-class citizen, and establish an increased level of sensitivity toward disabled persons' needs related to church gatherings; be it further

RESOLVED, that this Assembly request all Church of God congregations to work toward providing total accessibility for all facets of church worship and related activities, and endeavor to reach out to the disabled in their immediate communities, assuring spiritual accessibility as well; be it finally

RESOLVED, that the General Assembly call upon the leadership of our institutions of higher learning to examine the field of disability ministry and seek to activate appropriate academic curricula to equip present and future students with sensitivity and specialized training.

98. Freemasonry and Christianity (June 1994)

WHEREAS, the Church of God Reformation Movement has faithfully proclaimed that the Word of God declares Jesus Christ "the Way, the Truth, and the Life"; and

WHEREAS, the Word of God declares that no one comes to the Father but by the Son and that Jesus Christ is above every name whereby men must be saved; and

WHEREAS, Freemasonry is a Christless religion that omits the very name of Christ in its prayers and ritual and has a false view of God and the nature of God's salvation; and

WHEREAS, there is great danger that the Christian who becomes a Freemason will compromise Christian beliefs or allegiance to Christ (perhaps without realizing it); and

WHEREAS, there has been a lack of information and understanding of the true nature and bondage of Freemasonry and other similar secret lodges, societies, and organizations; and

WHEREAS, the secret nature of such lodges contravenes the Christian's open witness, and the secret nature of the oaths should be repugnant to the Christian; therefore, be it

RESOLVED, that the Church of God Reformation Movement reaffirm its historic position which proclaims that membership in secret societies and lodges which are oath bound is not compatible with the Christian loyalty to Christ.

F. Emphases, Studies, Celebrations

99. Declaration of Seminary Year (June 1960)

WHEREAS, this General Ministerial Assembly, upon the recommendations of the Budget Committee of the Executive Council and the Division of World Service, did last year (June 1959), designate the Special Project for the year 1960–61 to be the raising of $100,000 toward the erection of the first unit of the School of Theology building; and

WHEREAS, during the year 1960–61, when the campaign to raise this $100,000 will be in progress, those in charge of raising the fund wish to designate the year as SEMINARY YEAR IN THE CHURCH OF GOD, in order to focus the attention of the entire church upon the importance of training our young people for the Church of God ministry; be it

RESOLVED, that the General Ministerial Assembly hereby adopts the following proclamation:

To Every Member of the Church of God, Greetings:

Be it known that the General Ministerial Assembly of the Church of God and its several agencies hereby proclaim the year 1960–1961 as Seminary Year, during which time a special fund of $100,000 shall be raised for the erection of the first unit of the School of Theology building in Anderson, Indiana, for the training of ministers for the Church of God. Every congregation is urged to study this need and make provision to contribute toward this important work of the Church.

100. Greetings to the Zurich World Conference (June 1967)

In this 49th General Assembly of the Church of God, convened for the purpose of conducting the business of the Church, and the 78th International Convention, we as ministers and laymen pause to acknowledge our brethren in all countries of the world. We especially send greetings to you who are attending the Fourth World Conference in Zurich, Switzerland.

We feel a bond of love for you which is stronger than the tensions, misunderstandings, and estrangements which are so common between nations and cultures. The work of God in Christ has made us brothers and fellow workers.

The Assembly by a standing vote expresses to you its deepest Christian love and warmest fellowship. We live in a troubled and explosive world. Poverty, hunger, disease, illiteracy, social inequality, and rebellion are a part of our times. We pledge our faithful stewardship and cooperation with our brethren throughout the world in endeavoring to bring the peace of Christ and his deliverance, never letting up on the elimination of these evils.

While you are gathered in Zurich, we pray that the Holy Spirit will be real to each of you and that he will bring a flowing together of hearts so that you will truly experience fellowship at the deepest levels.

Where possible, we ask that delegates take our greetings and Christian love to the church in their home countries.

It was moved, seconded (Charles Weber-Albert Donaldson), and carried by a standing vote that these greetings be conveyed to the Fourth World Conference of the Church of God, Zurich, Switerland. [See entry 149 for a brief history of the World Conferences.]

101. Declaring a Year of Evangelism (June 1970)

WHEREAS, the Church of God has been invited to participate in the projected 1973 nationwide evangelism thrust, along with other religious communions; and

WHEREAS, the Board of Church Extension and Home Missions has offered its services in initiating the 1973 evangelism emphasis for the Church of God; and

WHEREAS, the Division of General Service sees great value in a carefully planned emphasis on evangelism, which will bring together interested agencies of the Church in a coordinated effort; and

WHEREAS, the Division of General Service has given its enthusiastic endorsement to the projected program and encourages the Board of Church Extension and Home Missions to initiate the planning, involving all interested agencies of the Church of God, for our participation in the Year of Evangelism Emphasis; therefore, be it

RESOLVED, that the Executive Council designate 1973 as the Year of Evangelism Emphasis, and that it seek the concurrence of the General Assembly by resolution, seeking its approval and support by urging each minister and each local congregation of the Church of God to cooperate fully in this program; and

RESOLVED, that we, the members of the General Assembly, do hereby concur in the action taken previously by the Division of General Service and the Executive Council in regard to the 1973 Nationwide Evangelism Thrust; and be it further

RESOLVED, that we pledge our enthusiastic cooperation in this concerted effort to make the Christian witness more vital and relevant in American society.

102. Call for a Consultation on Doctrine (June 1970)

The General Assembly sessions this year have helped us not only to see and handle our duties, but also to see and know our strong differences of opinion. Many of the expressed differences concern agency programs and decisions that were vigorously debated.

WHEREAS, some of the expressed differences reflected a possible problem of attitudes as well as opinions; and

WHEREAS, many of the differences reflect theological and doctrinal problems that need to be openly and honestly faced by this Assembly; and

WHEREAS, some of these problems grow out of evidently changing-patterns of our preaching, teaching, and publications across several decades; therefore, be it

RESOLVED, that we urge a serious restudy of the theological and doctrinal message of our Movement; and that the Executive Council and the School of Theology examine the feasibility of calling a "Consultation on Doctrine" to allow mutual discussion among us as leaders in faith and practice.

The intent of the Consultation will not be to prepare a creed or definitive statement of our position, but rather to hear and examine anew the doctrinal concerns that are important to our life and work as a movement.

Editor's note: For a review of the process that followed passage of the above resolution and a summation by William E. Reed of the useful purposes eventually served, see pages 527–31 of *The First Century*, volume 2, edited by Barry L. Callen (Anderson, Indiana: Warner Press, 1979).

103. Plan for a Centennial Celebration (June 1972)

WHEREAS, the Church of God, with general agencies in Anderson, Indiana, and with congregations in forty or more countries of the world, will reach its centennial at the end of this decade; and

WHEREAS, the Church of God around the world will want to celebrate its centennial in a way that pays tribute to those who have preceded us in this work and, at the same time, present an appropriate challenge to those in generations to come; therefore be it

RESOLVED, that the General Assembly, on this 21st day of June, 1972, concur in the recommendation of its Executive Council in confirming the time period for the Centennial Celebration as beginning with June, 1980, and extending through October, 1981; and be it further

RESOLVED, that the Executive Council be instructed to proceed through its committee on planning for an observance of the centennial in a manner commensurate with our spiritual heritage and our unrealized hopes.

104. Call for an Emphasis on Church Growth (June 1976)

WHEREAS, there is a continuous need for the Church of God to urgently and aggressively address its attention and resources toward a more adequate fulfillment of the commission given by Jesus Christ to His church; and

WHEREAS, in the last few years, there has developed a wide range of tools, techniques, and methods for stimulating church growth; and

WHEREAS, we believe God by His Holy Spirit is prompting the Church of God to intensify its efforts in a major evangelistic effort to win new persons to meaningful discipleship; therefore be it

RESOLVED, that the General Assembly of the Church of God, meeting in June, 1976, go on record, and hereby do, as endorsing a major effort within the church to stimulate church growth; and be it further

RESOLVED, that:

1. Such a church growth effort be launched July 1, 1978, and continue through June, 1980, in the midst of our centennial celebration, and that the program for church growth be designed and administered by a strategy committee as named earlier in this report;

2. The passage of this resolution mandates and pledges wholehearted support on the part of all national agencies of the Church of God in the United States of America for full cooperation and participation in a united effort for church growth;

3. The costs of this effort, as determined by the Strategy Committee, shall be funded through the budget of the Division of General Service by a grant approved by the Budget Committee, and included in the 1977–78 World Service Budget;

4. Members of the General Assembly who vote for this Resolution also pledge their full support to utilize the ministry and tools produced by the Strategy Committee for their congregations and areas;

5. The Strategy Committee will bring to this Assembly in June, 1977, a progress report on its work to date, and in June, 1978, the committee will bring a report setting forth specific and detailed goals for congregations, state and area assemblies, and national agencies, and a follow-through plan for reaching the projected goals;

6. The Division of General Service will bring to the 1981 General Assembly a summarization report on the effectiveness and accomplishments of the church effort.

105. Prayer and Plans for the 1980 World Conference (June 1977)

WHEREAS, it is the judgment of this Executive Council and General Assembly that immeasurable good has occurred as the result of the several World Conferences of the Church of God that have been conducted over the past several years [see entry 150 for a brief history of the Conferences]; and

WHEREAS, the different World Conferences have had a unifying effect upon the Church of God in many different nations and have served to clarify our thinking on many crucial issues to broaden our understanding and appreciation for persons in the Church of God in other parts of the world; and

WHEREAS, this Assembly has in many ways across many years given strong encouragement and support to the development of the several

World Conferences; therefore, be it

RESOLVED, that this Assembly extend to the World Conference of the Church of God a warm, cordial invitation to have the 1980 World Conference of the Church of God in Anderson, Indiana, in conjunction with the Annual Convention of the Church of God in June of 1980; and be it further

RESOLVED, that we instruct the executive secretary of the Executive Council to carry our Christian greetings and assurance of prayer and support to delegates meeting in the Strategy and Planning Consultation to be held October 17–26, 1977, in Nairobi, Kenya, East Africa; and be it further

RESOLVED, that we express our corporate concern for the success of this consultation and our promise of prayer for the guidance of the Holy Spirit by a standing vote of affirmation.

106. Goal-Oriented Plan for the Future (June 1983)

Editor's note: During 1983 final plans were being made for the major Consultation on Mission and Ministry scheduled for April, 1984, in Indianapolis. Many members of the Assembly were concerned that the Church of God did not seem to have a definite sense of direction as it prepared to move into the final years of the century. They also were hopeful that the substantial effort being invested in this coming consultation would result in more than a few generalizations that would not focus and energize the movement's ministries. A motion, therefore, emerged from the Assembly floor calling upon the coming consultation to work toward a specific goal-oriented plan for the coming years in the life of the Church of God. The Assembly adopted this motion. (For results of this consultation, see entry 122.)

107. Church Planting (June 1984, 1988)

WHEREAS, God has richly blessed the Church of God reformation with substantial congregational growth through the first century of its existence; and

WHEREAS, the General Assembly has established the Board of Church Extension and Home Missions to develop and provide services; and

WHEREAS, there is an urgent need for a more intensified effort in planting new churches among the Hispanics, Asians, Africans, Arabs, and more than 80 million unchurched Americans; and

WHEREAS, states and districts have assemblies, officers, state coordinators and Boards of Church Extension and Kingdom Builders to help do church planting and congregational revitalization; and

WHEREAS, the state coordinators, the national Board of Church Extension and Home Missions and the national Board of Christian Education have cooperated in selecting a State/National Task Force to seek ways to increase the planting of new churches; therefore, be it

RESOLVED, that the General Assembly recognize and affirm:

That the Church is most obedient to her calling when reaching the lost and unchurched of our nation and world;

That planting and nurturing new churches is biblical and an effective way to evangelize the lost;

That the ministry and support of church planting, as being done by state and district Boards of Church Extension and Kingdom Builders, continue to be done;

That there is a need for each indigenous congregation to consider sponsoring a new church; and,

That some persons are called and gifted as leaders for starting new churches and that they be urged to cooperate with a state and district Board of Church Extension and Kingdom Builders. And be it further

RESOLVED, that we recommend that the General Assembly enthusiastically accept and endorse the national strategy of church planting for the Church of God in North America for the next two decades as one of the major recommendations, goals, and ministries for the Church of God.

Editor's note: In the 1988 Assembly it was reported that since the 1984 action 106 new congregations of the Church of God had been launched. They were located in 36 different states or districts, representing a good beginning to a central and long term task. See entry 115.

108. Declaration of a Year of the Hispanics (June 1984)

WHEREAS, there has been a great influx of Hispanics in the 1970s and 1980s, principally in the southwest portion of the United States and in all major metropolitan areas; and

WHEREAS, Hispanic people constitute one of the largest and most rapidly growing minority groups in the United States; and

WHEREAS, an urgent need exists to evangelize and minister in Christian love to these new immigrants of Hispanic origin; and

WHEREAS, the Church of God is in a special position of responsibility and opportunity to broaden and increase its growing ministry among Hispanics; and

WHEREAS, there is great need to become better acquainted with Hispanic culture and language and to celebrate this contribution to the Church of God; and

WHEREAS, the Board of Church Extension and Home Missions, meeting in its annual session the 26th day of April, 1984, recommended to the Executive Council that 1986 be recognized by the reformation movement as a time for special attention focused upon the Hispanic community; and

WHEREAS, the Executive Council concurred in its meeting on May 10, 1984; therefore, be it

RESOLVED, that the General Assembly designate 1986 to be celebrated as the "Year of the Hispanics" and encourage general agencies and state organizations of the church to find ways to evangelize and minister within Hispanic communities.

109. Year of the Sunday School (June 1987)

Editor's note: In grateful recognition of the two hundred years of significant ministry of the Sunday school movement, the Board of Christian Education and the Publication Board jointly sponsored the following, which was affirmed gladly by the 1987 General Assembly.

WHEREAS, the Sunday school is a vital outreach and nurturing arm of the Church of God; and

WHEREAS, the Sunday school provides regular opportunity for teachers and learners to study the Bible for discovering God's instruction for contemporary living; and

WHEREAS, the Sunday school provides a time and a setting for unified and systematic study of Church of God doctrine and heritage throughout the Movement; and

WHEREAS, the Sunday school represents a rich history of strong lay involvement, enlisting the largest group of volunteer workers in the church; and

WHEREAS, the Sunday school provides opportunities for the training and development of leadership in the church; and

WHEREAS, the Sunday school is a basic component to church planting and growth strategies; therefore, be it

RESOLVED, that all agencies and congregations of the Church of God give support to the Sunday school and its leaders by declaring September, 1987 through August, 1988 to be "The Year of the Sunday School"; be it further

RESOLVED, that each congregation set September 13 as the date for launching of the Sunday school year; and be it further

RESOLVED, that we support the Sunday school through the use of "Journey With the Word" curriculum for the Church of God; and be it further

RESOLVED, that we enlist our Sunday schools in the Decade for Sunday School Development; and be it further

RESOLVED, that we emphasize the Sunday school through church growth and planting strategies.

110. Year of Revival in the Church of God (June 1987)

WHEREAS, the forces of Satan and sin continue their destructive assaults against the cause of Christ; and

WHEREAS, the Scriptures teach that true spiritual revival in the Body of Christ will not only restore God's blessing, power and healing to the Church, but will also bring healing to the land that has become sick unto death; be it, therefore,

RESOLVED, that the Executive Council of the Church of God designate as soon as possible, hopefully 1988–89, a "Year of Revival"; and be it further

RESOLVED, that the International Convention Program Committee for that year consider focusing on the "Revival" theme; and be it further

RESOLVED, that this resolution be sent to every national agency and that these agencies be encouraged to pick up on this emphasis in their planning and publications; and be it finally

RESOLVED, that during this time particular emphasis be given to the ministry of intercessory prayer and fasting.

111. Day of Prayer and Fasting (June 1987)

WHEREAS, there are many kinds of pressures that all persons, clergy and laity face as they minister in the Kingdom of God; and

WHEREAS, there is much disorientation about the morality, testimony, and lifestyle of Christians currently being witnessed by the world; and

WHEREAS, there is such an obvious need to reach this continent and the world for Jesus Christ; and

WHEREAS, the leadership needs of the church are so very great (the New Testament Church provides our example, see Acts 13:2–3); and

WHEREAS, the ministry opportunities to affect the spiritual and moral destiny of many people are numerous; and

WHEREAS, the Bible tells us that "our struggle is not against flesh and blood, but against the rulers, against the authorities, against the powers of this dark world and against the spiritual forces of evil in the heavenly realms" (Eph. 6:12) and we need divine help to stand; therefore, be it

RESOLVED, that the first Wednesday of each month during the 1987–88 fiscal year be a Day of Prayer and Fasting; and

RESOLVED, that every congregation of the Church of God be encouraged to promote and observe this Day of Prayer and Fasting; and

RESOLVED, that this program be administered by the office of the Executive Secretary of the Executive Council of the General Assembly of the Church of God; and

RESOLVED, that this observance begin July 1, 1987.

112. Year of Christian Higher Education (June 1988)

Refer to entry 59 for the content of this resolution highlighting the ministry of higher education in the life of the church.

113. Year of Canadian—United States Partnership in Ministry (June 1988)

WHEREAS, the Church of God in Canada has always been an integral partner in fulfilling the mission of the Church of God Reformation Movement in North America; and

WHEREAS, the population of Canada is approaching 30 million people comprised of many socio-ethnic cultures; and

WHEREAS, the nation of Canada has ten provinces and two territories, with the Church of God having 53 congregations located in six provinces; and

WHEREAS, the Canadian Church of God has established and supported the Christian higher educational institution, Gardner Bible College, to prepare laity and pastors for ministry and service, and has contributed numerous missionaries who have served in overseas assignments with the Missionary Board of the Church of God; and

WHEREAS, an urgent need exists to evangelize and plant congregations of the Church of God in Canada; and

WHEREAS, there is a great need to become better acquainted with Canadian congregations, and to recognize their contribution to the Church of God; and

WHEREAS, it is desirable to strengthen cooperation, improve relationship, and foster interdependence between the Church in the United States and Canada; therefore, be it

RESOLVED, that the two Canadian Assemblies along with the Board of Church Extension and Home Missions, Anderson, Indiana, recommend that the year 1990 be recognized by the Church of God in North America as a time to better understand the need and opportunities to evangelize and plant churches in the nation of Canada; be it further

RESOLVED, that the General Assembly designate 1990 as the "Year of Canadian—United States Partnership in Ministry" and encourage general agencies, state and area assemblies, and congregations to build supporting relationships with Canadian churches.

114. National Association's Diamond Jubilee (June 1991)

WHEREAS, the National Association of the Church of God with offices in West Middlesex, Pennsylvania, had its inception in August, 1917, when a group of saints, known as "The Brothers and Sisters of Love," held their first camp meeting in West Middlesex; and

WHEREAS, the National Association (hereafter identified by NA) since its beginnings 75 years ago has grown from a small farming community with rolling hills and wooded land to a camp ground site with modern cottages, retreat and recreational facilities and buildings with an assessed evaluation of more than two million dollars; and

WHEREAS, the primary motive in starting the NA was a desire of "The Brothers and Sisters of Love" for fellowship with those who believed in and practiced holiness; and

WHEREAS, the pioneers of the NA had no intent to start a schismatic movement apart from the international work of the Church of God in Anderson, Indiana, but rather to meet the needs among the Black saints for worship, fellowship, and service, and to enlist and develop its people without racist overtones and segregation control; and

WHEREAS, the NA is a vital and significant organization in the life of the Church of God and continues to make valuable contributions to the national and international life and ministries of the Church of God; and

WHEREAS, the impact and influence of the NA upon the Black community of the Church of God has been significant and immeasurable in terms of its scope and ministry, and constituency in the urban centers of our nation; and

WHEREAS, the NA has served as a catalyst for social change and cohesion to a significant number of the Black constituency of the Church of God and, at the same time, the NA has raised the social and political consciousness of the Church, resulting in some positive changes in race relations, employment, and attitudes; be it, therefore,

RESOLVED, that the 1991 General Assembly of the Church of God join the NA in celebrating its Diamond Jubilee by encouraging local congregations, state and regional assemblies, and national agencies to participate in the week-long celebration scheduled to take place during the Annual Campmeeting at West Middlesex, Pennsylvania, August 11–18, 1991; and be it

RESOLVED, that all local, state, and national Church of God publications be encouraged to promote the NA Diamond Jubilee Celebration in their newsletters, magazines and other appropriate publications; be it further

RESOLVED, that this Assembly declare August, 1991, to July, 1992, as the year of the NA throughout the Church of God; be it also

RESOLVED, that all pastors and congregations be encouraged to acquire and read the NA's Diamond Jubilee Historical Publication; be it finally

RESOLVED, that local congregations, regional and state assemblies, and the national agencies join in partnership with the NA to seek ways to evangelize the world, seek to solve racial problems, resolve church conflict, empower the poor and disadvantaged, and utilize our material and human resources for the up-building of the Kingdom of God.

115. Vision 2 Grow! (June 1991)

Rationale:

Jesus Christ, our Savior and Lord, commanded: "Go therefore and make disciples of all nations, baptizing them in the name of the Father and of the Son and of the Holy Spirit, and teaching them to obey everything that I have commanded you" (Matt. 28:19–20 NRSV);

The Mission Statement of the Church of God affirms that we seek "to enable persons ... to experience the redemptive love in its fullest meaning through the sanctifying power of the gospel and know Jesus Christ as Savior, Master and Lord";

In the nineties, looking forward to the next century, by faith and vision we believe:

• The Church of God has an opportunity to grow, to win more persons to Christ and help them find their place in the fellowship and ministry of a local church;

• Visionary, courageous, and trained pastoral and lay leadership can be enlisted and are essential to growth;

• The Spirit of God is convicting persons of sin and calling the church to be intensely involved in ministries of evangelism and to meet other human needs;

• The rapid change in the structures of society and in culture provides the church with a unique opportunity to proclaim and demonstrate the gospel.

Goals:

1. Church Growth—The Charge for the Future!

In response to the Great Commission, and in recognition of God's desire to increase the Church, we seek to:

A. Plant 60 new congregations each year.

B. Increase U.S. A.M. worship attendance to 200,000 by 1995 and to 225,000 by 2001, with similar growth in Canadian churches.

C. Renew biblical foundations, strengthen the family, and provide avenues for spiritual maturity.

D. Strengthen congregational response to world need.

E. Target 15 pastors of growing congregations to serve as partners in developing Vision 2 Grow! strategies.

2. Leadership

In response to the need for effective and visionary lay and clergy leadership we seek to:

A. Establish an intentional and focused effort for recruiting ministers.

B. Strengthen present tracks of ministerial enlistment training.

C. Create alternate models for in-service training and support.

D. Challenge and enable pastors and lay persons to: (1) Provide visionary leadership; (2) Exercise their unique gifts; (3) Be faithful to the trust placed in them.

Editor's note: In earlier years other Assembly actions had focused on similar concerns. See entries 101, 104, and 107.

116. Celebration of Ethnic Sunday (June 1992)

In October, 1492, Columbus' landing on San Salvador in the Bahamas was a historic event that triggered a tidal wave of global change that even today continues: the collision of the two worlds, the old and the new. This year our nation will commemorate 500 years since Columbus "discovered" the Americas. To celebrate while ignoring the pain of the natives who were already present when Columbus arrived is to be insensitive to our call as Christian peacemakers.

WHEREAS, we are a people called by God to be ambassadors of reconciliation for Christ; and

WHEREAS, millions of Americans, descendants of the Indians, Hispanic, Black, Asian, and other minorities feel the birthday of their country has been slighted by the so-called "500-year birthday celebration" of the Americas; and

WHEREAS, historians past and present have generally ignored the separate histories of minorities in the United States; and

WHEREAS, our Executive Secretary has challenged us as leaders to "be actively involved in our local communities in breaking down the barriers that destroy the lives of men and women and children who were created in God's image";

THEREFORE, the Spanish American Council of the Church of God in the U. S. A. invites the total Church to join us in a celebration of ETHNIC SUNDAY on October 4, 1992, whereby we can promote our unity in diversity by:

• Inviting minority pastors and leaders for pulpit exchanges, conferences, or seminars to enhance greater cross-cultural understanding;

• Planning workcamps into local communities or overseas to encourage people reaching out and working together;

• Promoting regional prayer services or prayer vigils in order to intercede for racial harmony in our cities, towns, and nation;

• Giving monies to our university, colleges, and other institutions of higher learning designated for minority scholarships.

Though Different in Race,
We Are One By His Grace.

Section III
Churchwide Consultations

All Board Congress and Planning Council (1963)
Consultation of the Church of God (1970)
Yokefellow Statement (1974)
Dialogue I on Internal Unity (1981)
Dialogue II on Internal Unity (1981)
Consultation on Mission and Ministry (1984)
Glossolalia and the Church's Life (1986)
Task Force on Governance and Polity (1987–92)
Mission of the Church of God (1988)
Cross-Cultural Consultation (1993)
Leaders' Visioning Retreat (1995)

Section III
Churchwide Consultations

117. All-Board Congress and Planning Council (1963)

Editor's note: The following is excerpted from the final report of the Findings Committee of the All-Board Congress and Planning Council, 1963.

On April 30—May 2, 1963, an All-Board Congress and Planning Council of the Church of God was convened in Anderson, Indiana, to facilitate and focus wide discussion on crucial issues then being faced by the movement as a whole. Some 260 persons participated in this intense and searching experience, including all national board members, selected national staff persons, all full-time state coordinators, and one representative from each state. In October 1963, the Findings Committee of the Congress summarized the results as follows.

We call for a clearer, more relevant expression of the existing theological foundations upon which this movement stands. We see the need for a rebirth of doctrinal emphasis, starting with the pulpit ministry and extending through all phases of the Church's life. Such a rebirth, we feel, should be undergirded in our educational work by clearly stated expressions of our faith published in readily available forms and appropriate for our people of all ages and at all stages of their Christian development.

We are discontented with where we have now arrived in the promulgation of our doctrinal position and see the need constantly to call up our teachings for reevaluation, particularly to see how they communicate living truth centered in a living Christ. In this way and through constant vigilance we would hope to avoid arriving at a dry and rigid creedalism which would undermine individuals whose faith is growing in an atmosphere of Christian fellowship and freedom under God. Serious theological discussion should be carried forward.

We recognize the need to maintain and build up a greater sense of unity among ourselves, achieving better and more harmonious working relationships. Our witness must begin with a more adequate demonstration of what we teach.

We recognize that we are not alone in our concern for unity. We have found, in working with our fellow Christians of other groups, kindred minds and spirits. We feel the need to increasingly express toward others the unity we teach, extending the loving fellowship and remembering that this is the basis of unity rather than intellectual uniformity.

While we feel the need to cooperate with other Christian groups, we are not looking toward mergers. We feel the need for more serious study on unity, perhaps by a duly appointed commission, which would find ways to enter into more serious dialogue with our Christian brethren. We must maintain the polarity of our position, expressing it more adequately and clearly while, at the same time, accepting our brethren as equals and as Christians.

To seek distinctiveness as a kind of denominational rationale is unjustifiable. At the same time, a genuine demonstration of Christian unity and of vital personal experience is an invaluable contribution in today's Christendom. If we are to make any distinctive contribution, we want to make sure it is of this kind. Perhaps any distinction should lie precisely in not setting up distinctives in the denominational sense.

We feel that our openness toward fellow Christians and to the truth, our conception of membership by salvation, the absence of creedalism, and our emphasis upon the dynamic nature of living relationships in Christ offer us some opportunity for Christian witness. It may be that our combination of teachings is significant, unity being possible only on the basis of truth and experience emphasized in this movement across the years.

As a church we need to know who we are, and why. It is possible to live on the memory of a few strong personalities who were able to rally a good force about them and make the mistake of taking their concepts of truth and attempting to confront today's situations with them. We may be united to one another and our rich heritage rather than united in Christ. We dare not become so preoccupied with ourselves that we feel that we must grow as a movement, forgetting that our mission may be to permeate society as others are doing, leaven that will benefit the whole loaf.

We register much concern that in the midst of our day-to-day ministry, in the press of pushing a program here and a project there, we have not given enough thought and prayer to developing and keeping sight of great, overarching goals. We feel our need of these to steer our everyday operations, to coordinate our efforts and measure our progress, and to draw us on as we take a long view of all the work that lies before us. We look toward such goals as means of helping us gain an enlarging sense of mission. Only in the light of such clearly defined major goals can we wisely discern the specific objectives we need to set before us. The big goals should not just lie in the haze of the horizon, but should be clearly drawn and carefully communicated.

A great theology, clearly understood, and great overarching goals, clearly conceived, mean little in themselves unless they are carefully harnessed to help the Church and its people carry forward significant ministry. We call for an increasingly adequate structure to serve as a channel for implementing our mission. We see a need for a broad study of national, state, and local structure in order to strengthen the work of the Church at every level in a coordinated way. We feel that increased lay representation is called for at all levels.

We see the need for strong local fellowships of the people of God to be of fundamental importance to the witness and outreach of the movement. Our total evangelistic thrust, our general sense of mission, our missionary out-reach demand strong local congregations.

The fact that a large percentage of our churches are perennially small, weak, and apparently lacking in resources to produce growth, was seen by the Congress to be a paramount concern.

The need to strengthen leadership, both layman and pastor, was felt to be of central importance. A better understanding of the autonomy of the local church was considered of basic importance. How can this freedom be used wisely in matters of congregational discipline, interpersonal relationships, seeking counsel, and the acceptance of guidance in choosing pastoral leadership?

We recognize the disturbing fact that the pastoral image needs upgrading, both within the Church and in our culture, that frequently the "parson" is no longer the important leader in the community, that often neither the man nor his congregation are thought to be of real importance in the community. There is need to face openly the relationship of "educational attainment" and the image of the pastor. There is need to understand the forces in society which help to create anti-clergy attitudes.

We recognized the growing and valuable role of our seminary in both the enlistment and training of pastors. Closer communication between the seminary and the local church and state-level organizations was seen as desirable.

Some means of in-service training for pastors was recommended. Continued, strengthened, and improved services on the part of the Division of Church Service was encouraged. Stronger state-level organization and better means of examining candidates as well as establishing higher standards of registration and ordination are desirable.

There is a strong feeling among us that we must seek and find a deep spiritual renewal if we are to find adequate motivation for the task ahead. It is not always more knowledge, better techniques, better training, or more tools we need—most of our people know more now than they are willing to use. There is definite agreement that we must cease striving for status or respectability as a church and return to a love for people that constrains us to give ourselves in Christian service because we care about the spiritual, physical, and social needs of others. This also will lead the church to be passionately concerned about winning others to Christ.

Evangelism is seen to be at the very heart of the Church. However, it is obvious that we are not getting the message to enough people fast enough. While in the early years of our movement we grew very rapidly, we seem to be settling down to the way of least resistance.

Major concern has been expressed regarding our knowledge of the world and its needs. Sometimes the sickness of the world communicates itself to the Church more than the Church communicates its life-giving message to the world. It would seem that we are using the language and meanings of another day to communicate with a modern and fast-moving generation. We need to say the same old message in new and different terms or at least bring this generation of new Christians up to date on our language.

We confronted the pressing need to involve the total ministries of the church, the need for full recognition of the scriptural concept of these ministries, and that of heightening the interest of the whole church in the so-called "lay ministries" beyond the usual "church work." A clarification of the lay and pastoral ministries is needed. Various kinds of preparation and training are needed to prepare the church to receive and adequately demonstrate the gifts of the Spirit in the total ministries of the church.

We need a strong emphasis on redemptive fellowship in the church. Often our acceptance of other denominations and even members of our own congregations has been conditional, based on whether or not they agreed with "Church of God" thinking. Perhaps we have forgotten the great inclusiveness of "being in Christ." People are going to church where they can receive help, healing, comfort, as well as where they can hear the

Truth preached. We need to be mindful of the needs of the total man.

It would seem that our ministry must be concerned with local, state, national, and even international problems of a social nature. Sometimes the ministry of the Church is not appreciated because we have seemingly closed our eyes to situations which exist, such as racial segregation. We have not been without our own problems as a movement. Perhaps we need to spend time and prayer eliminating our own problems before we talk too loudly.

118. Consultation of the Church of God (1970)

Editor's note: The 1970 Consultation of the Church of God was constituted (much like the one in 1963, see entry 117) with representation from the general agencies and from the state assemblies. It met with full awareness of the 1963 Congress, the findings of that earlier meeting having been widely distributed and discussed and the delegates having been given a review of those actions which had been taken to implement the findings.

An opening presentation of "the state of the church" suggested three focal points to keep in mind during the discussions:

1. The scriptural and theological base and imperative inhering in the mighty act of God through Jesus Christ, which gives the church its very life;
2. The social and practical reality of our time when people are hurting and lost and when Christians are called to incarnational involvement;
3. The relative and changing position of the Church of God movement within Christendom as it is expressed in fellowship and united witness.

The major work of this Consultation was to be done in six areas: (1) Social Concerns; (2) Unity; (3) Lay Ministry; (4) Evangelism; (5) Missions; and (6) Leadership. Coordinators had been appointed for each area and asked to prepare "projections" as a basis for study, analysis, and evaluation. Each area had three work groups with sharing times among the groups. Following are some of the issues addressed and points of the consensus reached.

1. Social Concerns

Issues: (1) What balance of social and individual emphasis? (2) How can we make the gospel relevant to all persons? (3) How can the church minister effectively in missions, evangelism, and unity, without seriously undertaking to bring reconciliation and equality within its own ranks?

Consensus: (1) Initiate creative programs relating to social concerns and encourage church agencies to do more; (2) Anticipate and plan rather than merely read; help black churchmen prepare for primary executive positions in the church; (3) Redefine and strengthen role in eliminating racism; (4) Disseminate success experiences in elimination of barriers; (5) Actively support churches and pastors who are attempting to overcome racism; (6) Develop and circulate courses of study setting forth biblical imperatives in social concerns; (7) Become a catalyst, prompting churches and pastors to programs of action; (8) Executive Council should clarify the function of the Commission on Social Concerns, giving it economic support and administrative integrity; (9) Continue dialogue between white and black churchmen that goes beyond polite conversation.

2. Christian Unity

Issues: (1) Where is the Spirit leading us in intra- and interchurch unity in the 1970s? (2) What is the nature of the unity we seek? (3) What opportunities and obstacles to unity confront the movement? (4) How can the Church of God best contribute to the ecumenical movement?

Consensus: (1) Polarities recognized were: inclusive vs. exclusive fellowship; social concerns vs. evangelism; "come-outism" vs. cooperative involvement; cardinal beliefs vs. tradition; diversity vs. uniformity; delegated assembly versus general assembly; (2) Recognition of racial divisiveness and the need to press for the removal of it; (3) Need to rethink sainthood and servanthood; (4) Find ways to utilize a larger variety of ministries; (5) Remain a nonjoiner but initiate more conversations with other groups; (6) Clarify responsibilities of the Committee on Christian Unity; (7) Officially endorse cooperative endeavors overseas; (8) Share insights on unity wherever doors are open.

3. Lay Ministry

Issues: (1) How can laymen best be supported in their own call and ministry in the everyday world? (2) What kind of training do laymen need to maximize their opportunities? (3) How can we broaden our base of planning and strategy to allow for their active participation at the planning, decision-making level?

Consensus: (1) Laymen do want to be significantly involved in the decision-making process; (2) Pastors should see their role more as opening up opportunities and giving guidance rather than trying to do everything themselves; (3) Institutes for laymen on college campuses for task-oriented study are needed; (4) Training institutes of longer duration for retired persons could prepare them for full or part-time leadership; (5) Study should be given to ordaining for lay ministries and the relation of that to baptism; (6) Lay ministry should be more than merely assisting in some "church work"; it should help identify authentic calls and support people in them.

4. Evangelism

Issues: (1) Are we an evangelistic people or have we gained mostly by those coming from other groups? (2) Are our methods of evangelism largely pulpit-centered and adequate for today and tomorrow? (3) What is evangelism, what are the essential ingredients? (4) Can we distinguish between personal evangelism and "gimmickry?" (5) Is our structure conducive and adequate for effective evangelization?

Consensus: (1) Admit that we have not been very evangelistic and need to seriously address this lack; (2) An evangelistic church is one characterized by warm fellowship, effective preaching, involvement with people and community, and a practical program of evangelistic outreach; (3) The time is overdue for evangelism as the primary thrust of the church; (4) Techniques of some interdenominational groups could well be utilized; (5) Special attention should be given to the inner city.

5. Missions

Issues: (1) With the rapidly changing scene in other countries as well as in our own, how can we better address the total task? (2) How can we achieve wider understanding and more informed cooperation in the church? (3) How can we best coordinate existing interest in the church and deploy it in a manner consistent with sound missionary policy? (4) What employment should be made of experienced (perhaps retired) people for specialized needs?

Consensus: (1) Schools are vital on the mission fields; perhaps some relocation is advisable; (2) Missions should be approached on an international basis, perhaps through some kind of international board; (3) Lay people, with orientation and training, should be used at strategic places;

(4) There is need for skilled staff personnel in securing large gifts; (5) Missions conventions should be encouraged and guided by the Missions Board; (6) Active recruitment of youth for missionary work is needed; (7) Missionary work means sharing in the ghetto as well as overseas; (8) We suffer a credibility gap in missions unless we find solutions to division at home; (9) To avoid the "brain drain," we should foster advanced education of nationals in their own countries.

6. Leadership

Issues: (1) What is the authentic role of the pastor? (2) Do we need a more structured approach to pastoral "placement?" (3) What is the rightful role of women in leadership? (4) What relationship exists between lay leadership development and the preparation of pastors? (5) What will be required of the leader in the new urban society? (6) Should the General Assembly agree on criteria for leadership? (7) What relation is there between leadership of the Holy Spirit and a reasoned, even structured approach to leadership development and deployment?

Consensus: (1) Pastoral leadership is crucial if competent laymen are to be actively involved in God's work; (2) There is a shortage of pastoral leadership, not quantitative but qualitative; (3) Ministerial drop-out is a serious problem. We need an effective support system for pastors; (4) There should be some youth representation on the Executive Council; (5) Leadership by the Holy Spirit mixes with human understanding and rational processes; (6) The minister should be "married to the mission, not to the church"; (7) Members of credentials committees should be trained with a code developed for their work; (8) We must help the church to think in terms of ability, not color; (9) Youth should be encouraged to select freely those with whom they wish to associate, regardless of racial differences.

119. Yokefellow Statement (1974)

Editor's note: Eighteen members of the Division of General Service and seven state coordinators gathered at Yokefellow House in Richmond, Indiana, May 9–10, 1974, to give prayerful consideration to the specific objectives to which they judged the attention and resources of the Church of God should be brought to bear in the immediate years leading up to the movement's centennial celebration in 1980–81. They called for and pledged themselves to objectives in five areas.

1. Identity

We affirm the reformational role of the Church of God movement and, in keeping with this affirmation, call the church to repentance, cleansing, and reconciliation—both among ourselves and toward God—to the end that we may reestablish and renew our covenant relationship with God and each other, restore the biblical root system of our heritage, and thus nourish those things that draw us together as a people on mission for God in today's rootless and fragmented world.

In order to accomplish this, we covenant together that we will stress through every available channel the crucial importance of responsible study and exposition of the Holy Scriptures in all of our preaching and teaching, with particular emphasis upon the centrality of Jesus Christ in his body, the Church, and upon the fulfillment of his mission in the world.

2. Relationships

In keeping with the historical dedication of the Church of God movement to Christian unity, individual freedom, and brotherhood, we affirm the importance of the unity that exists among us. While recognizing individual creativity and initiative, we call for responsible commitment to the Church's total mission at every level of its life and work, from the local to the world-wide, as our supreme objective. In our united opinion, this objective calls for:

1. Complete obedience to Christ and his Word;
2. Recognition of the dignity and freedom of human personality;
3. Commitment to each other as members of the Body of Christ;
4. Loyalty to, and support of the church's institutions and programs which we have created together;
5. Openness to the continuing revelation of God's Spirit in our common life.

It is our belief that the New Testament sets forth the ideal that all Christians should be able to learn from one another. We maintain, moreover, the conviction that this movement represents a force of reformation leadership within Christendom with its emphasis on ecumenicity based on unity rather than on union. To this end, therefore, we encourage through every means possible the establishing and maintaining of work relationships with other like-minded groups on the national, state, and local levels.

3. Ministry

The major purposes of the Church of God movement, so far as its origin and continuing life are concerned, must be clarified sufficiently to strengthen our ministerial and lay leadership in their preaching and teaching roles, with particular emphasis in the following areas:

1. To be more creative to discover, train, deploy, and conserve leadership;

2. To initiate programs and processes that are biblically centered for understanding and addressing social ills and injustices;

3. To promote the Christian ministry as a viable, exciting vocation and insist upon quality training;

4. To challenge our finest young men and women to give themselves in ministry;

5. To develop support systems for clergy where ministers and/or members of their families can find adequate counsel during marital, financial, physical, emotional, or vocational stress.

In keeping with the purposes of the Church of God movement, we urge that doctrinal concepts be periodically reviewed for strengthening the church's convictions. We further urge that the motivating force for ministry be rediscovered in order that the Church of God may have purpose for continued being.

4. Integration

The Church by nature is one; therefore, the Church must continuously work its way through and beyond racial relationships to functional unity. It must be recognized and admitted, in doing this, that racist attitudes are incompatible with the Christian gospel of oneness, brotherhood, and love. As we work toward functional and visible unity, the following objectives should be kept clearly in mind:

1. Continue to emphasize the positive things which are being done to include persons of different racial and cultural origins and backgrounds in the decision-making processes at all levels of the Church's life and work;

2. Increase dialogue among persons of all races and cultures with a view toward helping local congregations of the Church of God become more effective and inclusive in their evangelistic and missionary outreach programs in the homeland and abroad;

3. Encourage and make possible the enrollment and training of youth from minority and ethnic groups included within the membership of the Church of God in our church-related colleges;

4. Further explore the structuring of state, regional, and national organizations of the Church of God in order to more truly express the oneness of the Church in the fulfillment of its mission in the world;

5. Recognize that attitudes relating to race must always be interpreted in light of the social environment and climate in which the Church carries forth its mission, but without any compromise with the principles of the Christian gospel.

5. Polity

We affirm and recognize that the local congregation is the primary unit of ministry and outreach for fulfilling the Church's mission in the world, the stabilizing of the home, and in alleviating the tensions that undermine society. In order to strengthen the local congregation, we urge:

1. Better leadership preparation at all levels;

2. Stronger emphasis on personal and group study of the Word of God as a complement to public proclamation;

3. Development of greater stewardship commitment by individuals and congregations.

We further plead for the development of more precise lines of responsibility, cooperation, and communication between the local, state and national organizations of the Church of God that will reflect our interdependent relationships. Some areas in which this could serve a useful purpose are:

1. Providing for a greater degree of participatory democracy in the life and government of the Church;

2. Cooperative planning, programming, goal-setting, and budgeting;

3. Congregational and ministerial certification and credentials;

4. Establishment of new congregations and agencies.

120. Dialogue I on Internal Unity (January 1981)

Editor's note: The period 1980–1981 saw significant controversy in the life of the Church of God. To assist helpfully in bringing the most significant issues into focus and in bringing representatives of varying viewpoints into direct and prolonged discussion about these issues, the Board of Directors of the Executive Council convened a dialogue on internal unity. Present were thirty leaders invited because of their leadership roles in the national, state, and local ministries of the Church of God. The group decided upon its own agenda, choosing three major areas with the first, biblical inspiration and authority, receiving the most attention. The results of searching and intense discussion were mailed to all members of the General Assembly. They were as follows:

Issue 1: Biblical

How can the Church of God more adequately understand our position on the authority, inspiration, and nature of the Bible?

- Where are we agreed in our view of Scripture?
- Where are we not yet agreed?
- How much diversity can we have and still maintain unity?

<u>Affirmations—We Are Agreed That</u>:

1. The Bible is the inspired Word of God—the source of authority for Christians in faith, doctrine, and practice (2 Tim. 3:16–17).
2. The Bible is fully trustworthy and without error in its revelation of the will of God concerning man in all things necessary to salva tion and Christian living.
3. We must depend on the Holy Spirit's guidance in interpreting the Scriptures.
4. The individual and corporate study of the Bible is essential to effec tive discipleship and mission in the world today.
5. Our technical differences pertaining to Scripture in no way call into question our commitment to the authority of Scripture.
6. In our view of Scripture there are still areas where we hold divergent views. This does not jeopardize our fellowship or our Christian commitment.

Issue 2: Structural

What form of structure or polity can best serve the Church of God as it moves into its second century as a reformation movement in such areas as:

- The selection of leaders to serve national corporations, state organizations, and local congregations?
- The establishing of channels of communication through which more adequate information can be shared with the General Assembly by those who serve in leadership positions and who are accountable to the Assembly?
- The place of lay persons in the decision-making processes of the church—nationally, state, and local?

Some Recommendations

1. That a study be made of General Assembly functions which include frequency, location of, and duration of meetings; the nature and format of the agenda. (Consider dialogue need and rotation of location.)

2. That a review be made of the nature of accountability of boards and agencies, Executive Council and its subordinate units and related para-church groups, and to develop guidelines by which that accountability can be expressed to the General Assembly.

3. The study should involve widespread participation of the church at large.

4. Recommended to the Board of Directors that it encourage the Committee on Long Range Planning to initiate a continuing process which will allow all ministers of the church to share their views regarding the costs and priorities of the several agencies.

5. Use state and regional meetings as settings for communication seminars (to inform how national agencies function and means of access to them).

6. To develop a design for prayer support groups for individual agency personnel and their work.

7. A serious concern is expressed that our colleges are essentially unrelated and competitive. Some initiative should be taken to speak to this major problem.

Issue 3: Relational

What kind of unity do we seek in regard to social and moral issues as we are confronted by the mandates of Scripture regarding these? More specifically, are we seeking agreement of stance on the various contemporary social, moral and ethical issues?

(a) as a united voice of the church?

(b) as a common view of the world?

(c) as a common interpretation of Scripture?

(d) as a test of fellowship?

(e) as a measure of acceptability of leaders?

Some Recommendations

1. We recommended the development of scholarly statements on crucial social issues confronting the church. These can be printed resources, tapes or video-tapes which can be used in church study groups. These should present the various sides so that persons can "think" through what

their own stance is. Positions of respected Church of God leaders should be clearly stated.

2. Develop a pattern of bringing together the best minds from the diverse points of view to dialogue in depth on selected issues. Resulting information and conclusions could be used in preparation of resources for #1.

3. Explore ways in which existing meetings may be used to dialogue on the crucial issues faced in ministry; i.e., General Assembly and ministers meetings.

4. Make a better effort to include the conservative voice in deliberations on social issues from which study resources and position papers may be produced.

121. Dialogue II on Internal Unity (December 1981)

Editor's note: The General Assembly was kept well informed about the results of the second Dialogue, convened in December, 1981, by the Executive Council. Paul Tanner, Executive Secretary of the Council, reported to the Assembly that "issues of general interest did provide a free and open exchange of views, but there was no overriding issue as experienced in Dialogue I." The twenty-eight participants representing fourteen different states decided to discuss three subject areas. They came to the following points of consensus and recommendations.

Issue I: Priesthood of Believers

Consensus

1. The Scripture does support an orderly process in the work of the Church, but does not prescribe a specific polity.

2. We believe in the priesthood of believers, but this concept does not determine the specific numerical composition of the General Assembly.

3. We value increased involvement of Spirit-gifted lay persons in the General Assembly of the Church of God and its various structures.

4. The present proposed model for increasing lay participation in the General Assembly will not likely be accepted by the Church.

Recommendations

1. That lay participation be selected from and by existing formal assemblies.

2. Unless the Bylaws Committee can come up with a proposal that

gives greater evidence of acceptability, that they request a year's further study.

Issue 2: Leadership Development in Higher Education

Consensus

1. We have a genuine appreciation for the richness and diversity among our institutions of higher education and express concerns only out of a sense of stewardship for these resources.

2. We sense a great deal of frustration among ourselves over the competition and independency of action on the part of our educational institutions and other problems relating to the need for overall coordination and supervision of our higher educational process.

Recommendation

That the Board of Directors of the Executive Council appoint a committee to study ways similar communions structure their institutions of higher education and make recommendations for the corporate structuring of our approach to higher education.

Issue 3: Church of God Response to World Issues

Consensus

The Church of God has a biblical mandate to be involved in world issues by caring and doing.

Recommendations

1. Need to cultivate greater awareness of what is being done and should be done, by focusing on these in church publications and news media.

2. Upgrade image and work of Commission on Social Concerns by changing the name and assure that the membership is more inclusive (not only those of vested or concentrated interest) to increase its effectiveness.

3. Suggest that the 1983 International Convention Program Committee develop a theme emphasis to speak to a response to world issues, with speakers who can/will focus on the positive, evangelical Kingdom—now.

4. Suggest that the editor of Vital Christianity consider an issue with the theme of Church of God World Responsibility in the areas listed.

122. Consultation on Mission and Ministry (1984)

Editor's note: An intensive study and evaluation of the structure and function of the Executive Council was commissioned during the mid-1970s. Among the issues that emerged in that study was one expressing the need for the Church of God to be involved in long-range planning in a more aggressive and coordinated way. Up until that time the only instance of coordinated effort at long-range planning at the national level was lodged with the Division of General Service.

Restructuring was decided on and included the termination of the Division of General Service and the formation of the Committee on Long Range Planning. Very early in its work this new committee established its own priorities. It quickly recognized that it could not, on its own, formulate goals for the work of the church. This recognition gave rise to the idea of a national consultation that would be broadly representative of the total church in all of its diversity. Initial approval for such a consultation was given by the Executive Council in May, 1982.

Selected Church of God leaders from across the United States and Canada (total of 135) convened in Indianapolis April 2–5, 1984, for provocative and stimulating dialogue. The event was identified as a major Consultation on Mission and Ministry. It was the most representative and ambitious attempt of its kind in Church of God history. What follows is a brief summary of the central concerns and goals projected by this Consultation for the Church of God movement to the end of the century.

Area I

Concern: Truth—Here We Stand!

Purpose: To affirm the biblical foundations for the mission and ministry of the church and highlight central biblical teachings.

Goal: To establish the Bible as the authority for the faith and life of the church. We live in a time when traditional authority is questioned and an increasing number of persons, even in the church, are biblically illiterate. The Bible must be accepted as authoritative in the church and its contents must be taught and preached with clarity, discipline, and integrity.

Goal: To witness to those biblical truths central to the particular mission of the Church of God movement. The effectiveness of the ministry of the Church of God depends heavily on its own understanding of its distinctive mission as a particular fellowship and movement among God's people. The biblical truths central to this distinctive mission must be clarified, taught, and lived out.

Goal: To understand the church as a covenant community called to servanthood. The church today lives in an unstable and materialistic society. To be a faithful, influential and relevant witness in the world, the church must become a covenant community dedicated to the service of persons for the sake of Christ. This will require a biblical understanding of covenant and servanthood. It also will require sacrifice, even suffering.

Area II

Concern: Into All the World

Purpose: To broaden the church's understanding of world concerns and to motivate the church to fulfill its mission and ministry in the world. It is possible for the church to live in the world, but remain aloof and "not a part of the world."

The church is called to act within the world but not let the world squeeze it into its mold.

Let the church be the church—the model of ministry, care, and concern guided by its understanding of the world in which it lives and works.

Goal: To work toward global awareness and to recognize our responsibility to the whole world in Christian action and concern for world issues.

Goal: To sensitize the Church of God to the cultural distinctives of all persons in our world and to affirm their God-given dignity.

Goal: To become involved as the people of God who work for change at those points where the gospel speaks to the world in which we live.

Area III

Concern: Mission—Good News!

Purpose: To understand the mission of the church to present the gospel to every person through the power of the Holy Spirit at work in us.

Goal: To develop a statement of the mission of the Church of God Reformation Movement. The Church of God has always been a people on mission, a people with a purpose. As we seek to clarify our own understanding of our unique message and mission, state it forthrightly and communicate it to others, we will be able to live it out more effectively. [See entry 125 below for such a mission statement.]

Goal: To equip persons to evangelize, nurture, and bring to maturity all persons who are lost from God and separated from one another. As we become more sensitive to the many ways persons are separated from God and each other, we will become increasingly motivated to lead them to

Christ. In response to the Great Commission we will go out in the power of the Holy Spirit to make disciples. We will continue to teach and equip one another for this task.

Goal: To challenge the Church of God to redemptive action in relation to the social issues of our time. To serve Christ is to serve in the arena of human need. Our ministry of reconciliation must take us into the middle of the world's problems with redemptive action. We will respond to Christ's call to "preach good news to the poor ... proclaim release to the captives and recovering of sight to the blind, to set at liberty those who are oppressed!" (Luke 4:18).

Area IV

Concern: A Living Church

Purpose: To live out a ministry that fulfills the mission of the church as the people of God.

Goal: To prize the family as the basic unit in God's design for human relationships. The family, vital to every person's fulfillment, is an endangered species. Fast-paced living is emptying homes, making them temporary storage places and little more. But the family is of God's design, and we are stewards of this resource. The Church must help families to live in wholeness.

Goal: To strengthen the competence and effectiveness of ministerial-leadership in the church. The care and feeding of leaders is essential to the living church. Many, however, are crippled in effectiveness, wounded in the line of duty, unprepared, undisciplined for the challenges of a changing world. The church must offer the guidance and support to heal our healers.

Goal: To understand the biblical foundations for accountability and inclusiveness in ministry. Congregational freedom has not offered redemptive or useful ways to bring accountability to ministry. Conflicts often become diseases of destruction rather than building blocks for new strength. Women are being called, trained, ordained for ministry, but few are called to local pastorates.

Goal: To inspire all believers to use their gifts in the ministry of the church. Preparation and call of lay persons to a ministry of the common life is needed to release some of God's best, but least discovered resources for ministry. Lay muscles will mobilize the church.

Goal: To mobilize the church to implement the national strategy for church planting as adopted by the General Assembly, June, 1984. A surge of renewal for the movement will happen as we plant new churches. Seven hundred and seventy-three new congregations in ten years is a goal which can revitalize the movement, but only by a massive strategy of cooperation. The involvement of everyone is needed to achieve such a goal.

Area V

Concern: Being the Body of Christ

Purpose: To develop mutually interdependent relationships that enable the church to be effective in fulfilling its mission and ministry within the whole body of Christ.

Goal: To affirm the value and to strengthen the practice of interdependence within the Church of God. Throughout our history we have experienced a growing understanding of the importance of interdependence to the successful achievement of our goals. For both practical and theological reasons we know that "we really do need each other."

Goal: To determine and develop the best structures that best express interdependence and enable ministry and mission in the Church of God throughout the world. There is always more than one way to get a job done. Throughout our history we have sought to be sensitive to the Holy Spirit and responsive to the needs in creating structures to do the work of the church. We will continue to create structures that reflect our need for interdependence. [Note international examples highlighted in entires 150, 151.]

Goal: To establish specific time-related goals to be implemented through the church's interdependent structures. We increasingly sense the need for setting specific goals for implementing our mission and ministry. For the goals to have meaning they must be the result of the widest possible involvement of the church at all levels. We sense a special call to give attention to growth and evangelism goals.

Goal: To expand ministries through voluntary relationships with church groups outside the Church of God reformation movement. Our quest for Christian unity brings us into relationships with all members of the Body of Christ. Through voluntary relationships we can often achieve our mission more effectively and expand our ministries.

Goal: To lift up the responsibility of every congregation for ministry to the whole world, affirming our interdependence in recognition of the enormity of the task of global evangelization. The task of global evangelization is enormous. The common mission we share calls us to live out our Christian unity and to experience interdependence as we seek to fulfill our common discipleship in the world.

123. Glossolalia and the Church's Life (June 1986)

Editor's note: During the 1985 General Assembly a resolution was presented from the General Assembly of Ohio. It called for the establishment of a study committee "composed of qualified individuals from the academic and pastoral fields to study the work of the Holy Spirit as related to glossolalia in light of Scripture, our historical perspective, and present happenings in the Church of God movement." The resolution was referred to the Executive Council through which a study committee was named. In June, 1986, the committee submitted an extensive report. The Assembly received it with appreciation and commended "for careful study and guidance throughout the Church of God the biblical guidelines, observations, and recommendations contained in this report." In part they were as follows.

With particular reference to the gift of tongues, the following are understood to be biblical guidelines for its definition and exercise:

A. A gift of tongues is listed in the New Testament as one of the gifts which a given believer might receive as God chooses. Defining and governing the exercise of such a potential gift are important and difficult tasks in the context of the life of the contemporary church and in light of the limited biblcal teaching on the subject.

B. A gift of tongues, however defined, is not given to all Spirit-filled believers (1 Cor. 12:28–30) and is not the evidence of the infilling of the Holy Spirit. Paul's discussion of evidence, as seen in 1 Corinthians 12—14, clearly states that a life of love is the essential evidence. Chapter 14 must be understood in the context of chapters 12 and 13, particularly 1 Cor. 12:1–3 and chapter 13.

C. Which gift or how many gifts a person is given is not a factor in that person's salvation or sanctification. What is a factor is the reception of the Gift, that of the Holy Spirit (Acts 1:8 and Romans 8:9). A gift of tongues, therefore, should not be regarded as proof of spirituality on the part of the speaker. Any insistence to the contrary lies outside biblical teaching and leads easily to distortion in the meaning and intended use of spiritual gifts.

D. A gift of tongues, according to the instances recorded in Acts, probably was the supernaturally-given ability to speak in human languages not previously learned by the speaker. If so defined, the purpose of this gift was (1) to provide a tool for the multilingual proclamation of the gospel and/or (2) to provide a sign of the universal nature of the Christian faith.

E. A gift of tongues, according to the teaching in 1 Corinthians, is less clear in its nature. While it could have been a deterioration of the phenomenon of tongues at Pentecost or an extreme emotionalism related to local pagan practices, it may well have been a gift to some Christians of the ability to speak in the presence of God, which speaking required interpretation in public worship (1 Cor. 14:2). Whatever its nature, its manifestations in Corinth involved a range of problems which called for strict pastoral discipline. The problems centered in wrong personal attitudes, a misunderstanding of spiritual gifts, and unacceptable public practices. These problems were addressed by the Apostle Paul in part through the giving of the following guidelines.

1. Unintelligible speech in public worship is unacceptable (1 Cor. 14:9).

2. A gift of tongues should be seen as the least of the gifts because the person who so speaks without interpretation (unless in private) addresses God and does not directly edify the church through exercising the gift. A gift like prophecy, the ability to communicate clearly the word of God, is to be valued as a greater gift (1 Cor. 14:1–12, 19).

3. A gift of tongues should not violate the assumption that Christian worship services should be characterized by dignity, orderliness and self-control (1 Cor. 14:23, 32, 40).

4. A gift of tongues, if exercised in a public service, requires the presence and exercise of another gift, the gift of interpretation. Because the purpose of spiritual gifts is the upbuilding of the church, this latter gift is needed to bring the former back into the realm of common understanding and edification. If a gift of tongues is exercised publicly, it is to be governed by the following (1 Cor. 14:26–32):

a. Only two or three persons may so speak in one service;
b. Never should more than one person speak at the same time;
c. Someone must always interpret the speaking or it is not appropriate to proceed;
d. There should be no confusion, only decency, order and edification.

The following are offered as biblical guidelines for local church life.

1. Local congregations of the Church of God are urged to give careful attention to acquainting persons with the traditional beliefs and practices of the Church of God regarding glossolalia (particularly the biblical guidelines stated above).

2. Congregations also are urged to teach the central importance of the work of the Holy Spirit in the lives of believers and in the process of genuine Christian worship.

3. Corporate authority over individualistic assertiveness in congregational life is vital. Submission to each other in the Spirit of Christ is a key to harmonious church life.

4. Persons who feel that it is important to promote private manifestations and/or public demonstrations of a gift of tongues in violation of Biblical guidelines should not expect leadership positions in Church of God congregations.

5. Any proposal for major change in a congregation's worship style or practices should be implemented with sensitivity to the whole congregation and not merely in response to the preference of a few, including the pastor. Congregations contemplating such a major change might well seek counsel first from respected Church of God leaders outside the congregation.

6. While not wishing to build walls between Christians, serious concern is expressed about the negative effects on local congregations coming from well-financed Christian groups promoting charismatic concepts and practices opposed to the Biblical guidelines stated above.

124. Task Force on Governance and Polity (1987–1992)

Editor's note: The Task Force on Governance and Polity was established by the June, 1987, General Assembly and given the charge "to undertake a wide-ranging analysis of present governance and polity traditions, assumptions, structures, and relationships; to develop recommendations for enhancing the effectiveness of governance and polity—congregational, state and national—to the end that mission and ministry are strengthened." The assignment became one of five years, with substantive progress reports made to the Assembly annually. The fourth report was given in June, 1991. It detailed "emerging priorities" and identified as a basic issue "the tension between authority and autonomy." While the final report would come in 1992, the 1991 report presented five recommendations, all of which were approved by the Assembly. These follow.

1. Expanded Lay Membership in the General Assembly.

We recommend that all categories of present membership ... be maintained.... We further recommend that the following persons who are properly named and present in any meeting shall be members of the Assembly, effective with the General Assembly of 1993:

- one layperson from each congregation, AM attendance to 100;
- two laypersons from each congregation, AM attendance to 500;
- three laypersons from each congregation, AM attendance to 1,000;
- four laypersons from each congregation, AM attendance over 1,001.

We further recommend that this action receive a full evaluation and after three years of operation, with the Executive Council directed to design and conduct the evaluation, recommend action related to continuation, and bring that recommendation to the 1996 General Assembly for ratification.

2. Establishment of a Mission and Ministry Triennial.

We accept the general recommendation ... regarding establishing a Mission and Ministry Triennial ... and request the Task Force to develop further details and projections in its 1992 report. [This Triennial was further recommended in 1992 and rejected by the Assembly.]

3. Expectations of the Executive Council.

1. Act as the central corporate body for envisioning church-wide direction, formulating goals, and initiating follow-up to established directions and goals.

2. Be the central coordinative body for national ministries of the Church.

3. Provide a viable and strengthened linkage between national and state ministries.

4. Call national agencies to accountability with respect to those directions and goals which the General Assembly or Executive Council has approved or established.

5. Oversee the performance and management of the legal, administrative and financial responsibilities of the Council in its relationships with the national agencies, national and international conventions, and other segments of the work of the Church of God.

4. Executive Council: Membership, Name, Meetings.

(Tentative thinking on changes in the Council's membership, name, and meeting time were presented. The Assembly concurred in general and asked for definitive recommendations by 1992.)

5. Renewal Among National Corporations.

We recommend that the following take place in 1991–92:

• That the Task Force continue to nurture constructive dialogue among representatives (staff and boards) of these national corporations; and

• That the Executive Secretary of the Executive Council, within the spirit of the earlier recommendations concerning that office, initiate fresh cooperative consultations among the national corporations, built around the service clusters listed above; that new programming be cleared through these consultations.

Editor's note: The final report in 1992 contained nine additional recommendations, all approved except the proposed Triennial. One was altering the name of the Executive Council to Leadership Council. Another was authorizing a study of possible restructuring of the national work of the church.

125. Mission of the Church of God (June 1988)

The mission of the Church of God is to be a caring community of God's covenant people under the Lordship of Jesus Christ and the leadership of the Holy Spirit:

• To proclaim the love of God, through Jesus Christ, to all persons;

• To enable persons throughout all the world to experience redemptive love in its fullest meaning through the sanctifying power of the Gospel and know Jesus Christ as Savior, Master, and Lord;

• To call persons to holiness and discipleship;

• To equip persons to be servants of Christ in the world;

• To live as citizens of the Kingdom of God here and now, work for justice, mercy and peace, and abide in the Christian hope;

• To build up the whole body of Christ in unity.

Editor's note: This statement was developed by the Committee on Long Range Planning, endorsed by the Executive Council and General Assembly, and "commended to the Church as a resource and working document in the pursuit of its multi-faceted ministries."

126. Cross-Cultural Consultation (November 1993)

Editor's note: Under the sponsorship of the Leadership Council of the Church of God, a Cross-Cultural Consultation was conducted in Anderson, Indiana, on November 9–11, 1993, at the North Anderson Church of God. It's primary purpose was to provide a broadly-based group from a variety of cultural and ethnic backgrounds a forum to discuss hurts and healing, to consider commitment to each other, and to the common mission, to celebrate our unique distinctives, and to review ways to strengthen one another in ministry. The Consultation included the goals of communication, intentional commitment, building appreciation, rejoicing in victories won, planning together, and considering models of intercultural ministry underway.

The more than 100 persons in attendance included Black, Hispanic, Indian American, Middle Eastern, Asian, and White representatives. Also represented were all national agencies, the Board of Directors of the Leadership Council, the Commissions on Christian Unity and Social Concerns, the national Long Range Planning Committee, the Divisions of World Service and Church Service, Area Administrators from states and areas, WOMEN OF THE CHURCH OF GOD, the National Association, the Hispanic Concilio, the Native American Mission, and presenters of cross-cultural ministry models.

The Consultation gave primary attention to patterns of credentialing of ministers, expressions of racism and empowerment, concerns for interrelated worship and structure, desire to fully understand schisms in the Body, efforts to bring healing to hurts, and other such matters of faith in action. Early attention was given to knowing about and appreciating the stories of life and ministry each brought to the Consultation.

Concluding attention was given to possible action steps by which the total church might be strengthened to reach across cultural and ethnic lines to demonstrate for society the oneness of Christians on mission and to model how diversity and distinctiveness can be valued and utilized in a united witness. It was hoped that such consultations would be repeated at state and regional levels to bring a continuing sensitivity to this need.

127. Leaders' Visioning Retreat (January 1995)

Editor's note: In light of the Assembly's decision in 1992 not to approve a Mission and Ministry Triennium, this ad hoc retreat of about 120 church leaders sought to fulfill such a purpose, at least on a one-time basis. It convened at McCormick Creek State Park in Spencer, Indiana, January 16–18, 1995. The purposes were:

1. To fashion a statement of the unique purpose and mission of the Church of God as envisioned by participants in attendance;
2. To review Vision 2 Grow, past and present, and to project future direction;
3. To seek spiritual renewal and encouragement through worship, study, and fellowship.

From the process emerged a "Vision/Action Statement." It read:
<u>The Church of God Exists To</u>:

- Worship the Lord;
- Reach the Lost;
- Disciple Believers;
- Equip for Ministry;
- Celebrate the Unity of the Body of Christ;
- Live out the Love of Christ.

Three obstacles to fulfilling this vision were identified as: (1) Structure at the national level; (2) Leadership empowerment; (3) Lack of finance. Plans were designed to begin addressing these.

Section IV

Reflections on the General Assembly

Section IV
Reflections on the General Assembly

128. Reflections on the Future Role, Membership, Meetings, and Agenda of the General Assembly (Barry Callen)

The year 1980 saw the reformation movement of the Church of God celebrate its first century of existence and ministry. Much has changed and much has been accomplished over these many years. The General Assembly has acted often to create, encourage, and direct new forms of ministry at the national level. It also has spoken its conviction on a wide range of crucial issues that have faced the Church of God and society at large.

Now is a good time to review the process and implications of all of this activity and to think carefully about the future of the Assembly. Given all the material in this book about the nature and actions of the Assembly in the past, let us look to tomorrow. How can the Assembly be an effective guiding force as the movement faces a new century?

A. *Role of the General Assembly.* In light of the historic stance of the Church of God against the dangers of denominationalism, the Assembly has been careful to call itself "voluntary" and to deny itself "ecclesiastical authority." But there always is pressure for some influential and concerned person or body to seek the Assembly's formal view on a teaching, and even ask that such a view be binding on bodies accountable to the Assembly. It is easy for some persons, lacking any effective alternative, to look to the Assembly for such judgments or binding. Should the Assembly continue to resist assuming such authoritative roles? Would the integrity of the reformation movement be compromised if the assembly would assume such roles? Should the Assembly speak to or for the church—or should it speak at all on controversial issues? How can the Assembly better avoid becoming the stage on which attempts are made to circumvent the legally vested governance functions of the several national agencies? How can national coordination of ministry bring increased effectiveness without hindering local initiative, freedom, and creativity?

B. *Style of the General Assembly.* Some annual meetings of the

Assembly, reflecting periods of turmoil in the church, have been characterized by the presence of tension and debate. The 1981 report to the Assembly by the Executive Secretary of the Executive Council, for instance, expressed concern over the "recent politicizing of our General Assembly. To coalesce and muster persons to come with a block vote seems more the ways of man and less the leading of the Holy Spirit." Will the Assembly become increasingly like the conventions of national political parties, trying to hammer out a platform, or can it retain an orderly and trusting atmosphere in which all persons function as humble servants of God and not as persons maneuvering for some political advantage? Is the Church of God movement really different from other church bodies in the way it does its business? In what way should and can it be different? Various actions in recent years (e.g., the 1995 bylaws change establishing Assembly ratifications rather than elections) suggest a wholesome maturing of the Assembly.

C. *Membership of the General Assembly.* The Assembly began as a fellowship meeting of ministers. Its first formal action in 1917 stated that only ordained ministers of the Church of God could vote. Through the years, however, there has been much discussion about appropriate membership guidelines. Should the Assembly be delegated, not because of a desire to restrict the participation of ministers, but because geography has seemed to limit the participation of some ministers, giving the ministers of some states a disproportionate representation?

D. *Meetings of the General Assembly.* As the organized ministries of the church have grown in number and complexity over the years, the Assembly has assumed more business functions. Reports, ratifications, ballots, budgets, and resolutions have come to use most available time. The sheer size of the Assembly now necessitates considerable formality. The few hours of meeting time each year are sandwiched among the scores of events of the International Convention. Serious group prayer, in-depth exploration of issues, and careful long-range planning have become difficult in this setting. Should, therefore, Assembly meetings convene in groups for longer periods rather than in the Assembly itself? Should Assembly sessions be at a time or place other than during the International Convention which is held annually in June in Anderson, Indiana? Do not recent Assembly actions to increase lay participation militate against any separation of the Assembly from the International Convention in Anderson, Indiana?

E. *Agenda of the General Assembly.* Recent years have seen in the Assembly a parade of resolutions on subjects of concern to one group or another. It has been assumed that such formal statements by the Assembly are appropriate and meaningful actions. Should this practice of making pronouncements on a variety of timely subjects continue to be an important function of the Assembly? How accessible should the floor of the Assembly be to the concerns of small groups within its membership? Regarding the stating of "general reformation principles" (see entries 29–32), where is the line between declaring appropriately the central truths that make us the people of God and acting inappropriately by establishing creedal positions and building denominational fences? Does not the restriction of meeting time limit significantly the nature of the Assembly's possible agenda? Since a regularized supplemental gathering has been judged too costly (Triennial proposal rejected in 1992), what are the workable alternatives?

Part Two: Ecumenical Vision, Initiatives, and Partnerships

I. The Church Unity Vision: Past and Present

II. Churches of God: General Conference (Winebrennerian)

III. Christian Churches/Churches of Christ

Part Two: Ecumenical Vision, Initiatives, and Partnerships

I. The Christian Unity Vision: Past and Present

129. A New Approach To Christian Unity (Charles E. Brown)

Excerpted from *A New Approach to Christian Unity* by Charles E. Brown (Anderson, Ind: Warner Press, 1931), pp. 149ff. This is a classic statement of the unity vision typical of the earliest decades of the Church of God movement.

<u>Step One</u>. The first formal step necessary to get back to the freedom and unity of the apostolic church is to drop all official creeds insofar as they are official and authoritative definitions of denominational belief. The argument is made that it is foolish and absurd to expect to get away from creeds. Every group of people has its unwritten creed; and even every thinking individual has a personal creed. How vain then to think of escaping creeds by laying aside the great historic creeds of the church.

This argument overlooks a serious point. It is admitted that each thoughtful person has a creed. I admit that I have my own creed, in its way, and on some points as definite as the historic creeds of the churches. But my personal creed is not a division maker. No other Christian in the world is compelled to sign it in order to have fellowship with me. It is inclusive, not exclusive.

Again, my creed is capable of change. I can sit down with a devout Christian and after a few words of prayer we can discuss the Christian faith; and I may arise from that conference with my creed slightly amended. It is doubtless then a better creed; but I did not have to violate a solemn oath to change it a bit; neither did I become a heretic. But many persons are tied up so tightly to official creeds that if they change their own personal creed they have violated a solemn oath. This puts them in a difficult position; for if a man has taken an oath not to believe the truth when he hears it, he will take good care not to hear it; but if he should hear it, sometimes he is compelled to believe it in spite of his oath. Thus it may be seen that there is a world of difference between an official creed, the standard of faith of a denominational corporation, and the private, personal creed of the individual Christian.

The apostolic church unquestionably had an unwritten creed. It was the living and growing faith of the church. But this creed never caused division until it narrowed and hardened in the course of centuries into the official, written creed of a human corporation. Therefore, the first step to Christian unity is to disengage oneself from the historic creeds completely, reverencing them as much as he wishes, believing them as much as he can, but receiving them as mere relics of Christian theological history, and not as standing walls of isolation.

Personally I am an old-fashioned Christian; and I very much suspect that I actually believe the historic creeds much more strongly than the majority of the ministers of the respective denominations; but I would consider it sinful to arm myself with one against my brethren. The will of Christ, the fellowship of all Christians, and the unity of the church are far more precious to me than any human creed ever written.

Step Two. The second formal step to restore the unity of ancient Christianity is the total abolition of all formal organic denominational divisions among Christian people; not to merge the denominations, but to abolish them is our duty.

This will doubtless sound like anarchy to those dear old souls who have never thought through the inescapable evils of denominationalism. It will shock those who love the historic organizations of men better than the blessed unity of the body of Christ. It will seem revolutionary to the "stand-patters" who spend their time looking back to the good old days of the past. But to all such we would say there is a true place for conservatism in the kingdom of God. Let us look back to the good old days when the church had visible organic unity. Let us remember that the denominations are only a comparatively recent development in the two-thousand year history of the church. All signs point to their eventual abolition and the gathering of God's people once again into the blessed peace and unity of the ancient church.

I shall be asked how the practical business of the church could ever be carried on in such a system. To begin with, it is perfectly all right to organize the agencies of the church according to the very best examples of systematic and orderly management of business. We have divine authority for this.

When the Greek-speaking Jews complained because their widows were neglected in the daily ministration, the apostles committed the matter to the church and the church chose several believers to handle the problem (Acts 6). Notice that the church, and not the apostles, chose them. Also, the Gentile churches appointed a committee to bear their gifts to the poor saints at Jerusalem (1 Cor. 16:3; 2 Cor. 8:19, 23). This is ample authority for organizing and managing efficiently such bodies as missionary societies, church schools, publishing plants, and the like, for which a denominational organization is usually considered essential. But one can search in vain for any evidence that the apostolic church was organized as a human corporation in the sense that denominations are organized today.

Step Three. The apostolic church was organized by the inward urge of the Spirit of God, which led men to undertake the work of preaching and the like, and led the believers to recognize and encourage their call. Where believers could not sense the existence of the call by the instinct of the indwelling Spirit, there was not much danger involved in allowing such a person to exercise himself in some other way till his calling became manifest to the sanctified judgment of the assembly of believers.

The church can only regain her lost visible unity by rallying around our Lord Jesus Christ. In the past there have been cries to rally around this doctrine or that creed, or to rally to this or that battle-cry. Now the call is to come alone to Jesus Christ. "The scepter shall not depart from Judah, nor a lawgiver from between his feet, until Shiloh come; and unto him shall the gathering of the people be" (Gen. 49:10).

Doctrine is very important; but more important it is to get back to the supreme Person, who is the source of all true doctrine. He has said, "I am the way, the truth, and the life." When all Christendom gets back to him it will be one. There will then be plenty of time to compare and study doctrines, when the clamor of debate has given place to the silence of the humble and earnest pupils in the school of Christ.

130. Establishment of a Commission on Christian Unity

Editor's note: See entry 14.

131. Schismatic Tendencies in the Movement (Val B. Clear)

Excerpted from Val Clear, *Where the Saints Have Trod* (Chesterfield, Ind: Midwest Publications, 1977, based on his earlier doctoral dissertation). Even a movement on behalf of Christian unity occasionally suffers from its own internal disunity.

The first sizeable division in the history of the Church of God movement came in 1899. Data for analysis are weak and sparse. It was defined as a doctrinal dispute over the nature of sanctification, whether it could occur simultaneously with regeneration. Because the rejected view was earlier taught by Count Zinzendorf and the Moravians, the heretical doctrine was termed Zinzendorfism, and was officially repudiated in 1899 by the annual assembly. The senior historiographer of the movement (Charles E. Brown), who was a minister at that time, estimates that half of the ministers left, but by 1906 most of them had returned. No permanent group developed from the break.

Shortly thereafter another period of unrest developed, aimed primarily at liberalizing practices in dress and diet. Christians were clearly told to "lay aside all filthiness and superfluity of naughtiness" (James 1:21) ... but many leaders were weakening by wearing neckties, lace collars, dresses with unnecessary gatherings, showy combs, and gaudy print. The editor of the Gospel Trumpet tended to side with the conservatives, and most of what was published was critical of the liberals. Even so, one article did appear in which the writer observes: "In some localities a preacher is not of much use unless he says much about the 'old paths'.... If the old paths are construed to mean merely what we preached ten or fifteen years ago regardless of the gospel, then they are nearly 2,000 years too young to be binding on the consciences of men.... Above all things, holy brethren, let us not judge one another nor find fault with one another...."

The issue finally centered around neckties and the editor reported that "a few ministers ... have but little if anything more than 'necktie' religion.... On the other hand, some have 'anti-necktie' religion." The editor apparently sided with the "anti-necktie" faction, but their opponents subsequently prevailed. As a result of the 1913 camp meeting in Anderson, the anti-necktie group began to publish a periodical, The Herald of Truth, which is still being published in Guthrie, Oklahoma, under the title Faith and Victory. This group persists, but in an extremely stunted form. It is likely that not one percent of today's members of the Church of God movement are aware that the schism ever occurred or that this schismatic group exists.

About a decade later, rumblings of unrest were heard again. The spokesmen were a missionary, G. P. Tasker, and a pastor, Fred Bruffett. Both of these men had been "highly esteemed in the past ... still loved by practically all who know them." Tasker had developed doctrinal views at variance with the consensus of the church at home, and had mailed booklets in large numbers from India to laymen and ministers in the States. Bruffett's attack was on a broad front, but particularly focused on centralization of authority in the central boards and the growth of power in the ministerial assembly. A small circle of supporters gathered about Bruffett and Tasker, but no permanent conflict group persisted.

There have been other occasional local eruptions of protest limited to a few leaders, most of which never became a separate protest group. One, however, started in Indiana in 1943, and snowballed until it became a major threat to the central organization, which spent virtually all its efforts for several years in defending itself against the onslaughts of the "Watchman-on-the-Wall" controversy.

Literally tons of material were circulated and accusations were myriad, but most protests centered around two general complaints: (1) Anderson leaders were relaxing personal, moral, ethical, and religious standards; and (2) the organization of the Church of God movement in Anderson had reconstructed the evils of organized Protestantism from which it originally withdrew. It was accused of being an "ecclesiastical octopus" with a voracious appetite for power.

The General Ministerial Assembly appointed a committee to investigate the charges. When it presented its inconclusive report, both sides claimed vindication. The agitation continued. At one time there were reportedly 1,100 names on the schismatic mailing list and several hundred congregations. The new group sent its own foreign missionaries, set up its own school, and organized administrative boards.

The General Assembly finally did take official action and withdrew recognition of the protesting leaders as ministers of the Church of God movement. These disfellowshipped leaders promptly interpreted this as proof that their claims were accurate, that the parent body was apostate, and that the new group was really the remnant of the original movement, now preserved in freedom and truth. The new group continued to call itself "Church of God." One interesting comment by its leader is very pertinent to this discussion. He said: "It was a mistake ever to declare a last reformation. While the truth that was brought out in 1880 must never be lost, yet the people who embraced the truth, most of them have today forgotten it ... have repudiated it. It remains therefore for God to sound out clearly and distinctly a clarion call...." Later in his life this leader relaxed his criticism and was reinstated in the parent body.

At the present time [1977] there are only undercurrents of dissension in the Church of God movement. A few ministers have joined counterparts in traditionally non-charismatic denominations such as the Presbyterian and Episcopal Churches in experimentation with glossalalia. For the most part, these have found it difficult or impossible to continue in the Church of God ministry [see entry 123 on glossalalia]. A larger minority has clustered around the conservative group publishing the *Reformation Witness*. Some distance appears to be developing between Gulf-Coast Bible College and the liberal arts colleges. But all of these tensions appear to be only eddies in the onflowing stream. The Church of God movement has reached the quietude of middle age and is busily engaged in building new churches, in educating young people to occupy pews and pulpits, and in trying to find a raison d'etre for itself in a world that has changed rapidly while the movement has been growing to maturity.

132. Options for the Movement's Future (John W. V. Smith)

Excerpts from John Smith's *The Quest for Holiness and Unity* (Warner Press, 1980), pp. 439–443.

One item with major unresolved issues for the future of the Church of God movement comes under the general heading of relationships. In light of the movement's central emphasis on Christian unity, these issues become particularly important. It must be remembered that despite, its strong irenic focus, the Church of God was born and developed in a very polemic atmosphere. Enemies were readily and specifically identified—even invited. Attacks by and on these adversaries were vigorous and frequent. If, as many sociologists affirm, a certain degree of conflict is essential to group formation and growth, then the early Church of God movement had the basic ingredients for a solid self-identity and rapid expansion. Unity as a doctrine or an ideal for the church was itself a source of conflict because it was opposed by loyal "sectarians" who were offended by the call to "come-out" of their denominations and stand together in an open fellowship of the Spirit. In this context the message of Christian unity was a call to action and combat.

Then the religious climate began to change after 1910 when the glow of ecumenism sparked by the Edinburgh Missionary Conference began to grow brighter and burst into a light by 1948 with the formation of the World Council of Churches—a development in which the Church of God had been totally uninvolved. For this movement it might have been thought of as having won a war without having been in a single battle, but that was not the case. The launching of a worldwide ecumenical movement was not regarded as a victory, and there was not rejoicing over the fact that a great segment of Christendom had come to the point of openly questing for the same goal the Church of God had upheld for two-thirds of a century. Instead, the changing external climate sparked the beginning of a time of internal assessment within the movement itself.

The Church of God movement had lost its enemies and with their passing came a sense of wonderment resulting from the erosion of a sharp definition of identity and purpose. This condition set off an avalanche of self-analysis studies by young Church of God scholars. The popular response to what was happening outside the Church of God was for it to become critical of the ecumenical movement regarding its methodology, for its truncated view of union rather than unity, and, along with other conservative evangelicals, for its involvement in social and political issues. In the ultimate sense, however, there could be no denying that the Church of God and the cooperating "sinful sectarians" were aiming at the same target.

To complicate the situation, the noncooperative stance of the Church of God led it to a position of relative aloneness in the Christian world. At the same time that the movement was losing its enemies, it was not cultivating many close friends.... There were no real allies to join forces with in doing battle with the major evils of the world. So at its first century's end [1980] the movement found itself with a rather fuzzy identity as related to the rest of Christianity, without specifically identified enemies, and without any formally declared friends. In this uncomfortable context it is difficult to find exciting ways to give emphasis to the doctrine of Christian unity.

In facing this situation the Church of God movement has several options. At least four possible courses regarding its unity stance seem to be open to the movement as it looks toward the future.

Option One. The first option is simply to continue as in the past—preach unity vigorously, get emotional about the biblical vision of the one holy church, write articles and books about it, tell others that "we believe in it," and then wait for it to happen, taking little or no responsibility to implement it or further its achievement. Stated this way, such a position appears idealistic, even dreamy and unrealistic. This, many would quickly say, is the best way to insure that Christian unity will never be realized. The voice of practicality would say that such a stance should be altered and that the movement should quickly find ways to become involved in the multitude of opportunities to further the cause of unity.

On the other hand, there still is the possibility that there may be some validity to what Church of God leaders have been saying for many years about being "leaven in the lump," about being dedicated to a "unity of the Spirit" approach, and about the inadequacies inherent in the federation or council-of-churches path to unity. It could be that the nonjoining stance might be, in the long run, a greater witness to real unity than to be linked on a marginal basis with many other groups. Careful scrutiny and evaluation might determine that the historic stance is an option that is both tenable and defensible or that only slight modifications need to be made.

Option Two. The second option would be to seek out compatible allies and work with them in all ways that would enhance the spread of the gospel and increase the impact of the church's mission in the world. This is already being done in selected areas such as curriculum, foreign missions, and stewardship education. The possibilities for enlarging these cooperative arrangements are almost infinite. Such a posture allows a high degree of selectivity regarding both what and with whom such relationships are established. Probably it would cut costs and increase overall effectiveness in the cooperative areas. If this option were selected, the movement's aloneness would be mitigated. It would be possible to do this without violating the nonjoining principle. It is a viable option, but obviously not a major step on the road to Christian unity. Such arrangements are nice, but they really do little to solve the deep problem of Christian disunity. [See entries 142–146 for a brief overview of the recent Church of God dialogues with the Churches of God: General Conference and the Christian Churches/Churches of Christ.]

Option Three. Another option would be to reassess the historic nonjoining stance and to affiliate with selected interdenominational organizations with which the movement could feel comfortable. The long and often advanced argument, that the Church of God cannot join any organization because its polity does not provide for any corporate body which has authority over the various congregations, would need to be dealt with in such a manner that it would be clear to all just what commitments were being made. The General Assembly itself could join any of these ecumenical organizations, and it is true that this would not obligate any congregation to any greater extent than it desired—a condition which is true for any action of the Assembly. This would pose no problem for any of the ecumenical organizations, for they would simply list the General Assembly of the Church of God as a member rather than the Church of God. Properly understood, it should pose no problem for the movement either.

Once this hurdle was passed, the next big question would be which interdenominational group(s) to join. Unfortunately, there are competitive and rival councils and associations. Theologically, the Church of God movement would find greater affinity with groups such as the National Association of Evangelicals and the Christian Holiness Association, and there has been considerable involvement of Church of God persons in the meetings and continuing programs of groups like these. On the other hand, there has been an even longer involvement in program departments, divisions, commissions, and committees of the National Council of Churches. Recent restructuring within this body has eroded the opportunities for nonmembers to be included, so that participation there has been considerably lessened in recent years. Even so, relationships have been good and the spirit of openness and freedom of expression have created good feelings on the part of participants, even though there might be strong disagreement with some National Council pronouncements and programs....

<u>Option Four</u>. There is one other possible option. Being a Christian unity movement, the Church of God could enter the ecumenical arena "full blast"—joining all interdenominational organizations whose "basis" would not require a compromise of cardinal biblical teachings. Standing where it does in the theological spectrum, and with relatively wide acquaintance already in the various camps, the Church of God may be in the unique position of serving as a bridge across the wide chasms created by these polarized clusters in national and world Christianity. The full implications of such a move are difficult even to imagine, but it is an option and all the avenues of reformation have not yet been traveled. It would take a great deal of finesse—and courage—to make this choice and act upon it.

133. Where Do We Go From Here? (June 1983)

Excerpts of "A Statement of Concern and Guidance to the Church of God (Anderson, IN) from this movement's Commission on Christian Unity," published by the Commission.

This statement grows out of a necessary assessment of where we are in fulfilling our voiced concern to foster and assist Christian unity. It is issued after considerable study and in the spirit of responsible love.

For the greater part of our history as a reform movement, our people took pride in the comfort and security of being "all just alike." We dressed alike, talked alike, lived alike, learned alike, prayed alike, and worshiped alike. Patience was limited toward any who dared to differ, because to tolerate differences was like drifting from the moorings or "letting down the standard." But as more and more believers were attracted to our fellowship and more and more instances of difference were evidenced, the church had to begin dealing with backgrounds and theological positions that were not all alike. The church became painfully aware of groupings to the left and right on what had been the acknowledged center in worship style, prayer manner, musical expressiveness, dress code, social class, and educational concerns. Again and again our seriousness about Christian unity was being tested.

It is time to deal seriously with our concern to relate to other believers and exemplify unity. We must learn how to implement our concern in the midst of different doctrinal emphases, patterns of race and and ethnic expectation, different educational levels and intellectual concerns, different income groups, age differences, and orders of worship. The need before us is to work toward an intentional togetherness, to exercise a "willed movement toward each other." We must seek to understand each other in order to relate with greater creativity.

We must work deliberately to remove any barriers which separate us from other confessed Christians, and we must do so both as individuals and congregations. God intended that his people be one in fellowship and we must do this by bypassing all structures of our organizationally diverse group traditions. The boundaries of God's revealed truth about Christian unity have not been reached. All who have "light" are under mandate to share it with others—and to receive "light" from them as well, offering and receiving more in the spirit of love.

The willingness to recognize every true believer as belonging to God's church is a must. So is the need for us all to remain open to the Scriptures, studying what is taught there with eyes that look beyond our own tradition and group background. True believers have a common participation in the grace of God and are under the guidance of the one Spirit. All are blessed by the overarching will and love of a common Lord. To recognize this will help us overcome denominational differences and flow together with a concern for the will of the Lord. Separated believers lack the unity needed to take the good news of salvation to all nations. As individual Christians and local congregations, we must search for productive ways to experience oneness with other confessed Christians; only thus can we visibly show what it means to be the church and serve to the glory of God and the good of the world.

The church has benefited from the enthusiastic preaching and inspirational singing and courageous approach to mission long associated with the Black congregations. The church has benefited from the vision and tested operational skills of its White majority. The church has benefited from the work stamina of the Women of the Church of God, the outreach of the Men of the Church of God, and the experimental ministries of the paramission groups. The church has profited from the intercultural sensitivity and theological insights of the Church of God in other countries, the questing spirit of its many minorities, and the heritage concern often associated with fellowship groups. It has been enriched by the excitement of the newly-converted and the wisdom of experienced believers. We can have a fresh life and a contagious witness at such a time as this, if we are willing to live and learn together, searching the Scriptures anew to be guided by what the Lord is saying to us all.

Our movement traditionally has considered itself as being a non-structured reform movement, and the very words "sect" and "denomination" have been so abhorrent that there is an evident reluctance to consider any formalized relationship with any other church group. For many, the thought of relating ourselves with other groups in any formal way seems foreign to our historic self-image and what we believe our group represents as a reform movement.

The question is: How can our group that seeks to epitomize the whole church dare to identify with one or more of the "fragments" of the church without denying the vision we hold of the true church? This has been and is a very real obstacle to any consideration of our formal togetherness with other church groups. To seek to work cooperatively with any group which we have previously regarded as a "sect" has been viewed as a compromise of our own idealized self-image, a reduction of the Church of God to being only one among other "man-made organizations," and thus to sell short the concept of the church presented by the New Testament writers. So there has been a strong theological and psychological resistance against even considering the possibilities open to us to pursue or accept more formal relations with other Christians in life and work for Christ.

Practically and functionally, then, all of our presently authorized agencies can participate in cooperative work with other church groups. The fact is that all of our agencies have long done so. In curriculum preparation, in facilitating missionary assignments both at home and abroad, in higher education endeavors, in missionary education, in stewardship education, to name only a few areas, our agencies have entered into working agreements and participated in cooperative programs on a rather wide basis and at very significant levels across many years.

Without question, these contacts have been our most immediate ways to relate with other Christian groups so far, and these contacts have done more to make us and our work and witness known nationally and internationally than any other single activity in which we have engaged.

The Commission calls the Church of God movement to recognize that at many points we are indebted to others beyond our fellowship. We have benefited from our sharing with them. The time has come to state this plainly, and to rejoice over opportunities to experience unity in working with other believers in some of the causes listed above.

It is time for us to think soberly and respond creatively as we face God's call for his people to be one. As contacts continue to be sustained and initiated with other church groups, and as our basic togetherness of faith and love is clearly seen and experienced, we must be ready to do what agape love demands and what unity inspires.

God has chosen to use us as a particular people within both the wider church and world at this time. God is still guiding, but we must follow. The challenge is still "holiness and unity," not just the one or the other, but both. We are called to model them so that the church which is seen by the world will be an effective representative of Christ. Such is the challenge and opportunity confronting the Church of God movement in its second century of ministry.

134. Inter-Church Cooperation

Editor's note: For the content of this action of the General Assembly regarding relationships to other church bodies (June, 1985), see entry 25.

135. The Wisdom of Fraternal Guests

Editor's note: Between 1987 and 1994 the officers of the General Assembly took initiative to bring some ecumenical perspective to its annual meetings. They invited a series of "fraternal guests" to observe, evaluate, and then address the Assembly, with their addresses then published in the *Yearbook of the Church of God.* These guests were Clyde VanValin, Bishop of the Free Methodist Church (1987), Myron Augsburger, Mennonite college president and theologian (1988), Billy Melvin, Executive Director of the National Association of Evangelicals (1990), David McCord, pastor and president of the North American Christian Convention (1991), B. Edgar Johnson, retired General Secretary, Church of the Nazarene (1993), and Dennis Kinlaw, Old Testament scholar and past president of Asbury College (1994). The following is a condensed presentation by Barry Callen of the perspectives of these Christian leaders on the General Assembly of the Church of God, and of the movement itself.

Humorously, David McCord reported that, "as one of our great American philosophers, Yogi Berra, has said, 'You can observe a lot just by looking.' " The observation most commonly made by these fraternal guests might be described as the "enthusiastic ethos" of the Assembly. McCord, for example, reported: "I like the enthusiasm of your singing and worship. I appreciate very much the fervency of your prayers and the joyous fraternal spirit that I have discovered here." Clyde VanValin spoke of a "winsome style" by which "you celebrate easily and joyfully" with a distinctive "unity within diversity." He said that "you are an anointed people of God" who appear to feature "a trust in the integrity of each other without the need of an authoritarian hierarchy."

Myron Augsburger reported observing "the spirit of praise and joy" functioning with a "spirit of freedom and openness" and a special "sense of community." B. Edgar Johnson noted the role of music in strengthening this community. He referred to the song "O Church of God" as the movement's "national anthem." When he first heard it sung by the

Assembly, "I couldn't help but feel enthused.... I've since had the opportunity to read the words and I enjoyed and appreciated them very, very much." Dennis Kinlaw observed that "wherever God is among his people, music develops.... There is within you a sense of loyalty to your tradition.... Pay any price to keep it, not to sanctify the past, but don't you lose those roots."

Kinlaw, however, issued an important caution along with his observation about roots. He called on the Assembly to develop further its sense of church history *before* Daniel Warner in the late nineteenth century. In the body of Christ "we've got four thousand years of history and if you are a part of that kingdom, all of that history at its essence belongs to you.... Any denomination that is less than a hundred years old is a sect by definition."

Affirmations of distinctive emphases of the Church of God movement were common in the statements of these ecumenical guests. VanValin, for example, spoke of the movement's focus on Christian unity as "a message that we all need to hear expounded and demonstrated." Augsburger characterized this unity emphasis as something "the Christian world needs to understand because it is far more biblical and far more dynamic than an organizational ecumenicity. It is an ecumenical spirit." With this affirmation, however, there also came a challenge.

VanValin put the challenge in question form: "What if you exported more frequently and fervently your message, your music, your vision of the body of Christ throughout the whole evangelical movement? We need that message and we welcome it." Billy Melvin was direct and specific: "I wonder why I have not seen more involvement by the Church of God in the community I represent—the National Association of Evangelicals. I believe with all my heart that the Church of God has something to share with those larger bodies of Christ. You have some great rootage and great fruitage in your fellowship." Beyond sharing, Melvin noted, "I believe you could also learn from this experience as you would share in the larger body of Christ."

Other affirmations clustered around the subject of holiness. As a Mennonite, Myron Augsburger wanted to be sure that "we are not just talking about whether I smoke or drink; we are also talking about how I feel toward the poor and the dispossessed and the issue of violence." Melvin warned similarly that the world today "is not so much interested in our talk as our walk. He affirmed the longstanding emphasis of the

Church of God movement on holy living, noting that "few evangelical denominations that I know have done as beautiful a job in involving our Black brothers and sisters and other ethnics and minorities as you have in your [Church of God] fellowship."

A final affirmation centered around the concept of "movement" that is highlighted by the Church of God tradition. VanValin called for a retaining of this focus and pointed with admiration to the International Convention of the Church of God that convenes annually in Anderson, Indiana—of which the General Assembly is a part. He observed: "The Convention and the Assembly, the camp meeting, this week-long annual event ... is the glue that holds the Church of God together. You do not depend on structures and processes, form and legislation to make you who you are so much as you depend on this gathering." Added Kinlaw:

> I love the vision that brought you [Church of God movement] into existence, the one that transcends denominational lines, but, more than that, the one that champions the unity of the body of Christ. I think what promoted this was a deep sense of "seek ye first the Kingdom of God and His righteousness" in which Kingdom loyalties were put ahead of all other loyalties. You've got an organization now, but don't lose that trans-organizational vision. You must lead the way in sharing it so that the rest of us that are trapped can see somebody who cares more about the Kingdom of God than they care about their own organization. The Kingdom is first. Now, that's part of who you are.

Kinlaw warned the movement never to lose the heart of its heritage: "Don't let anything stop within you that hunger for the Spirit to work in your midst."

There were other observations and cautions in the area of the church organization. Augsburger observed that the Church of God movement is "wrestling, as we [Mennonites] are, with what it means to be persons who have a polity of order without selling oneself out to institutionalization." Melvin openly wondered "if perhaps so much emphasis in the Church of God movement has been placed on independence of the local church that there has not been sufficient emphasis on the interdependence of the whole church. You are moving to a point in time when you are going to have to work harder with what it means to interrelate one with the other as local churches." Edgar Johnson offered this advice:

> If we depend on organization for success, we may fail; but if we don't organize we may fail too.... There is a problem with lack of structure. It could be like a body without a skeleton, lacking direction. Probably some of your expressed fears about structure in the church's life may be carried over from a long-ago problem—maybe a problem in the thinking of the early founders of the Church of God movement that may not exist today.

Perhaps the observation and caution of Myron Augsburger serves best as a general summary. To the Assembly of 1988 he said:

> You use movement language; I like that. Movement means something that is dynamic, something that is happening. The risen Christ is moving among us, the Holy Spirit is doing something. That also means that I (we) have to become flexible and be willing to be vulnerable—not act as though I (we) have captured the Kingdom. To date, the Church of God movement has visioned rightly and worked diligently in this regard.

136. The National Association: A Positive Force
(James Earl Massey)

Editor's note: This is an excerpt of a chapter by Dr. Massey in *National Association of the Church of God: Diamond Jubilee,* Wilfred Jordan and Richard Willowby, co-editors (Warner Press, 1991), pp. 3–5.

It is a fact of more than passing significance that the Church of God has long had the active presence of a larger number of African-Americans within its life than any of the holiness-oriented church bodies, and, in addition, a larger number than any of the mainline denominations reporting a black constituency. Why? First, some statistics are in order.

Among the holiness denominations which have had primary contact with African-Americans are the Christian and Missionary Alliance Church, the Church of the Nazarene, the Pilgrim Holiness Church, the Holiness Christian Church, the Salvation Army, and the Church of God (Anderson).

Although the separate history of any one of these groups has not always reflected the best social arrangement with their black members, it is interesting that blacks did not break away from any of these church groups to form independent organizations—as was the case with segregated blacks in the Methodist Church, for example. Part of the reason for not separating might lie in the fact that most of the named groups have had so few black members in comparison with the white majority.

The holiness body that has had the most fruitful results for its message among African-Americans is the Church of God. Although its black constituency has experienced social trauma at critical stages of wider social strain in the nation, there has not been any widespread interest on the part of blacks in breaking away from the larger group. In fact, the relationship between African-Americans and the Church of God movement as a whole has been remarkably stable, with an obvious pattern of calculated responsiveness in the midst of threatening strain. It is important to understand what stands behind this result. One of the reasons for this continued involvement of blacks in the life and work of the Church of God is the appealing and promising ideal of the unity of believers. This message has kept thoughtful members, both black and white, mindful of the need to keep working at reducing the points of tension and strain as they have arisen.

Early on, the unity emphasis in the message of the Church of God appealed strongly to African-Americans who were otherwise beset by restrictive segregation patterns in the land. The message of unity provided promise for needed affirmation of self-worth, on the one hand, and needed social togetherness, on the other. Unlike other church groups whose doctrinal positions accented nonrelational themes and teachings, the central theme of the Church of God movement was a relational one, the unity of believers. When social relations within this movement have been under strain, the challenge of the unity ideal has always been present as a prodding factor toward correction and reform. To be sure, the sad fact of race distancing and polarization in Church of God history can be documented as readily as that result in other church groups; but the unity ideal never has allowed that separateness to stand unchallenged. Rather, the announced ideal has stirred the most thoughtful to seek a remedy for the problem and to bridge the distances that have developed.

But there is another reason why African-Americans within the Church of God have remained openly relational despite times of racial tension in the larger body. That reason is the organizational entity known as the National Association of the Church of God (West Middlesex, Pennsylvania, initially formed as a camp meeting organization in 1916).

The National Association has been a social means for black assertiveness and black group pride. The National Association has at times functioned as an active witness against racist influences at work in the church; it has been the social entity to protest when the church was not as socially responsible and active as the unity ideal seemed to demand. It is not too much to say that, at nearly every time when social and racial awareness needed to be increased within the Church of God, the National Association helped to effect this result, sometimes offering distinct strategies for dealing with race issues, always involving persons who were interested in making needed changes.

That the Church of God has both gained and held African-Americans within its communal life has been duly noted by other church bodies, but the reason for such sustained togetherness is more than doctrinal; it is based in part upon a system of relating that includes recognition of voluntary associations within the church that nurture ethnic identity and group pride and grant opportunities for training and enrichment. It is in these areas of benefit that the National Association of the Church of God has historically shown a strategic influence during its eighty years of existence.

Across the years the National Association has continued to play a major role in helping to effect many changes and developments in both the African-American congregations that support and depend upon its ministries and the Church of God movement generally, within which it remains one of the most vital and vibrant voluntary associations. Aware that the Church of God has been like most of the other religious groups in America in having to deal with the sad influences imposed by conditions of faulty social customs and limiting stereotypes, the National Association has worked steadily to help the whole church deal with its deficiencies and challenges at the point of race and develop a sustainable fellowship in keeping with the social implications in the Church of God message about the holiness of life and the intended unity of believers.

137. Christian Unity: A Statement About Its Meaning and Expressions (James Earl Massey)

Editor's note: This is an excerpt of a paper given by Dr. Massey to the Doctrinal Dialogue Task Force (Christian Churches/Churches of Christ and the Church of God), Cincinnati, Ohio, May, 1993.

Two things are central in the Christian experience of unity: first, the awareness that we belong together, and second, the spirit to fulfill what belonging together requires. The whole matter is summed up in this expression: "a shared life." This is the ideal that was given to guide us, and it also argues for a function to which we must remain actively open.

The concept of unity is, in my opinion, best expressed in our time as community. The word "community" can keep us moderns from thinking singly about an institutional form or our organizational structures. "Community" immediately reminds us that unity is more than a theological concern and a spiritual given, that it also is a social result dependent upon our personal and willing involvement.

This fact of denominational families and denominated organizational forms is one of the most familiar facts in contemporary religious life. It is also, however, one of the most problematic facts in light of the biblical mandate for Christian unity. We all know that there is something essentially problematic about the boundaries our institutional differences and loyalties have made between us. Some formally-fixed boundaries (doctrinal and otherwise) are so delimiting that they hinder a holistic view of the universal Church, while some others are more loosely structured because of a wider perspective generated by the biblical ideal of unity.

Denominated organized forms can be honorable and effective, but only if these are not honored as ends in themselves. If fellowship and mission are given prior place in the organizational life and purpose, with the group's work being more basic than the group's structure, then that denominated group need not be a barrier to unity. Whether any denominated group is a barrier to or an agency of the biblical unity ideal depends largely upon how and why the group began, what it teaches and promotes, and the spirit that characterizes its life. If that spirit is one of openness and cooperativeness with respect to other believers, then the group can serve the purpose and spirit of the wider Church. But if the spirit of a denominated group is closed, competitive, and argumentative, then that group—whatever its beginnings and orthodoxy—is in need of renewal and reform.

Separately structured group life is not necessarily schismatic. The human family involves multifaceted forms and varieties of cultures, so it is only natural that the richness expressed in creation would be seen as well in the variety of responses humans make in organizing to promote the gospel and its claims. Diversity is not evil, only the spirit of divisiveness is. As Paul pointed out in First Corinthians 12:12–27, diversity of members in the body is not incompatible with the unity of the body.

Three attitudes are necessary on our part if we are to make Christian unity visible. The first attitude is one of *acknowledgment*: Since the New Testament tells us that all true believers belong to the Church, we must refuse to see other believers through eyes clouded by discriminating categories of placement. Ours must be an attitude that accepts all other believers despite the "historical accident" of their differing denominational backgrounds. The second attitude is one of *affirmation*: We must promote an atmosphere of participation and belonging. Every Christian believer has a legacy in every other Christian believer. The third attitude is one of *participation*: We must make common cause with each other. Any lingering and understood loyalty to tradition notwithstanding, the relational imperative of agape-love is set for sharing and cooperative mission. Christian love never stops prodding us to transcend what is parochial and local; it works ever and always to help us think and pray and plan and work with the wider world in view.

There is far more to Christian unity than meets the eye, much more than we experienced at first or have experienced since we believed. There are deeper levels in fellowship than we have dared to open ourselves to experience. We need to take another look at the concept of unity, and then take still another look. The seeing will search us, stir our hunger for more, and test our openness to venture. There is more in the doctrine and experience of Christian unity than we have yet seen or lived. May God grant us the wisdom and courage to go on and live it.

138. Celebrating Christian Unity Today

Editor's note: Following is an edited digest of the presentation made by Gilbert Stafford to the World Forum of the Church of God, Sydney, Australia, July, 1995.

What are the things that bind us together? We have a common Bible, a common Lord, a common commitment to making disciples, a common desire to be people of the Spirit, a common urgency about living the holy life, a common desire to be church together. We agree that the Bible is the book of God's revelation in written form, that Jesus is the Lord and Savior, that disciple-making is the church's mission, that the Holy Spirit is the church's source of power, that holiness of life is the church's mode of life, and that believers only are the true church.

I am convinced that we need to return to the study, preaching, and teaching of the Bible's message on unity. The New Testament has no dearth of passages setting forth Christian unity as part and parcel of the divine will for the church. By regularly preaching and teaching from them, we emphasize again and again that unity is a biblical mandate, and not simply the idealism of the early leaders of the Church of God movement or of contemporary ecumenists. Since Christian unity is a New Testament theme, it is a subject with which Christians as Christians need to wrestle.

By definition, unity of any kind presupposes diversity. If there were no diversity, we would not have unity, but sameness. The key question has to do with the limits of diversity. The short answer is that the limits are transgressed whenever the church ceases being the church. Any diversity which contradicts the essential nature of the church is unacceptable.

The most basic understanding of the church is that it is the circle of Christ's disciples (see Matt. 28:19–20). Furthermore, it is the fellowship of those who both believe in the atoning death and resurrection of Jesus Christ and live dead to sin and alive to Christ (see Rom. 6). The church, then, is the universal circle of those who have a personal relationship to the risen and living Lord Jesus Christ, believe that he died for our salvation and rose again, and are committed to the life of Christian holiness (i.e., dead to sin and alive to Christ). These are the biblical tests of fellowship.

In the course of time, however, the church had to identify itself in opposition to heresies. In doing so it fleshed out these basics in terms of formalized understandings about Jesus' relationship to his heavenly Father and to the Holy Spirit, resulting in Christian trinitarian thought, and about Jesus' personhood, that he is fully human and fully divine, yet one person. So, for us to be the church which continues to stand against these ancient and contemporary heresies, we must affirm the Trinity and the two natures of Christ.

What I have said to this point has to do with the church as Christian church. But what about our particular fellowship of the Church of God (Anderson)? What theological diversity can we tolerate? In order to answer this question I believe that we need to make a distinction between the teaching ministry of the church and the general fellowship of the church. What I have said up to this point applies to the general fellowship of the church as Christian church. That means that within the general membership of a local congregation, we cannot allow for a diversity which denies any one of the following: our call to Christian discipleship, Christ's atoning death and resurrection, Christian holiness, the Trinity, or the two natures of Christ.

The question is whether agreeing on these fundamental matters is sufficient for being involved in the teaching ministry of the Church of God (Anderson). I think not. As a particular fellowship of Christians we have doctrinal understandings which are part and parcel of who we are as a church. To disagree about these "Church of God" perspectives does not mean that one is not a Christian, as is the case of the matters mentioned above. It simply means that these are matters about which equally devoted Christians may disagree. I have in mind such widely held understandings of the Church of God as: salvation is synonymous with membership in God's one church; it is God's will to do a perfecting work in the lives of believers prior to death; the kingdom of God was inaugurated by Jesus Christ, is manifested in hearts made pure by faith, and will be brought to consummation at the return of Christ when world history will end and the saints will be gathered into heaven; and believers' baptism by immersion, the Lord's supper, and feet washing constitute the basic ordinances of the church.

These matters are deeply rooted in our history. If we are to continue being a distinctive tradition of Christians, our teaching ministry needs to be broadly united regarding these issues. But what about participation in the life of the church? Should all members of local congregations be required to adhere to this broad consensus? I answer No, because it is not these matters which determine whether one is a Christian in a biblical and historical sense. These matters do not have to do with the essential being of the church, but they do have to do, we believe, with the well-being of the church. If this is the case, and I believe it is, then these must not be tests of Christian fellowship in the same sense that the matters mentioned earlier are. Rather, Church of God perspectives are matters for which we are called to be good stewards in the interest of the well-being—not the essential being—of the whole church. If, then, we are divinely called to be good stewards of these perspectives, our teaching ministry needs to have enough unanimity about these matters to enable us both to share them with others and be agents of orderly thought in our own churches.

How can the Church of God cooperate with others without losing its distinctiveness? This is where we need to plow some new ground. Originally we were a come-out group in that we called those who had seen the light regarding the church to "come out from among them, and be ye separate, saith the Lord." Consequently, deeply ingrained in our historical life is not only a passive distrust of other church groups, but an overt war against them. However, in the course of time another stream of thought developed among us which is much more appreciative of the broader Christian world.

The Church of God (Anderson) ought to be making itself available to other church groups for the purpose of asking the following question both of them and of ourselves: What changes do all of us need to make in order to be the one church which is pleasing to God? Others can see things in us which need to be changed, things which we cannot see in ourselves. They have contributions to make to us, and we have contributions to make to them which in God's spiritual economy perhaps only they can make to us and only we can make to them.

Involvement with other Christians does not rob us of our identity; it enhances it. Cooperation with other believers does not destroy our distinctiveness; it expresses it. Participation with others of like precious faith does not endanger our tradition; it enriches it. Interaction with other church groups is not dangerous to our spiritual health; it nourishes it. The Christian mission is too important for any of us to be satisfied with the perpetuation of our own little slice of church life without being willing to become deeply involved with the whole cause and people of Christ. Unity is a biblical mandate, not a Church of God relic.

139. Together We Go (Barry L. Callen)

Editor's note: This doctrinal essay appeared in VITAL CHRISTIANITY, November, 1995.

This key entry appears in the personal journal of Daniel Warner on March 7, 1878: "On the 31st of last January the Lord showed me that holiness could never prosper upon sectarian soil encumbered by human creeds and party names, and he gave me a new commission to join holiness and all truth together and build up the apostolic church of the living God. Praise his name! I will obey him." Warner wrote a year later that "the God of all grace has most emphatically taught us in his word that his church is one, as the Father and Son are one, and that a manifestation of this unity is to be the world-saving salt of the church."

With these motivating insights, Warner became the primary pioneer of the movement of the Church of God, a gathering among God's people of some believers who know that they belong together by God's grace and that their obvious togetherness in the Spirit is crucial to effective Christian mission. In the early years of this movement this holiness-unity vision challenged many human compromises in the church and determined to find a better way to be God's people in the world. It still is the case that unity is a biblical mandate, not simply the idealism of our early leaders or of contemporary ecumenicists.

In the twentieth century the Christian community has given dramatic new attention to the problems of a divided Christian church. The Church of God movement has chosen not be involved for the most part. Why? Unfortunately, there has been at least a trace of arrogance by some of us who have felt that we already represent adequately what ought to be. There has been occasional fear that the movement might become contaminated by public association with Christians who represent differing traditions of belief and practice. There has been much insistence that the movement not support any preoccupation of Christians with solving the disunity problem the wrong way (theological compromises and denominational mergers).

But now the time for such criticizing of others is mostly past. Warner's was a prophetic voice that now must be translated into constructive action. We are both to tear down old obstructing walls and build new relationship bridges. For this movement of the Church of God, the need now is to develop its particular gifts to the glory of God, while respecting and benefiting from the divine gifts of other Christians. After all, every Christian has a legacy in every other Christian. We experience that legacy only as we receive each other and move eagerly beyond our group boundaries.

Believers who choose to be isolated from other believers get stunted by their isolation and soon are open to idolatries of their own making. Even a movement dedicated to Christian unity can destroy its own genius by failing to move creatively within the larger body. It is time for this movement to do more moving. Christian unity is first a gift of God and then the achievement of those committed to its fullest realization. True oneness comes only as the Spirit breathes the new life of holiness and as disciples dare to take appropriate uniting actions as inspired by the Spirit.

The unity of the earliest Christian churches was a unity of spirit which grew out of the shared experience of God's Spirit. Christians are to have the one Spirit poured out on them (Rom. 5:5), making them members together of the one body of Christ. This oneness of the body is a consequence of sharing the one Spirit (1 Cor. 12.13).

Today individual congregations of Christians should act as representatives of all of God's people. Evangelizing should be done as the church (the whole body of Christ) and for the church. New believers belong first and foremost to the church and not to a denomination that may recruit and nurture them. When a congregation baptizes a new believer, that baptism should be into the whole church, not merely a sectarian piece of it. The invitation to the Lord's supper should be issued as representatives of the whole body to any in the body wishing to participate—after all, it is the Lord's table, not ours!

A united church, living in creative togetherness, is a sign of the already coming Kingdom of God. The church is to be a united community of faith in a very divided world of unfaith. Christian mission is so important that none of us should get stuck in protecting our own little group at the expense of being involved deeply in the whole cause of Christ. There is a place for church structures; but that place is not for them to lead lives of their own.

Dating back to the vision of pioneers like Daniel Warner, this simple line of thought should still lead us forward. The center is Christian mission. Holiness enables authentic unity, which in turn increases a credible witness to the world. The authority and power all belong to God. In fact, it's God's Church!

140. Position Statements from Within the Recent Life of the Movement

Editor's note: At the request of the Commission on Christian Unity, Barry Callen compiled this list of recent statements about Christian unity emerging from within the life of the Church of God movement.

1. 1963. All-Boards Congress and Planning Council: "We need a strong emphasis on redemptive fellowship in the church. Often our acceptance of other denominations and even members of our own congregations has been conditional, based on whether or not they agreed with 'Church of God' thinking. Perhaps we have forgotten the great inclusiveness of 'being in Christ' " [from the final report to the General Assembly of the Findings Committee, June, 1963].

2. 1970. Consultation of the Church of God: "Consensus: (1) Polarities recognized were: inclusive vs. exclusive fellowship; social concerns vs. evangelism; 'come-outism' vs. cooperative involvement; cardinal beliefs vs. tradition; diversity vs. uniformity; delegated assembly vs. general assembly. (2) Recognition of racial divisiveness and need to press for the removal of it. (3) Need to rethink sainthood and servanthood. (4) Find ways to utilize a larger variety of ministries. (5) Remain a non-joiner but initiate more conversations with other groups. (6) Clarify responsibilities of the Committee on Christian Unity. (7) Officially endorse cooperative endeavors overseas. (8) Share insights on unity wherever doors are open" [report to the General Assembly, June, 1970].

3. 1974. Consultation on Doctrine: "As we have examined the theological and historical root system which has produced the movement, we have recognized the humanness of the pioneers of the past, while, at the same time, recognizing the rightness of direction which they gave to the movement. A reexamination of their posture regarding the nature of the church and the role of the Church of God as a reforming movement has given additional evidence that the Church is of God and that God is still working in his church to call sinners to repentance, Christians to unity, and the world to judgment." See the significant section "The Unity of the Church" in this Consultation's printed report to the General Assembly, [June, 1974, pp. 23–29].

4. 1974. Yokefellow Statement: "It is our belief that the New Testament sets forth the ideal that all Christians, operating in true humanity, should be able to learn from one another. We maintain, moreover, the conviction that this movement represents a force of reformation leadership within Christendom with its emphasis on ecumenicity based on unity rather than on union. To this end, therefore, we encourage through every means posssible the establishing and maintaining of work relationships with other like-minded groups on the national, state, and local levels" [report to the General Assembly, June, 1974].

5. 1979. The *We Believe* statement of the School of Theology, Anderson University: "The dividedness among Christian people today is not just unfortunate; it is inappropriate and wholly unacceptable. Unity is clearly God's will for the church.... The goal is less a contrived peace treaty among deeply divided church organizations and more a radical reconsideration of what is an appropriate network of relationships among brothers and sisters in Christ."

6. 1983. Commission on Christian Unity: "Where Do We Go From Here?", a printed booklet presented to the General Assembly as "a statement of concern and guidance to the Church of God (Anderson, Ind.) from the Commission on Christian Unity," June 1983 [see entry 133].

7. 1984. Consultation on Mission and Ministry of the Church of God (Indianapolis, April, 1984, see entry 122). This Consultation established as one of its priority areas of concern the task of the church to really function as the church. One stated goal for the movement to the end of the twentieth century is "to expand ministries through voluntary relationships with Christian groups outside the Church of God Reformation Movement and seek to live out the vision of unity through broader interdependent relationships that serve mutual needs for training, fellowship, and witness."

8. 1985. Committee on Long Range Planning and Executive Council presented the following "for information and guidance" to the June, 1985, General Assembly: "... supports the historical stance of the Church of God Reformation Movement to seek intentional inter-church relationships through which its own ministries are strengthened and which provide opportunity for the Church of God Reformation Movement to live out its message of Christian unity through enriching the entire Body of Christ."

9. 1988. The General Assembly adopted the resolution, "Inter-Church Cooperation," June, 1988 (see entry 25). It reads in part: "Inter-church relationships should be seen as opportunities to serve and witness in light of the distinctive heritage of the Church of God reformation movement. We have something important to share as well as receive in any such relationship."

10. 1988. Mission Statement for the Church of God Movement. The General Assembly endorsed a mission statement for the Church of God in June, 1988 [see entry 125]. It includes: "To build up the whole body of Christ in unity."

11. 1995. Leaders' Visioning Retreat. See entry 127. This retreat of leaders of the Church of God (Jan. 1995) affirmed that the Church of God exists, among other things, to "Celebrate the Unity of the Body of Christ."

141. Publications Related to Christian Unity

Editor's note: A major new bibliography of published materials and select unpublished theses/dissertations related to the theological tradition of the Church of God movement (including the subject of Christian unity) is found at the end of Barry Callen, *Contours of a Cause: The Theological Vision of the Church of God* (Anderson) (Anderson University School of Theology, 1995). Following are selections from that larger listing.

1. Charles Brown, *The Church Beyond Division* (Warner Press, 1939).

2. Barry Callen, "The Church of God Reformation Movement: A Study in Ecumenical Idealism," M.Th. thesis, Asbury Theological Seminary, 1969.

3. Barry Callen, *Thinking and Acting Together* (Warner Press, 1992)—especially the General Assembly statement on "Inter-Church Relationship Guidelines."

4. Barry Callen, "What We Have Learned," unpublished paper (Open Forum with the Christian Churches/Churches of Christ), Central States Ministers Meeting, St. Joseph, Mich, 1993.

5. Barry Callen and James North, "Open Forum: A Meeting of Two Movements," VITAL CHRISTIANITY (Feb. 1993) (appeared simultaneously in *Christian Standard*).

6. Barry Callen, *It's God's Church!: Life and Legacy of Daniel S. Warner* (Warner Press, 1995).

7. Barry Callen, *Contours of a Cause: The Theological Vision of the Church of God Movement* (Anderson) (Anderson University School of Theology, 1995).

8. Barry Callen, "Daniel S. Warner: Joining Holiness and All Truth Together," *Wesleyan Theological Journal* (Spring 1995).

9. Val Clear, "Reflections of a Postsectarian," *The Christian Century* (Jan. 16, 1963).

10. Wilfred Jordan, ed., *The Shining Light* publication (Jan.–Feb., 1995) features the reconciling ministry of Samuel G. Hines.

11. Juanita Leonard, ed., *Called To Minister, Empowered To Serve: Women In Ministry* (Warner Press, 1989).

12. James Massey, *Concerning Christian Unity* (Warner Press, 1979).

13. James Massey, "A Positive Force," in Wilfred Jordan and Richard Willowby, eds., *Diamond Jubilee: National Association of the Church of God* (Warner Press, 1991), 3–5.

14. James Massey, "Christian Unity: A Statement About Its Meaning and Expressions," unpublished paper, Open Forum Doctrinal Dialogue, May 21, 1993.

15. Cheryl Sanders, "Ethics of Holiness and Unity in the Church of God," in Juanita Leonard, ed., *Called to Minister, Empowered to Serve: Women in Ministry* (Warner Press, 1989).

16. John Smith, "The Approach of the Church of God (Anderson, Ind.) and Comparable Groups to the Problem of Christian Unity," doctoral diss., University of Southern California Graduate School of Religion, 1954.

17. John Smith, "Holiness and Unity," *Wesleyan Theological Journal* (Spring 1975).

18. John Smith, *The Quest for Holiness and Unity* (Warner Press, 1980).

19. John Smith, *I Will Build My Church: Biblical Insights on Distinguishing Doctrines of the Church of God* (Warner Press, 1985).

20. Gilbert Stafford, "Experiential Salvation and Christian Unity in the Thought of Seven Theologians of the Church of God (Anderson, Ind.)," doctoral diss., Boston University School of Theology, 1973.

21. Gilbert Stafford, "We Celebrate Our Unity," unpublished paper, World Forum of the Church of God, Sydney, Australia, July, 1995.

22. Merle Strege, *Tell Me The Tale* (Warner Press, 1991).

23. Merle Strege, *Tell Me Another Tale* (Warner Press, 1993).

24. David Telfer, "Sociological and Theological Foundations for Church of God Ministry in Ethnic Minority Communities in the United States," doctoral diss., Iliff School of Theology, 1975.

25. Cecil Watson, "An Analysis of the Schismatic Tendencies in the Church of God Reformation Movement," masters thesis, Anderson University School of Theology, 1957.

II. Churches of God: General Conference (Winebrennerian)

142. Conversations in Recent Decades: Church of God (Anderson) and Churches of God: General Conference (Barry L. Callen)

Editor's note: Within the evolution of the Commission on Christian Unity (see entry 14), several "ecumenical" contacts were pursued, at least at the getting acquainted level. Included were meetings of Church of God leaders with leaders of the Church of the Brethren, the Evangelical Covenant Church of America, and especially the Churches of God (Winebrennerian). In this latter case there was recognition of "major commonalities and heritage," acknowledgment of some difference in polity and doctrine (especially on the subject of "sanctification"), and by 1969 serious discussion about the practicalities of "flowing together." Following is a brief summary by Barry Callen concerning the conversations with the Churches of God: General Conference.

Daniel Warner, primary pioneer of the Church of God movement, originally was a minister of the Churches of God (Winebrennerian). His experiences with and final break from this body are detailed in Barry Callen's *It's God's Church!: Life and Legacy of Daniel S. Warner* (Warner Press, 1995). The resulting separation of these bodies, both committed to Christian unity, has continued for over a century, although a series of events from 1941–1977 renewed a considerable level of constructive contact between them.

In 1941 the Churches of God: General Conference formed a Committee on Christian Unity for the purpose of seeking "close cooperation or definite organic unity" with selected other church bodies. That same year the Gospel Trumpet Company (Church of God) began customizing its Sunday school literature for use by the Churches of God. This publishing relationship lasted about thirty years.

During the years 1955–1959 the young School of Theology in Anderson (founded in 1950) initiated faculty/student dialogue with the Churches of God seminary in Findlay, Ohio. By 1960 the Executive Council of the Church of God had formed a Committee on Conversations that met with its counterpart to explore the possibilities of even closer cooperation. Several joint ministry opportunities were pursued. In 1964 the dialogue was expanded to include the Brethren Church and the Church of the Brethren. Particularly between the Church of God and the Churches of God there were joint conferences, exchanges at the General Assembly and General Conference level, discussion of a joint hymnal, a merger of two congregations (Auburn, Indiana), discussions at the state level in Michigan and Pennsylvania, and even consideration of the seminary in Findlay closing and opening a foundation on the Anderson campus of the Church of God. There was the evident hope that at least these two bodies might "flow together."

For whatever reasons, little such functional flowing together actually occurred in the following years. Priorities tended to keep the paths of these two church bodies largely separate. The most recent meeting was at Anderson College in 1977 with about ten leaders from each group present. There was no talk of "merger," but tentative plans were made for a "Consultation on the Holy Spirit" (which never convened). Despite the considerable commonality of heritage, various experiments in joint ministries, etc., only a few mutually appreciative personal acquaintances (e.g., church historians Harvey Gossard and John W. V. Smith) have kept a certain warmth in this marginal relationship.

In 1995 two books by Barry Callen (*It's God's Church!* and *Contours of a Cause*) drew upon certain Churches of God (Winebrennarian) published sources, sought the critical perspective of Harvey Gossard of the Findlay seminary, and sought to present a fair assessment of the historic relationship between these two church bodies. Callen's earlier history of Anderson University (*Guide of Soul and Mind*, 1992) relied in part on consultation with Richard Kern who earlier had written the history of the University of Findlay. Also in 1995, Donald Dennison, pastor of the Indian Village Church in Auburn, Indiana, was named "Associate in Cross-Cultural Ministries," a Church of God (Anderson) minister called to administer the missions work of the Churches of God: General Conference.

Currently there are no unity dialogues between these two historically related bodies. Occasionally greetings are brought to each others assemblies and seminaries, keeping alive at least congenial contact in the relative absence of significant relationships and cooperative ministries.

III. Christian Churches/Churches of Christ

143. Open Forum: A Meeting of Two Movements
(Barry L. Callen and James B. North)

Editor's note: This news release was published both in VITAL CHRISTIANITY and *Christian Standard* in February, 1993, seeking to inform wider circles in both movements of this Open Forum dialogue to that date.

In the nineteenth century two different Christian movements began that had a common dream. They hoped that all children of God would come together in unity and work for the perfection and mission of God's people under the authority and guidance of biblical teaching.

These two reforming movements—one symbolized by the leadership of Alexander Campbell, the other inspired by pioneers such as Daniel S. Warner—became significant bodies of believers as they grew and matured. Congregations of the Christian Churches/Churches of Christ and the Church of God (Anderson) soon dotted the entire American landscape as well as spreading to many other countries. Leaders such as Campbell and Warner shared a similar vision of Christian unity, but the two movements they represented have remained apart.

Recently that awkward separation has been changing. For the last year, ministers of these two movements have been meeting together in Cincinnati, Ohio, to share their vision of the church, talk about mutual problems of local ministry, and learn about each other's strengths and idiosyncrasies. They have eaten together, prayed, joined in fellowship, and even argued together, and have planned joint worship times. The goal of all this has been to bring to fuller realization the prayer of Jesus that "they all may be one" (John 17:21).

In 1989, national meetings began to occur between leaders of the Christian Churches/Churches of Christ and the Church of God (Anderson). These meetings became known as the "Open Forum." The Open Forum actually began in 1984 as a brainstorming effort within the Christian Churches/Churches of Christ about how to get their congregations out of a lethargic plateau they were then experiencing. A number of individuals decided to call for a meeting of representative key leaders in the Christian Churches/Churches of Christ to probe ways to restore real "movement" into what is fondly called the "Restoration Movement"—a movement to restore New Testament Christianity to today's splintered denominational world.

After several successful meetings where issues of importance were discussed, members of the Church of God (Anderson) were invited in 1989 to come to Traders Point Christian Church in Indianapolis to worship together and discuss issues of common interest in church history, theology, practice, and the ordinances. What emerged from this first meeting was the realization that both groups have an overwhelming number of essential elements in common. Additional meetings involving hundreds of persons now have convened in Anderson, Indiana, in 1990 and in Lexington, Kentucky, in 1991. These friendly meetings have not been shallow and nonconfrontive, however. In spite of the numerous similarities acknowledged by the Christian Churches/Church of God (Anderson), there are still some significant differences between them.

Because of the differences, leaders in the national gatherings decided in 1991 that provision should be made for the scholarly, in-depth discussion of these issues, getting beyond the exploratory conversations held in the much larger Open Forum meetings. In August of that year, a Task Force on Doctrinal Dialogue gathered in Cincinnati, composed of equal numbers of individuals from the two groups. Formal papers were presented from both groups in this and subsequent meetings [see bibliography, entry 146].

Beyond abstract discussion of theological issues, however, these Task Force meetings have manifested a concern for the evangelistic mission of the church. In what ways can these two movements join together in common work for the advancement of the kingdom of God on earth? [Samples of accomplishments to date are listed in entry 145.]

144. What We Have Learned (Barry L. Callen)

Editor's note: What follows are excerpts of a paper delivered by Barry Callen to the Central States Ministers' Meeting of the Church of God, St. Joseph, Michigan, March, 1993. It highlights eleven lessons being learned by Church of God participants in the "Open Forum" process with the Christian Churches/Churches of Christ. This paper attempts to represent the thinking of the Church of God participants, the most active being Barry Callen, Keith Huttenlocker, Kenneth Jones, David Lawson, Vernon Maddox, Arlo Newell, Spencer Spaulding, and Gilbert Stafford.

1. *This Process Is Worth the Time.* The last thing any of us needs is more busywork, more routine and maybe unnecessary tending to organizational machinery. All of us are busy people and have to be convinced that such a new venture as this multi-year "Open Forum" process with the Christian Churches/Churches of Christ is not just more meetings and endless talk. Dialogue participants have dealt directly with the question, "Is it all really worthwhile?" Although the final verdict is not in, most of the participants have developed a growing conviction that this process may be ordered of God for some important ends. We judge it most worthwhile, even though many specifics of potential outcomes still are seen only dimly, if at all.

2. *Historical Perspective Increases One's Humility.* The Church of God movement, especially in its early decades, tended to dismiss as without value much of Christian church history. That history was seen mostly as centuries of apostasy now about to end with the gathering of God's true church and the return of Christ. In the train of bold reformers like Martin Luther and John Wesley, movement leaders rejoiced in the belief that God was introducing again the "early morning light." We saw ourselves being called to "cleanse the sanctuary" in a full and final way as the age was coming to a close. So it has been easy for us as a movement to value AD 50 and AD 1880, while generally lamenting most in between as a sorry state of affairs.

There now is a growing realization of the loss we have sustained by devaluing the long and rich "restorationist" tradition of which the movement is a part. Particularly in the United States, the Stone/Campbell tradition predated the Church of God movement and is full of common cause with it. There are some differences, to be sure. Some of these differences can be an enrichment to the movement. Why? In part because, in addition to any distinctiveness granted the Church of God movement by divine grace, the movement also is a product of a given time and place in church history. That time and place inevitably have had a significant shaping influence, an influence we have only begun to understand. Sharing with a dialogue partner who has so much in common with us sharpens our historical perspective and thereby enhances our self-understanding.

3. *We Too Have Some Walls.* Church of God participants in the Open Forum have learned that the structural and non-structural obstacles to real Christian unity are more subtle and complex than sometimes we have assumed. We all live in a day when traditional denominational walls are

eroding rapidly. Nevertheless, even free-church "restorationist" bodies that champion non-creedalism and Christian unity visions often themselves develop significant and stubborn "denominational" characteristics (products of humanity and history). For idealists like us, that is a hard lesson to accept.

4. *We Need To Practice What We Preach.* Why did some Church of God leaders become involved in this particular dialogue process? The answer is more than the fact that there was an opportunity and a direct invitation from leaders of the Christian Churches/Churches of Christ. For many decades our movement has set forth what we have judged to be the New Testament vision of Christian unity. We have declared our willingness to "reach our hands in fellowship to every bloodwashed one." Sometimes over the decades we have been accused of being sectish ourselves, not living up to our proclaimed ideal. In fact, we have not always modeled clearly what we have announced with the best of intentions. At first it was natural for our movement to focus on being critical of the obvious wrongs seen all across the denominationalized and demoralized Christian community. The positive building of a viable alternative, however, always is more difficult than the negative judging of what is so wrong. Some of us in the movement have learned only slowly that it is difficult to preach convincingly a commitment-based and fellowship-based vision of Christian unity without being intentional about seeking its actualization.

5. *Both Groups Resist the M Word.* Participants in this dialogue process have reminded each other over these last years that the *M* word, merger, is not on the Open Forum agenda. A structural uniting of our two church bodies is not our priority goal. We all know that immediate mistrust and spirited opposition would arise from within each of our constituencies if it were perceived that these dialogues were exploring seriously anything like a "denominational" merger. Neither body envisions such a union outcome as the way to achieve Christian unity. Neither body has a structure to make such a thing possible even if it were desirable. We have learned, nonetheless, that a certain "flowing together" is a possibility, probably even in some sense a divinely guided goal. Such meshing should focus on building relationships, enriching understandings, and discovering cooperative ministry opportunities.

We have become convinced that there are many important things that we and the Christian Churches/Churches of Christ can do to help each other in church life and mission. Without raising the specter of a "merger mentality," we can do much together to further the Kingdom's cause. We have learned, however, that moving over this fruitful frontier, whatever its components might turn out to be, will require a selfless attitude, and certainly an avoidance of "turf protection" by our several church institutions. History teaches that, right as it may be, this cooperative path is narrow and traveled successfully only by a few.

6. *Mission Is the Motive That Inspires our Dialogue.* Merger is not the goal, and a bad conscience about poor performance in past unity efforts did play a key role in beginning this dialogue process. The primary motive driving and sustaining this dialogue, however, has been a mutual concern for the better accomplishment of Christian mission. Mission is the motive. Mission is accomplished best in cooperation with brothers and sisters in Christ. The church is bigger than "us." Its mission will get done best when we decide to do it together.

7. *We Have Much To Learn If We Remain Open.* Driven by our commitment to accomplishing the church's mission, the Church of God participants in this dialogue have tended to learn one or two theological lessons in the process. One is that the movement should take more seriously its own stance of non-creedalism. The challenge for us is not to protect our current perceptions of truth (one way to define denominationalism) so much as it is to continue seeking the most adequate possible apprehension of truth in an open fellowship of maturing believers. Openness and maturing does not survive well in a context of defensiveness and suspicion. It is enabled by widening the circle of disciples who are searching for all that God intends for the whole church to know and be and do. Much overblown has been our movement's historic fear of theological contamination if we should involve ourselves seriously with Christians whose perspectives differ at points from our own. Some of us now are learning that we ought to believe more strongly that truth is not that fragile and that God still superintends the life of his faithful people. In the end, it is not light that yields to darkness, but darkness to light.

8. *Baptism: Study of an Apparent Doctrinal Difference.* Neither body involved in this Open Forum process is creedal in nature, nor by tradition is either "fundamentalist" in the rigid, doctrinaire sense of this term. Doctrinal positions, nonetheless, have been explored in considerable detail, with only a few found to be stubbornly troublesome between us. Theological "style" and emphasis occasionally vary between our groups, mostly products of our differing histories of origin. A key reason appears

to be the impact of aspects of the "Enlightenment" on one group and the more experience-oriented impact of American revivalism on the other.

The doctrinal dialogue portion of the Open Forum often has focused its attention on the subject of Christian baptism. Both groups believe baptism to be a biblical mandate and best administered by immersion. We agree that genuine repentance of sin is required prior to baptism, thus making this sacred practice not appropriate for infants. We agree further that there is no merit leading to salvation in the baptismal mechanics themselves—baptism is not what saves. With all this agreement, however, one key area related to baptism remains unresolved. Our dialogue partner tends to see the phrase "for the remission of sins" necessarily related closely to baptism, although by this association not meaning "baptismal regeneration." We have explored why the retention of this phrase with baptism is seen as so crucial by one group and why it is a matter of substantial concern for the other. Language certainly is one problem. Time and patient listenings are required to really hear and understand each other here. But language is not all of the problem.

One insight we have gained has been of some help. Our differing approaches to baptism and "the remission of sins," obviously a biblical phrase, can be explained in part by the differing "enemies" each group has been fighting over the decades. The Christian Churches/Churches of Christ is a movement that has been resisting "faith-only" revivalism and "liberalism" as represented to them by the Disciples of Christ wing of the restorationist movement. "For the remission of sins" has become a touchstone in their eyes for strict biblical obedience. The Church of God, on the other hand, has been resisting Roman Catholicism and her "Protestant daughters." Our movement has been very sensitive about anything that appears to retain for establishment Christianity a control over the dispensing of God's grace through given church rites, including baptism.

9. *We Suffer a Common Dilemma.* Both dialogue bodies have the dilemma of freedom-spontaneity versus efficiency-accountability in church life. Both groups resist a denominationalizing trend, but also seek some path to more efficiency and mutual accountability. Here is a central dilemma we share, one not easily resolved. While neither of us wants any more church structure, both are searching for better ways to be accountable and effective. No one has yet arrived at the ideal place. Are there ways that we can assist each other along this uncharted path? We are learning that there are.

10. *Testimony Is a Good Strategy.* A productive way to proceed in demonstrating the potential meaningfulness of this Open Forum is to take local and practical action. In Cincinnati, Ohio, for instance, pastors and spouses from each of these church groups now have become acquainted and mutually supportive. Professors and administrators from some Church of God schools have met some of their counterparts. Visits and guest lectures across group lines have begun. Such developments are encouraging and might be repeated elsewhere with good benefit. All of these Open Forum meetings and talk are helpful only when real relationships evolve and prove productive for the Kingdom of God. Some good things have happened and need to be told widely.

11. *Each Group Is Challenged To Widen the Dialogue Circle.* More dialogue participants are invited and more wisdom is needed. The bottom line is this—two similar groups of God's children have begun an honest quest for a fuller realization of the divine will for our day. The goal is elusive, but since it seems divinely motivated, the quest goes on.

145. What We Have Accomplished Together (Open Forum Dialogue) (David L. Lawson)

It is apparent that these years of discussion and mutual effort have been productive for the Church of God and the Christian Churches/Churches of Christ. We have developed a mutual appreciation and trust in our times together. We have discovered a broad expanse of consensus in our common faith and work and have expanded the number of persons who have first-hand acquaintance with the dialogue.

Beyond increased acquaintance and much writing and talking, we have found ways to be on mission together. Here are a few.

1. The Missionary Board of the Church of God has cooperated with the mission work of the Christian Churches/Churches of Christ to prepare a missionary couple to serve unreached peoples.

2. In one area of the world the Missionary Board of the Church of God, through its registration with that nation, was able to assist the Christian Churches' mission by conserving equipment and property which otherwise would have been lost.

3. Some local churches have found ways to work together. They have had some unity services on Sunday nights. In some cases, pastors and spouses have formed support groups among themselves.

4. There has been some shared use of facilities.

5. A Christian Church has hosted a singing group from one of the Church of God colleges.

6. A Joliet, Illinois, Christian Church reported a united vacation church school effort with a local Church of God congregation and described it as "a very effective ministry together," to be repeated.

7. Christian Churches colleges and area unity gatherings have invited Church of God persons as guest leaders or visitors.

8. Eleanor Daniel, Christian Churches faculty member then at Cincinnati Bible Seminary, attended by special invitation the 1991 Commission on Christian Higher Education meeting of the Church of God and offered excellent observations from her more objective viewpoint.

9. In promotion of Barry Callen's 1992 biography on Rev. Lillie McCutcheon, *She Came Preaching,* both *Christian Standard* and College Press agreed to assist Warner Press in reviewing the book, and College Press offered to highlight other books as well as help acquaint the Christian Churches with Church of God history and teachings.

10. Leroy Fulton, former president of Warner Southern College of the Church of God, was appointed to a key staff position at Pacific Christian College, was the first to include the Forum papers in a college library, recently presented to Pacific's faculty a lecture on "Who Is the Church of God?" and has begun through Pacific Christian College a preaching clinic including participants from both communions.

11. In recent annual meetings of the North American Christian Convention, leaders of the Church of God have been invited to bring greetings, pray, and lead seminars. Included have been Leroy Fulton, Keith Huttenlocker, and Barry Callen.

12. Barry Callen has been invited to speak in chapel sessions at Emmanuel School of Religion in Johnson City, Tennessee, and Lincoln Seminary in Lincoln, Illinois.

13. A Biblical Literacy Task Force, composed of leaders from the Christian Churches/Churches of Christ and the Church of God, has met several times to attempt together a biblical literacy campaign under the theme "Read For Your Life." Included have been: (1) Church of God leaders Sherrill Hayes, Board of Christian Education, David Shultz, Warner Press, Fred Shively, Anderson University, and David Lawson, Leadership Council, (2) with Christian Churches leaders Sam Stone,

Brian Clark, and Dick McKinley. The hope is to offer materials to local churches of both communions by January 1, 1997.

14. Invited to the 1995 International Convention of the Church of God was Pastor Bob Russell of the Christian Churches. He was asked to give leadership in an all-day Vision-2-Grow session. Warner Press featured several of Russell's books for sale at the Convention and worked with Standard Publishing in delivering this service to our ministers.

15. Sam Stone, editor of the Christian Standard, was present for an all-day conference led by Vision-2-Grow and Bob Russell. He was the guest of David Lawson and the Leadership Council of the Church of God.

16. Dean John Howard of Gardner College in Canada served for a considerable time as the interim pastor of a significant local Church of Christ in Alberta, Canada.

17. Barry Callen published three books in 1995, *It's God's Church!* (Warner Press), *Contours of a Cause* (Anderson School of Theology), and *Sharing Heaven's Music* (Abingdon Press). Copies of the first two were given by the Leadership Council to members of the working group on doctrinal dialogue for study and primary focus at the October 1995 discussion. The *Contours* book included numerous reflections arising from the years of the Open Forum. The third, on preaching, included a chapter written by Dr. Fred Norris, scholar of the Christian Churches. Dr. Callen also included an article by Byron Lambert in the Spring, 1995, issue of the *Wesleyan Theological Journal,* an academic journal Callen edits. The article's subject, Christian experience, has been one of frequent discussion in the Open Forum dialogues.

18. Dialogue members have noted and celebrated two new studies in the historical and theological heritage of the Christian Churches/Churches of Christ. One was *In Search of Christian Unity* by Henry Webb; the other was *Union in Truth* by James North.

19. The Institute for Servant Leadership has sought Christian Churches participation in preaching clinics held in Indianapolis and in Salem, Ohio, with good representation resulting. The 1996 clinic will replace the St. Joseph minister's meeting and offers excellent opportunity for expansion of this effort.

20. We have laid beginning plans for a joint publication drawing together the history and significance of the Forum and Dialogue. Authors will be James North and Barry Callen, one scholar from each fellowship.

146. Bibliography of Subjects Addressed Formally (Open Forum)

Editor's note: The Leadership Council of the Church of God has maintained a bibliography of the formal study papers delivered at the Open Forums and Doctrinal Dialogues. These dialogues between the Church of God and the Christian Churches/Churches of Christ have convened since 1989. As of October, 1995, the list contained sixty entries. The following are those focusing on the subject of Christian unity.

1. Bream, Harvey, "Unity Through Restoration" (April 1991).

2. Callen, Barry, "The Signs of Christian Unity in the History of the Church of God Reformation Movement" (March 1990).

3. Corts, David, "What Are the Signs of Christian Unity in the Acceptance of Others As Christians?" (March 1990).

4. Dwyer, Timothy, "Implications for Christian Unity in Acts 2:37–38" (April 1991).

5. Fife, Robert, "What Have Been Signs of Christian Unity In Our History?" (March 1990).

6. Fife, Robert, "Our Conception of Christian Unity" (May 1993).

7. Hines, Samuel, "Contemporary Possibilities for Christian Unity" (March 1990).

8. Huttenlocker, Keith, "Implications for Christian Unity from Acts 2:41–47" (April 1991).

9. Jones, Kelvin, "Of One Accord: My Vision for Christian Unity" (March 1990).

10. Jones, Kenneth, "Implications for Christian Unity in Acts 2:1–13" (April 1991).

11. Kelley, W. Ray, "Implications for Christian Unity in Acts 2:1–13" (April 1991).

12. Massey, James, "Christian Unity: A Statement About Its Meaning and Expressions" (May 1993).

13. Newell, Arlo, "Unity Through Holiness" (April 1991).

14. Pearson, Sharon, "What Are the Signs of Christian Unity in the Acceptance of Others as Christians?" (March 1990).

15. Phillips, Calvin, "The Signs of Christian Unity in the Practice of the Ordinance of Christian Baptism" (March 1990).

16. Reese, Gareth, "Implications for Christian Unity in Acts 2:37–38" (April 1991).

17. Scott, Mark, "Implications for Christian Unity in Acts 2:41–47" (April 1991).

18. Shively, Kay, Response to Knofel Staton: "The Teaching in Acts 2:17–18 and Its Implications for Christian Unity" (April 1991).

19. Staton, Knofel, "The Teaching in Acts 2:17–18 and Its Implications for Christian Unity" (April 1991).

20. Taylor, Larry, "My Vision for Christian Unity" (March 1990).

21. Taylor, Myron, "The Grand Design for Christian Unity" (March 1989).

Part Three: International Vision, Initiatives, and Partnerships

I. Historical Perspectives
II. Philosophical Perspectives
III. Assemblies and Countries

Part Three: International Vision, Initiatives, and Partnerships

Section I
Historical Perspectives

147. Early Efforts Toward a World Vision (John W. V. Smith)

Editor's note: The following are excerpts from chapter six of John Smith's *The Quest for Holiness and Unity* (Warner Press, 1980).

As would be expected, the initial thrust of evangelistic efforts by the "flying ministry" was concentrated in the United States. The calls for meetings were so numerous...that every available worker was traveling constantly in response to requests. There was little time to sit and dream of new worlds to conquer. It needs to be noted, however, that even during the first decade of the movement's history [1880s] there were several contacts and some overt efforts to extend the reform work beyond the national borders. By the turn of the [twentieth] century the international activity was extensive, and by the time of the first organization of any planned effort through the creation of a "missionary committee" in 1909 the work was global. This chapter will review the highlights of this period of spontaneous, unstructured expansion of the movement to worldwide proportions.

Since a great deal of the activity of the publishing work and the itinerant ministry was centered in the upper Middle West, it was only natural that the first international extension of the message was to Canada. The first contact made by the movement to this northern neighbor of the United States was through the printed pages of the *Gospel Trumpet*.

The first extension of the Church of God reformation movement beyond the southern border of the United States was initiated by Benjamin F. Elliott (1859–1926). In 1889 Elliott, a former Methodist preacher, began preaching in the streets of Santa Barbara, California. Around 1891 he became impressed with the need to spread the gospel to the Spanish-speaking people. In the fall of 1891 Elliott was led to go into Lower California (Baja Calif.), Mexico.

In addition to its extension to these North American neighbor countries of Canada and Mexico, the Church of God, by the time of the formation of the Missionary Committee in 1909, had spread to or had significant contacts in at least seventeen other countries. In the British Isles the movement was functioning in England, Scotland, and Ireland. On the European continent there were congregations or known adherents in Germany, Switzerland, Denmark, Sweden, Poland, and Russia. In Asia there were either missionaries or native pastors in China and Japan, and in India there was significant work developing from four widely separated geographic centers. Egypt was the the only African nation represented. The continent of Australia also had been reached and there were congregations on at least three islands in the West Indies: Jamaica, Trinidad, and Bermuda.

In reviewing this worldwide expansion without benefit of a sending agency or any other method of assuring the underwriting of travel expense and support, one cannot help being struck with some sense of amazement that such could happen. While it is true that there was a certain "naturalness" about much of the international activity—German immigrants went to Germany, Scots to Scotland, Swedes to Sweden—there was more than the desire to share a good thing with kith and kin. The same spirit which drove the "flying messengers" to crisscross the North American continent also motivated these global itinerants. They were in possession of a message which they believed all the people in the world ought to hear. Any place on the earth was a potential "field" for witness and evangelization simply because the people there had not yet heard. While being "burdened for" or "led to" a given place often was related to previous contacts or information, the "call" was considered to be God-sent and there was a willingness to respond with faith that the means would be provided. By 1909 more than two dozen people were "out there," by faith, sharing the message in at least twenty countries of the world.

148. Establishing the North American Missionary Board
(Lester A. Crose)

Editor's note: The following are excerpts from chapter two of Lester Crose's *Passport for a Reformation* (Warner Press, 1981).

The need for some form of organization to bring together and coordinate the missionary outreach of the Church of God reformation movement became evident by 1909. Twenty years of voluntary and independent expressions of missionary endeavor were now culminating in the formation of a Missionary Board. The Missionary Board became the second Church of God agency to organize on a national level [the first was the Gospel Trumpet Publishing Company].

Good as the early missionaries were who went out on their own under God, problems began to arise and multiply. This gave the church at home a growing concern for the well-being and future of its missionary expansion into new fields and the growth of work already existing. Many of these pioneer missionaries felt responsible only to God. Therefore, each one did what he or she felt should be done, seeking always the guidance of the Holy Spirit. But strained situations began to develop where there were more than one or two missionaries. Living in a new culture, many were unable to cope with new and strange situations arising. This caused differences among missionaries and sometimes between missionaries and native workers.

Financial support also was creating some misunderstandings. Missionaries went to the field on faith—faith that God would supply their needs. But some could tell the story of their work better than others, by letter or when they were home on furlough, and, therefore, they got more support. Churches became aware of these developing inequities, and pastors were asking questions and suggesting that there might be a better way. Also, new missionaries going out on their own were most of the time ill-equipped, not knowing how to care for themselves, how to live in another country so different from their own, or how to learn a language. Consequently, the inevitable happened.

Following is a quotation from George P. Tasker's diary dated June 12, 1909:

> On June 12, 1909, after an address on "Government in the Church," H. M. Riggle, after presenting our plans for a missionary paper, to be called the *Missionary Herald*, recommended that, "certain brethren should be recognized amongst us, by common consent, as having and exercising in behalf of the Church, the responsibility and care of the foreign missionary work. They should be capable of advising, instructing, encouraging and restraining." The names here presented, and that were acknowledged by the immediate rising to their feet of the entire assembly of ministers, were D. O. Teasley, J. W. Byers, E. E. Byrum, E. A. Reardon, G. P. Tasker, H. A. Brooks

and D. F. Oden. Brother Riggle then said, "It is intended that the entire ministry should cooperate with these brethren," to which all said, "Amen."

This was a bold step forward for a church that did not believe in organization. It was to provide purpose, meaning, and coordination to former independency. It was to make possible more systematic giving so that missionaries would receive more equitable remuneration for their services. It should be noted that all these brethren had been abroad except one. It was assumed that their observations and experiences would enable them to know better how to look after missionary funds and personnel.

In the first annual meeting of the new Missionary Board (June, 1910), twenty-seven missionaries were recognized: British Isles—4, China—2, Japan—4, British West Indies—2, Germany—4, and India—11. There were actually only nineteen missionaries because eight of those listed were evangelists. The first missionaries appointed by the Board during that meeting were N. S. Duncan and his wife, who were to go to Barbados. Duncan had been in Trinidad before. In order to have the necessary funds to go, he was selling his property in the United States. The Board also approved Charles E. Hunnex for service in China. The missionary family grew rapidly, and eight new missionaries were sent out during the next year. Within two years sixty-five regular missionaries were on the field: India—20, British West Indies—18, Denmark—2, Germany—6, Russia—5, Ireland—1, China—5, Japan—4, and Egypt—4. Actually, seventeen of those listed were evangelists or pastors, not missionaries in the strictest sense. Six new missionary homes were built and properties purchased.

Certain policies were being formulated for the benefit of the work. It was thought caution should be exercised "in the immediate establishing of orphanages." There was reason for this because so many wanted to start orphanages and the Board considered such an objective not to be the prime purpose of missions. Encouragement was given to those preparing for missionary service to take correspondence courses being offered by the Church of God Missionary Home in New York City. An early attempt was made to regularize the disposition of funds raised by missionaries home on furlough. The Board had to deal with the necessity of making a fifty percent cut in missionary allowances when the bottom dropped out from under missionary income early on. And it was thought best that "the native church should support its own native ministers in a native style."

To be sure that only true missionaries were sent to the field, a motion was adopted that only "apostles" should be sent.

In 1912 the Missionary Board moved all missionary correspondence from the general files of the Gospel Trumpet Company to missionary files in the Board's office. By 1914 the Missionary Board was in need of holding property and carrying on legal business. Therefore, it became incorporated under the laws of the state of Indiana, adopting a new constitution to conform to those laws related to the incorporation of a not-for-profit organization. It was necessary to add four members, making a membership of eleven. From then on the Missionary Board could register in other countries as an alien corporation in order to hold properties and do business.

From the very beginning it was considered imperative to have a missionary publication. D. O. Teasley was selected as editor of the *Missionary Herald*, which was a paper for missionary activities only. It drew together and united all efforts. It kept the church informed. In the opinion of some it helped to develop for the Church of God a modern missionary movement. Unfortunately, it existed for only three years, and in 1913 the *Gospel Trumpet* made an announcement that it would devote one issue per month to missionary emphasis.

149. History of World Conferences and World Forums, 1955–1995
(Barry L. Callen)

Only in recent decades has the Church of God movement established formal international settings for cooperative dialogue and ministry. The first and most prominent of these is the World Conference that to date has convened as follows:

1955, Fritzlar, Germany
1959, Essen, Germany
1963, Bochum, Germany
1967, Zurich, Switzerland
1971, Oaxtepec, Mexico
1975, Beruit, Lebanon—canceled, war
1980, Anderson, Indiana, USA (centennial)
1983, Nairobi, Kenya
1987, Seoul, South Korea
1991, Wiesbaden, Germany
1995, Sydney, Australia

A particularly historic convening was the 1980 World Conference in Anderson, Indiana. This was a celebration of the centennial of the Church of God movement and saw the first convenings of the World Forum and the International Dialogue on Doctrine (both meeting immediately prior to the World Conference itself).

The quadrennial event of World Conferences began in 1955 when the Church of God movement was active in only thirty-five nations. T. Franklin Miller, then the executive of the Board of Christian Education in the United States, provided much of the initial vision and leadership.

Shortly after World War II, during an International Youth Convention in Miami, Florida, the Church of God in North America was invited to hold in Europe a world meeting of the church's youth. The resulting meeting was in Fritzlar, Germany, in the summer of 1955. Fritzlar was and still is the home of the Bible Training School in Germany. Dr. Miller named Tom A. Smith, national youth director in the United States, to carry major planning responsibilities. His young counterpart in Germany was Willi Krenz, a ministerial student at Fritzlar.

Dr. Miller continued giving executive direction during the decade of the 1950s through sponsorship of the national Board of Christian Education in the United States. Financial assistance came largely from the national ministry agencies of the North American church. Leadership and financial responsibility for the conferences was turned over to the Executive (Leadership) Council in 1960. The Executive Secretary of the Council became the chief coordinator for these events. Charles Weber was director of all conferences in the decade of the 1960s. T. Franklin Miller continued to make many of the arrangements during that decade. William Reed directed the conferences in the 1970s, Paul Tanner in the 1980s, and Edward Foggs during the final decade of this century, all from their leadership posts in Anderson, Indiana.

World Conferences have been scheduled at four-year intervals, with the exception of 1980 when the meeting was scheduled at a five-year interval to coincide with the centennial celebration of the Church of God movement's beginning. In the Tenth World Conference (Australia, 1995), special recognition was given to Willi Krenz of Germany, participant in all Conferences and a planning leader of most.

Dr. Miller reports concerning that first meeting in 1955: "Deep emotional and spiritual tides flowed freely at Fritzlar. It was not only the first world meeting of Church of God people, but it was the first meeting of its kind to be held following World War II. Youth were present who had only recently fought on opposing sides. Leaders from seventeen countries gathered to build bridges of redemptive Christian love and to give themselves again to the supremacy of Jesus Christ. Friendships were begun there which have lasted across the years." One friendship was that of youth leaders Willi Krenz (Germany) and Norman Beard (United States). Together they would contribute much to future Conferences and to TRI-S, the international education program of Anderson University in Europe and elsewhere.

Following an evaluation of the 1955 event, it was agreed that this type of international fellowship and dialogue was needed and should continue. Essen, Germany, was selected as the site for a 1959 World Conference. The theme for the Essen meeting was "Jesus Christ Is The Lord." Eighteen nations were represented. All program materials were prepared in both the English and German languages. There were 212 registered delegates, with over 1,000 persons attending general services.

The stirring procession of national flags, which has characterized the opening and closing of all subsequent Conferences, first occurred at the Essen meeting. In those days commercial flags were not available, so they were hand-made by the women of the Essen congregation. Essen was also the first occasion to feature the graphic arts with an impressive backdrop to highlight the Conference theme. Essen also was the longest of the World Conferences to date, lasting over two weekends. All meal functions were held in the Handleshof Hotel and Sunday services were held in the town hall. Conferences were planned during the daytime hours, with buses transporting the entire delegation to churches in neighboring cities for mass meetings. The bonding that resulted in these eight days of preaching, singing, sharing, and fellowship impacted the delegates greatly.

The 1963 World Conference in Bochum, Germany, was especially noteworthy for two significant reasons. First, sponsorship changed from the Board of Christian Education to the Executive Council in the United States. Second, this turned out to be the last World Conference to be held in Germany for nearly three decades. The trend was toward a widening international focus. Since the Conference now was more an "all church" meeting than principally the gathering of the church's youth, it was judged by the Board of Christian Education that an agency more representative of the church's total constituency and concerns should assume responsibility. Since the Executive Council was now a staffed office of the General Assembly in North America, it was agreed that the Council should accept this assignment.

Twenty nations were represented in Bochum, Germany, in 1963. The 600 delegates gathered to discuss the theme, "One Lord, One Faith, One Task." Weekend attendance swelled to more than 1,000. This Conference was scheduled for Wednesday through Sunday, the pattern for all succeeding conferences except Seoul, Korea, which was Wednesday through Friday to accommodate the specific needs of the Korean church. Like the Conference in Essen, the Bochum meeting was held in an auditorium during the day and moved to the churches for evening services.

The World Conference moved to Zurich, Switzerland, in 1967. Said Harold Phillips: "This was quite a setting in which to explore the topic 'The Church: Her Nature and Mission', for just a few blocks away stood the church in which Zwingli lit reformation fires in the sixteenth century and not a few gave their lives as Christian martyrs." About six hundred delegates from eighteen countries explored the meaning of this theme. The program was built around the New Testament metaphors of salt, light, soldier, and servant. R. Eugene Sterner, program chair, said in his welcome to the delegates: "We come from every continent, from climates tropical and frigid, from both eastern and western hemispheres, to beautiful Switzerland, with its towering Alps and its peace-loving people. We come because we want to be together and because one overarching purpose dominates our lives—to make Christ known, and to become, in this troubled world, the penetrating, proclaiming, marching, serving church."

It was agreed in Zurich that four years hence another Conference should be held, this time in the western hemisphere. Thus the 1971 World Conference convened outside Mexico City in Oaxtepec, the beautiful site of earlier Pan American Games. Housing and meals were provided in the sports complex so that opportunity for fellowship and dialogue could be enhanced. The theme, "Called To Serve the Present Age," directed the 496 registered delegates in their thinking for the four conference days. A new record of international involvement was set with twenty-seven different countries represented. This was also a landmark meeting in that for the first time representative delegates from the various nations participated in the World Conference planning. This was a new plateau in internationalizing this worldwide event.

The planning committee elected in 1971 convened in 1973 to make preparations for the 1975 Conference. The site for the Conference was to be the city of Beruit, Lebanon, located on the eastern coast of the Mediterranean. To the great disappointment of all who were planning to attend, the meeting had to be canceled because of the outbreak of war in the Mideast.

According to T. Franklin Miller, "The most significant gathering in regard to planning since 1955 was the next meeting of the planning committee in 1977." It convened as the Worldwide Strategy and Planning Consultation and met in a conference center about 100 miles outside Nairobi, Kenya. For ten days the members listened to various points of view, took time for reflection, and sought the will of the Holy Spirit. It was in this 1977 meeting that world leaders of the Church of God movement drafted a design and further nurtured the growing idea that soon would become the World Forum.

The first World Forum met in Anderson, Indiana, in 1980 preceding the sixth World Conference. In this inaugural Forum major papers were delivered by Donald Johnson and Douglas Welch on the theme "International Partnership In Mission." It was unanimously agreed to continue the World Forum on a regular basis. It has preceded each World Conference since that time. Another first for 1980 was the convening of the International Dialogue on Doctrine hosted by the Anderson School of Theology (the Dialogue's history is told briefly in entry 150). The 1980 Conference set all records for Church of God international participation to that date.

Laura Withrow was chair of the program committee for the 1980 annual campmeeting held in Anderson. Barry Callen preached the keynote sermon for the World Conference and T. Franklin Miller acted as overall coordinator for the Conference, Forum, and Dialogue. More than 250 overseas guests from most of the countries where the Church of God was at work participated in this sixth World Conference. Willi Krenz of Germany and Carlton Cumberbatch of Trinidad were co-chairs of the planning committee for this historic event. Three thousand registered delegates attended the Conference to discuss the theme "Let the World Know." About seven thousand were present at general services, with an estimated 30,000 different persons attending at least one service of the eight-day event (including the annual Anderson International Convention). Simultaneous interpretation was utilized, translating all services into English, Japanese, German, and Spanish.

Nairobi, Kenya, was selected as the site of the 1983 World Conference.

It was held in the beautiful Kenyatta Conference Center in the heart of downtown Nairobi. Twenty-four countries were represented, with four hundred and thirty delegates from the United States. Because the Church of God in Kenya had about 100,000 members, delegates and guests from Africa swelled the attendance at general services to approximately 4,000 persons.

The World Forum in 1983 addressed the subject of "Strategies for Interdependence in Mission." Subjects for the sessions included: "A Biblical Basis for Interdependence in Mission," "How Do We Evangelize Together?" "How Do We Respond to Personal Needs Cooperatively?" and "How Do We Relate to Persons or Groups Seeking Affiliation With the Church of God?" Excerpts from the paper delivered by Douglas Welch are found in entry 151. The planning committee, chaired by Isai Calderon of Guatemala, had set the Conference theme "Partners in God's Action." The keynote sermon was delivered by Edward Foggs following an opening address and greeting to the Conference by the President of Kenya, Daniel Moi. The African choirs were a great blessing. Planned visits to African villages were a highlight for international guests. The Conference ended with a candlelight service.

A new planning committee chaired by Victor Babb of Barbados was named to prepare for the 1987 Conference scheduled for Seoul, South Korea. Represented on the committee were leaders from South Korea, Tanzania, Singapore, Germany, and the United States. The theme chosen for the World Forum was "Unity With Diversity." The World Conference theme was "Arise My People."

Church of God leaders from 52 nations gathered in Seoul, South Korea, in the summer of 1987, with all conferences, rallies, lodging, and food services under one roof, the Seoul Hilton International Hotel. Never before had so many nations been represented in a world gathering of Church of God people. The great increase, from 24 countries represented in Nairobi to 52, was due in part to a strategic decision by the Executive Council of the Church of God in the United States. Since this event was becoming more significant to the life and work of the Church of God all around the world, it was agreed that a way must be found to avoid lack of representation from any nation because of lack of funds.

Budgetary means were appropriated through allocation of World Service funds (United States) on an annual basis and from a premium registration charged North American delegates. Assemblies in every country were invited to send at least one delegate, with some subsidy provided as necessary for travel, food, and lodging. Most nations now not sending delegates were deterred for personal or political reasons, not financial. There were 700 United States delegates in South Korea and 300 registered delegates from other countries. About 2,000 persons were in attendance at the mass evening rallies to celebrate the theme "Strengthening Our Unity."

Planning committee for the Tenth World Conference, Australia, 1995.
(Back row, left to right) Norman Beard (USA), Edward Nkansah (Ghana), Norman Patton (USA), Edward Foggs (USA), David Lawson (USA), John Campbell (Canada), Nelson Junges (Brazil)
(Front row) Noboru Yamaguchi (Japan), Leonard Bradley (Australia), Willi Krenz (Germany), Lloyd Chilver (Australia)

Excerpts of the paper delivered by Donald Johnson to the World Forum are found in entry 152. Many of the Americans present were pastors and laypersons who came in tour groups. All travel arrangements were made by Norman Beard of Anderson University. To the South Korean experience were added tours to China, Japan, and Hong Kong before or after the Conference.

Program highlights included a footwashing service in the World Forum and the Lord's Supper in the World Conference. The same persons who carried flags in the opening pageantry wore banners and national costumes as they distributed the elements for the communion service. A 5:00 am morning prayer service was led by members to the Korean church, where such services are traditional and conribute to much of the Church's fervor and growth. The Korean Children's Choir of World Vision sang in one event and put on a cultural performance in another. They won the hearts of the delegates. The meeting closed with 2,000 delegates holding their candles high and pledging themselves to go back into their world of influence to more effectively share the gospel of Jesus Christ.

The year 1991 saw the World Conference return to Germany for the first time since 1963. The very first Conference had been in Fritzlar when the devastation of World War II was still very visible. Now the large gathering in Wiesbaden came soon after the infamous Berlin Wall had been torn down. The nation finally was united again—a fitting symbol for the goal of the international work of the Church of God.

The titles of the presentations in the 1991 World Forum reflected the global perspective and practical purposes of the Forum. They were: "Exploring Strategies for Mission in the 21st Century" (Edward Foggs, USA); "Biblical Strategies for Mission" (Arturo Schultz, Argentina); "Understanding Our World" (Eckhard Bewernick, Germany); "Exploring Mission Strategies for the Local Church" (Fouad Melki, Lebanon); and "Partners in Mission" (Leaderwell Pohsngap, India). Norman Beard again arranged all travel, sending hundreds of the delegates across Germany and into neighboring European countries either before or after the Wiesbaden gathering.

Most recently was the 1995 convening in Sydney, Australia, of the tenth World Conference and the fifth World Forum and International Dialogue on Doctrine. The World Forum convened from July 18–20 in the Sydney Hilton Hotel with the theme "Learning to Celebrate." Delegates were present from forty-eight countries. Major papers were

"We Celebrate Our Heritage" (Barry Callen, United States), "We Celebrate Our Message" (Nelson Junges, Brazil), "We Celebrate Our Mission" (Borman Roy Sohkhia, India), "We Celebrate Our Ministry" (regional reports from around the world), and "We Celebrate Our Unity" (Gilbert Stafford, United States). Edward Foggs, Forum coordinator, thanked regional assemblies for their efforts to help fund their own delegates and emphasized the importance of effective communication between the Leadership Council in the United States and the several assemblies in the matter of expediting Forum arrangements.

Gilbert W. Stafford

Barry L. Callen

The half-day International Dialogue on Doctrine then was convened by Barry Callen of the United States. It again was sponsored by the School of Theology of Anderson University. About sixty world leaders explored the theme "Christian Unity: God's Will and Our Role." Immediately following, in the convention center at Darling Harbor near downtown Sydney, convened the World Conference itself. Australian pastor Len Bradley brought greetings on behalf of the host country. Cleve Grant of Jamaica delivered a stirring keynote sermon, with Diana Swoope of the United States delivering a powerful closing message. Willi Krenz of Germany had chaired the planning committee's work for this Conference. One program highlight was a special offering taken to assist the Australian church in planting a new congregation in nearby Auckland, New Zealand, to be led by a young family commissioned from the Australian church.

From their beginning the World Conferences have been international gatherings of the church, ministers, laypersons, and youth. The main purposes have been to network, instruct, and inspire all participants. Since 1980, however, the World Forums have supplemented the Conferences with much smaller, delegated, task-oriented gatherings. As revised in Seoul in 1987 and reaffirmed in the subsequent 1991 and 1995 meetings, the objectives of the Forums are:

1. To foster acquaintance and fellowship with Church of God leaders from around the world;

2. To share the good news of what God is doing in the world through his faithful servants, but not to become authoritarian or elitist as to what others should do;

3. To experience the oneness and unity which exists interculturally within the Church of God;

4. To discuss needs and concerns as well as solutions and resources for fulfilling our ministry;

5. To consult with one another on doctrinal and theological issues, with the awareness that it shall not function as a supreme authority in these matters;

6. To provide opportunity for national Boards of Missions to seek harmonious working relationships in countries where work overlaps;

7. To arrange for future World Conferences through the selection of a Conference coordinator, a planning committee, and a location for the next Conference;

8. To think strategically regarding the work of the Church of God around the world.

At the Seoul meeting of the World Forum (1987), Donald Johnson, former executive secretary of the Missionary Board in the United States, presented the paper "Affirming Our Diversity" (see entry 152). This paper highlighted the maturing purpose of the Forum itself. Said Johnson: "It is right and proper for us to affirm our variety. Rather than conformity, we desire multiformity. The variety of resources, emphases, contributions, and of theological awareness is staggering. Our purpose is to identify our diversities and maximize them." Beginning with that first gathering in Fritzlar, Germany, in 1955, these many world meetings of Church of God people certainly have enhanced acquaintances, appreciations, and cooperative ministries.

150. History of the International Dialogues on Doctrine, 1980–1995
(Barry L. Callen)

The General Assembly of the Church of God in the United States and Canada recognized in 1970 that there were "theological and doctrinal problems that need to be openly and honestly faced by this Assembly." Since those problems, it was assumed, "grew out of evidently changing patterns of our preaching, teaching and publications across several decades," the Assembly acted in June, 1970, to call a major "Consultation on Doctrine." Its stated purpose was to enable "a serious restudy of the theological and doctrinal message of our movement" and "mutual discussion among us as leaders in faith and practice." Soon a design committee had adopted the following formal statement of purpose for the Consultation:

To explore biblically and historically the church's nature, mission, polity, and unity in order to find a common ground for the commitment of old and the nurturing of newer members of our churches.

The intent did not include any attempt to develop "a creed or definitive statement of our position."

Four papers were written and distributed widely, papers on the nature, mission, polity, and unity of the church. By 1974 about thirty area assemblies, involving a total of some 2,200 church leaders, had participated in dialogue on the substance and implications of these papers. A final report given to the 1974 General Assembly detailed five areas in which the Consultation was seen as having served a useful purpose. One was having provided a vehicle for the encouragement of persons of differing points of view "to sit together and discuss these differences without fear of judgment or ostracization."

If no adequate standing vehicle existed in North America for broadly representative, disciplined dialogue on doctrinal issues of common concern (thus such an ad hoc consultation process), neither did one exist in the international arena of the life of the Church of God. As a sense of need evolved for such serious dialogue internationally, the North American Consultation of the early 1970s was one available model, even a stimulus for launching the first International Dialogue on Doctrinal Issues in 1980 in Anderson, Indiana. This was a natural time and place because of the celebration of the centennial of the beginning of the Church of God movement and the convening of a World Conference (and the first World Forum). Anderson University, through its graduate School of Theology, committed itself to sponsoring this first and subsequent doctrinal dialogues as a service to the church worldwide. Drs. T. Franklin Miller, Barry Callen, and Gilbert Stafford of the School of Theology were instrumental in the Dialogue's beginning.

The faculty of the School of Theology developed during 1979–1980 a booklet titled *We Believe* for use by the Church of God on the occasion of its centennial celebration. It sought to state central theological burdens which for a century had been at the heart of this movement's theological tradition. The decision was made to use this booklet as a means of focusing discussion as the first International Dialogue on Doctrine convened in Anderson in June, 1980. Gilbert Stafford of the School of Theology acted as convener and began the dialogue by telling the participants: "Just because the Church of God has no written creedal statement does not mean that we do not believe much. We have thought very carefully about our doctrinal life. However, our idea of arriving at doctrinal consensus will not work unless there is doctrinal dialogue.... That is what this meeting is all about." Then the group heard and reacted to four papers which had been prepared in relation to various sections of the *We Believe* booklet. They were written by P. V. Jacob of India on "Salvation," Carlton Cumberbatch of Trinidad/Tobago on "The Church," Franco Santonocito of Italy on "Mission," and Byrum Makokha of Kenya on "Unity."

The 1980 Dialogue participants proceeded to share their perceptions of the most pressing doctrinal issues in their respective countries at the time. As a group they then prioritized these issues for future consideration. The general issue of greatest common concern internationally was "Pentecost and the Church." Thus, this issue was chosen as the subject for the second International Dialogue to convene in Nairobi, Kenya, in 1983. In August, 1982, in preparation for Nairobi, Koesuke Nishitani of Japan wrote a paper titled "What Does the Pentecostal Experience of the Holy Spirit as Reflected in Acts 2 Mean for the Life of the Church Today?" All expected participants received in advance from the School of Theology of

Anderson University (1) the Nishitani paper, (2) a guide to it prepared by Dr. Stafford, and (3) three formal responses to it prepared by Nelson Junges of Brazil, Martin Goodridge of England, and R. Eugene Sterner of the United States. When the Nairobi Dialogue had concluded, it was clear that there was need and desire to continue pursuing dimensions of these concerns, now in the third International Dialogue set to convene in Seoul, South Korea, in July, 1987.

In Seoul, Dr. Stafford, again serving as convener, clarified that the purpose was not to seek common agreement on an issue so that such an agreement could be considered standard worldwide in the Church of God. Rather, the purpose was said to be taking advantage of the meeting of so many church leaders in order to facilitate the sensitizing of each other to the thinking of the church around the world. The subjects under consideration in Seoul centered in the "gifts of the Spirit," with four thoughtful monographs written, sent, and studied by all in advance. They were: (1) "The Concepts of Gifts in the Letters of Paul" by Leaderwell Pohsngap of India; (2) "Tongues in the New Testament" by Franco Santonocito of Italy; (3) "Doctrine of Sanctification" by Eckhard Bewernick of Germany, and (4) the "Report of the Study Committee on Glossolalia" by the General Assembly of the Church of God in the United States and Canada. Dr. Barry Callen (United States) recorded highlights of the subsequent discussion focused around these four documents. This printed record was sent to all participants by the School of Theology.

Through a steering committee, Dialogue participants determined the desired focus of the next meeting, this time to convene as the Fourth International Dialogue on Doctrine in Wiesbaden, Germany, in July, 1991. That focus was to be "Sanctification." A four-year plan of preparation was laid, including (1) the writing, publishing, and mailing of key papers on this subject, (2) the gathering of responses to the papers by leaders from around the world, and then (3) the writing by Barry Callen of a paper reflecting the status of the discussion and suggesting aspects of the subject of sanctification which appear desirable for particular attention in the Wiesbaden Dialogue. On-site leadership was provided by James Earl Massey, dean of the sponsoring Anderson University School of Theology in the United States. A very stimulating and insightful discussion was launched by Fouad Melki of Lebanon who highlighted the paper he had written in the study booklet sent in advance to participants.

The fifth International Dialogue was convened in Sydney, Australia, in

July, 1995, again immediately prior to the opening of the tenth World Conference. Barry Callen acted as coordinator and discussion leader. His 1995 volumes *It's God's Church!: Life and Legacy of Daniel Warner* and *Contours of a Cause: The Theological Vision of the Church of God Movement* had been sent to participants in advance in order to stimulate reflections on the Dialogue theme, "Christian Unity: God's Will and Our Role Today." Jeannette Flynn of the United States served as recording secretary.

The half-day dialogue process in Sydney focused on five prepared reflection presentations, one each by Nelson Junges of Brazil, Willi Krenz of Germany, Bassem Malek of Lebanon, Leaderwell Pohsngap of India, and Gilbert Stafford of the United States. About sixty persons participated in exploring this topic so central to the heritage of the Church of God movement. It was clear that much about the issue of Christian unity had changed in the movement and in the Christian community generally since the movement's nineteenth-century beginnings. New challenges and opportunities lie ahead.

Consistent with the non-creedal and "movement" nature of the Church of God, these Dialogues have been times of serious theological study and interaction among interested leaders from around the world. They have not been intended to work toward formalized positions on given topics, positions to be thought of as "official" and urged on others. Rather, they have sought to be ad hoc settings in which the Spirit of God could better inform and inspire the teaching ministry of the church around the world.

Section II
Philosophical Perspectives

Section II
Philosophical Perspectives

151. International Partnership in Mission

Editor's note: The following are excerpts of a presentation made by Douglas Welch to the World Forum of the Church of God meeting in Nairobi, Kenya, July, 1983.

I will touch briefly on four areas which I see the Bible addressing in relation to the Church of God movement as a world body. How do these areas affect our common life? What changes in our interrelationships do they call on us to make? What new forms of obedience do they demand of us in our various contexts? Perhaps these areas of concern can become an integral part of our dialogue from this point on, both in this Forum and in other settings.

Selfhood

In the first place, there is the area of selfhood. It may seem that Paul was being self-contradictory when he insisted that "there is neither Jew nor Gentile," that there is only one body, not many, and then judged that Gentiles do not have to think and behave like Jews. But interdependence does not demand uniformity. It begins rather with diversity. If the whole body were only one part and functioned only as the one part functions, there would be no body. This diversity is to be recognized and celebrated.

Interdependence begins with the recognition of selfhood. Selfhood does not mean independence, for each part needs the whole to be truly itself. Nor does it mean self-sufficiency. No part can say to another, "So who needs you?" True selfhood has to do with full self-acceptance, with the recognition of the gifts one has to give. It has to do with being set free from the imprisonment of inherited structures, of church polity or organization, of theology, structures of domination and dependence. It is being set free from the need to dominate, to be preeminent, to maintain control, and to think and speak for others.

A part of the world community of faith, acting as if it can by itself represent the whole, that is, speak for it, speak to it, and speak of it, is a distortion of selfhood—both of its own and that of others. This includes the doing of theology. As Orlando Costas argues in *The Integrity of Mission* (p. 50), theology is not something we simply memorize and repeat. Theology is something we do. It is not equivalent to faith; it relates faith to the context of life.

For the spiritual wholeness and theological health of every part of the body, it is necessary that it have the benefit of the theological reflection, the doing of theology, of every other part of the believing community. If the doing of theology is relating faith to the contexts of life, then we shall all be vastly enriched by the diversity of theologies among us. All theologies will be accepted as pilgrim statements arising from differing sociocultural and historical contexts, but all speaking of our one faith and of our one Lord. For Africa or India or Japan simply to parrot the conclusions of American theological reflection is a denial of the selfhood which the Bible insists upon.

Community Building

A second area which the biblical material addresses by implication is that of community building among us. Our special problem in the West is our lack of a sense of world community. Very many of us have little knowledge of the world church and little inspiration to seek that knowledge. Ours is the problem of self-sufficiency. There is a strong, scarcely-realized feeling that we really do not need anyone else. We have it all; we know it all; and we understand it all. Our responsibility is simply to take it to the rest of the world.

It is urgent that, at this juncture in our history, we sit down together and discuss ways and means of informing ourselves more fully about each other. We must find ways of building community among us—koinonia. We need to build mutual acceptance and trust. We must be willing to be vulnerable with each other. We must allow each other the freedom to make our own mistakes.

Structuring for Missions

Thirdly, there is the area of structuring for missions. It is to be accepted as a biblical "given" that missions are a necessary part of our total mission as the People of God, a necessary part of our missionary obedience in Christ. But no longer can this missionary obedience be largely a movement from North America to the rest of the world. Geopolitical reality, if nothing else, makes that impossible in many areas of the world, particularly in Asia. It is not possible to send Western personnel to a growing number of nations. Even when it is possible, it is not always desirable. Such sending may violate the selfhood of other parts of the community.

Decisions which affect the whole community should not be made unilaterally. This is especially true in the area of missions. Every segment of the community is charged with the missionary mandate. And every segment is responsible for its own obedience to that mandate, both within its own borders and beyond them. Particularly in those efforts which take a part of the community beyond its own borders, there is need for consultation, coordination, and cooperation with other parts of the community. One segment of the community is violating the selfhood of all other segments when it acts unilaterally, both in decision-making and in missionary sending. No one part can take upon itself that right and that obligation on behalf of all the other parts.

Resource Sharing

Fourth, there is the very sensitive area of resource sharing. Here we refer to the total resources of the church: spiritual resources, human resources, and financial resources. It is in this area that the principle of reciprocity applies. We do not share the same things with each other. As Paul remarks in 2 Corinthians 8, it is fitting that we also should share our material resources with the churches elsewhere, for they have shared their spiritual resources with us. While we do not give and receive the same things, we must all both give and receive. But our philosophies and structures of resource sharing have made it impossible for some of us to give and for others of us to receive. Some of us feel we have nothing to give, and others of us feel we have nothing we need to receive.

We in the West have great spiritual problems with our affluence. Rather than enhancing the spiritual and numerical growth of our congregations, it seems to be doing quite the opposite. We can no longer say, "Silver and gold have we none." Neither can we say, "In the name of Christ, rise up and walk." We need non-Western believers to sit down with us and help us deal spiritually with our affluence. They must help us know how to share our human and financial resources in ways which do not create dependence, which do not stifle local initiative, and which do not violate selfhood. We all need to learn how to be servants.

Conclusion

The church desperately needs biblical renewal. But this does not mean simply reaffirming and enhancing our traditional ways of thinking and doing. It means reaffirming our obedience to the normative principles of Scripture. We speak much of the authority of Scripture, but waffle at the point of obedience. That is the ideal, we seem to say. But we must be practical. Things will not change overnight. Church people will not give to support programs not in keeping with their traditional views and practices. What the Scriptures infer is the ideal, and we affirm that. But much of it is simply not expedient, which is what we generally mean by practical. I ask then: Where is the authority of Scripture? Do we live only by that which is expedient?

Why is it that I get the uncomfortable feeling that what we usually mean by the authority of Scripture is that it is authoritative in the formulation of our doctrinal beliefs, rather than in the living of our life as a People of God? Our boast is that we teach only what the Bible teaches. But do we intentionally seek to live by the principles revealed in Scripture, principles such as those we have discussed here? It is at this point that we are too often guilty of bowing before the idol of expediency. For our Lord, right doing was always primary in relation to right doctrine. He did not say, "Affirm this and you will live." What he said was, "Do this and you will live."

The Scriptures challenge us to take seriously the total interdependence of the community of faith. This is not optional. It is therefore urgent that we sit down together, intentionally and as immediately as possible, to discover new wineskins for the new wine of the Spirit flowing in this age.

152. Affirming Our Diversity

Editor's note: This is an excerpt of the address by Donald Johnson to the World Forum of the Church of God, Seoul, South Korea, 1987.

Church of God missions throughout most of its 100 years plus has affirmed and rewarded unity, not diversity. The sending church in North America has responded best to the establishment of look-alike churches. It has been the similarities reported in the younger churches which have prompted us [in the US] to believe we were doing mission properly. The supporting church has responded with its dollars when both missionaries and Missionary Board reported on and pictured people around the world who sounded like, looked like, were structured like, and believed like its missionaries and the "home" church. It is not overly critical to observe that producing North American Christians has seemed at least as important as producing biblical Christians. This is part of the confessing we now need to do as North Americans.

The very fact that we are coming now to recognize and value our diversities, rather than only our similarities, is a quantum leap forward. It has not come about easily or quickly. As early as the middle 1950s, both missionary and national church leadership of the Church of God in the US were talking about the "indigenous church." Paternalism and colonialism were labels being dealt with by missions around the world. The Missionary Board of the Church of God responded by moving to "turn the church over" to local leadership. Missionary personnel decreased in numbers. Emphasis increasingly was placed on the education of local leadership. Encouragement was given to the development of locally written material. The Missionary Board dissolved its legal entities as national churches became incorporated in order to hold their own property. Mistakes were made, but the movement was in the right direction.

Two additional sets of circumstances began to emerge through the 1960s and into the 1970s. National assemblies were developing, strengthening and taking greater local leadership. As these assemblies emerged, the North American missionaries had to find a new identity. Their role changed from that of being supervisory to that of being colleagues in mission. Obviously, this did not happen with the same speed or to the same degree in each country, but the trend now was clear. Things finally were changing, and rightly so.

As National Assemblies with integrity and recognition emerged, the need of communicating with area neighbors followed close behind. It was time for the Church of God in one country to begin to be aware of others around them. Multinational assemblies began to be emerge [see entry 158]. The Missionary Board in North America was asked to help facilitate international gatherings of the Church of God. Planning sessions and strategy sessions were undertaken. Lester Crose describes these as "orbits of influence" in his book, *Passport For A Reformation* (1981). So, what had been the rather exclusive responsibility of the Missionary Board of the Church of God to be the coordinative clearing house for missions and the one entity relating to all countries in which a mission existed, now became the work, interest, and prerogative of various assemblies.

When the World Forum first convened in Anderson, Indiana, U.S.A. in 1980 [see entry 149], Douglas Welch and Donald Johnson were asked to write a paper addressing "International Partnership in Mission: A Missiologist's View and a Mission Administrator's View." In that paper a concept of *interdependence* emerged for the Church of God which has been enlarged, tested, and widely practiced since. The term interdependence implies that there are differences in our churches. Each has its own unique strengths to contribute to a truly international partnership. It is proper for us to affirm our variety. Rather than conformity, we desire multiformity. The variety of resources, of emphases, of contributions and theological awareness is staggering.

Our churches are an expression of our story. No one of us has the right to deprive others of us of our histories. We do not always think logically or theologically about our responses to the gospel; they are a part of our community life. I urge considerable tolerance as we open up to each other in the midst of our diversity.

153. The Three Frontiers

Excerpt from Louis Meyer, *Pioneering New Frontiers in North America: A Historical Overview of the Board of Church Extension and Home Missions of the Church of God, 1921–1991* (1992, 257–260).

The tasks assigned by the General Assembly to the Board of Church Extension and Home Missions in its original charter were clear, and in many ways timeless. Seventy years later, congregations still need assistance with building needs; new congregations still need to be developed; people still need to be confronted with the claims of the gospel and invited to claim their inheritance in Christ; and the church still needs to be challenged to reach out to hurting and forgotten people in the United States and Canada.

This is an agency of the church seasoned in living on the frontier. It has served the church well on many social, ethnic, programmatic, and mission frontiers. This rich heritage should serve it well as it continues to help the church be effective in the twenty-first century, where new frontiers will abound. With a clear sense of its assignment, with commitment and resolve, the unchartered waters ahead should be welcomed as a gift from God.

I have been asked to conclude this writing with a suggestion of some possible trends and frontiers I see facing the church and all its agencies in this, the last decade of this century, and in the coming century. What I have listed below is not a full treatment or development of any trend or coming event. It is simply a hint of what might be ahead, an arrow pointing in the direction of a possible future.

To serve effectively in the century ahead, the church must become far more proactive and less reactive. This Christian belief that God is the God of the future, as well as of the past, brings liberation. The desire to return to the past fades, while faith and confidence increase and enable believers to join with God, who is still creating and making all persons and all things new.

The Global Frontier. In June 1989, the world watched as a Chinese university student, alone, stood before an army tank in Tianamen Square, challenging its repressive mission. Because of instant satellite coverage, it was as riveting as though one were viewing the event in his or her own neighborhood. Indeed, it was in our neighborhood, our global neighborhood.

A key shortcoming in much thinking today is in the way the world is perceived. Many have not acquired the global neighborhood perspective. This is a challenging frontier for all individuals, institutions, religions, nations, and governments. Whether the world's critical need is environmental restoration, ecological balance, food production and distribution, peace and reconciliation, or meeting human spiritual needs, solutions based on a global perspective will bring more lasting and satisfying solutions.

To be effective in the twenty-first century, the Church of God also needs this enlarged perception of reality—the global community perspective. Proposals, plans, and strategies based exclusively on parochial or national boundaries will not suffice. This frontier will exact the creative energies and skills of all agencies of the church. Perceiving our mission as one to a global community will position the church for a positive and effective ministry in the decades ahead.

The Multicultural Frontier. Diversity is God's plan. This is evident in the changing seasons, the mountains and valleys, and in the people of the globe. Yet, human beings have not fully appreciated or come to terms with God's pluralistic creation.

Based on the 1990 census and other demographic studies, if current trends continue, by the decade 2040 European Americans will comprise less than half of the United States population. This country will be a nation of ethnic minorities with no single group as a majority. Such a frontier will challenge the church and all institutions of society. Those who begin now to access the information, assimilate it, and accept the multicultural realities as within God's plan will be far more effective in the twenty-first century. Anything done to promote and encourage cross-cultural understanding will help lay the foundation for a peaceful, reconciling world.

The Religious Frontier. There can be no true understanding of the causes of the world's wars, nor of finding paths to peace without taking into account the religious factor. Peace between the world's peoples will never be realized unless there is better understanding and peace between the religions of the world. Far too often, religion makes people fanatical, angular, and exclusive, rather than cooperative, understanding, and reconciling.

This will be an even more critical frontier in the next century. As the world's population increases, as nationalism continues to rise in many countries, as the United States and other nations become even more multicultural, the religious bodies and their leaders must play a greater role in developing the conditions for peace and justice. To do the work required of the church universal in the twenty-first century, all religions must endeavor, not to form a syncretistic faith, but to understand one another and discover how to work together. New roads must be built for joining ministries to alleviate some of the world's pain, suffering, and misunderstanding. The Church of God, with its enduring belief in Christian unity, could carve out an exciting niche for its work and mission on this frontier.

These frontiers are but examples of what appear to be exhilarating and challenging decades ahead. The Board of Church Extension and Home Missions has had enough experience in vanguard and frontier life to be of help to the Church of God as it pioneers this intriguing future.

154. Honoring the Six Rs of Heritage Celebration

Excerpt from the keynote address delivered by Barry Callen to the Fifth World Forum of the Church of God, July, 1995, Sydney, Australia.

Why should we celebrate the heritage of the Church of God movement on the occasion of this Fifth World Forum? There are at least six reasons, six Rs, six dimensions of true celebration.

1. We should celebrate by *Remembering* our heritage. Israel's identity was preserved in its remembering. God is known by what God does. To forget the history of God's actions is to fail to be God's people. The words of the Psalmist express generations of the faithful who determine not to forget: "I will call to mind the deeds of the Lord; I will remember your wonders of old" (Ps. 77:11, NRSV). The Church of God movement, like ancient Israel, is a "testifying" people. We are intentional recallers and grateful retellers of what God has done in Christ, for us, and among us as a movement of God's people.

The Church of God movement has been a people who seek to come-out of what now is wrong with the church because of a vision of what once was and again should be right with the church. We remember and honor the church's apostolic beginnings and seek to represent now that "early morning light." True identity relies on effective memory. Unfortunately, many people associated today with congregations of the Church of God do not know the historic vision and reforming burden of this movement. One essential for moving forward is intentionally staying rooted in the right past. When we stop to remember, we realize anew that there is much to celebrate. We must not forget!

2. We should celebrate by *Reassessing* our past. All that we remember is not worth repeating. According to one movement historian: "Tradition is important, but we are under no divine obligation to blindly accept a belief or a method simply because it is what has been said or done in the past. A Reformation Movement cannot reject the principle of continuing reform." According to another of our movement historians, the title "'reformation people" cannot be inherited, "cannot be passed on from generation to generation like the family Bible." Any legitimate claim to be a reformation people "must be made by each generation for itself."

We are to remember gratefully; but we remember adequately only when our remembering is accompanied by a Spirit-enabled discrimination of our memories. We celebrate not merely a proud past, but the presence of God's Spirit with us now, the Spirit who helps us evaluate what has been and apply what now should be. We are to be rooted in a remembered past, but not captured by it. The goal is effective mission now.

3. We should celebrate by *Reaffirming* our central convictions. Remembering and reassessing our movement's past will reveal much that is worth reaffirming. We should recognize that, if today we are tall, it is because we are standing on the shoulders of many great souls who have gone before us in the life of this Church of God movement. For instance, let us remember and reaffirm with joy the first world gathering of the Church of God movement. It convened in 1955 in war-torn Germany. Dr. T. Franklin Miller and Dr. Thomas Smith of the United States carried major planning responsibility, with youth leaders Norman Beard (US) and Willi Krenz (Germany) leading then and leading still. We celebrate these men of God!

There is a vision given to us by our movement pioneers that yet has power to send us on mission to a still divided church and a still unholy world. What, for instance, in the following should still inspire and motivate us as we remember, with discrimination, and with an eye to reaffirming what still should be? ...

Free from babel, in the Spirit,
Free to worship God aright;
Joy and gladness we're receiving,
O how sweet this evening light!

4. We should celebrate by *Reuniting* ourselves in thought and action. If together we will remember, reassess, and reaffirm, then together we can be effective in our current mission opportunities (thus the great importance of the World Forums, International Dialogues on Doctrine, etc.). Says historian John Smith: "As a movement grows and expands to many countries and cultures, there are inevitable tendencies toward the formation of definable, internal groupings built around special doctrinal interests, variant methodologies, racial and cultural differences, or certain leaders with particular appeal. These tendencies are not necessarily divisive, but they are potentially so." The more we focus on the vision the less we will "fuss" with each other.

The Church of God now is a worldwide movement that must learn increasingly to profit from its diversity, not be paralyzed by it. We always have said that unity does not mean that we all will look, act, and think exactly alike. Instead of being threatened by diversity among us, may God help us to celebrate it and channel it for God's glory. God's call is that we be united, not uniform. We represent differing cultures and God gives us differing gifts; but we are to be one people by the power of the Spirit.

5. We should celebrate by *Reaching Out*. Celebration is more than remembering, reassessing, reaffirming, and reuniting. To truly celebrate God's good news is to break free of self-preoccupation. This movement does not exist for itself, but as a witness to holiness and unity, and as an instrument of God's healing work in the church and the world. To date, the Church of God movement has kept too much to itself, thus risking self-preoccupation. Fearing the contamination of our doctrinal understandings, and thinking it wrong to look and act like the denominations, we have been too much isolationists with our unity witness. The irony of this now is quite apparent, and should end. It is time for this movement to take more risks and be more humble about the finality of its own wisdom apart from the wisdom of the whole Body of Christ. Let us celebrate the whole church!

We leaders in this movement should do more than just keep saying that "we reach our hands in fellowship to every bloodwashed one." We should actually reach out, build ministry bridges, celebrate our God-given solidarity with all our brothers and sisters in the faith, regardless of church labels and honest differences in biblical understanding. The 1984 "Consultation on Mission and Ministry of the Church of God" (USA/Canada) wisely set this as one key goal for today's movement:

> To determine and develop the structures that best express interdependence and enable ministry and mission in the Church of God throughout the world.... To expand ministries through voluntary relationships with church groups outside the Church of God Reformation Movement.... Through voluntary relationships we often can achieve our mission more effectively and expand our ministries.

Within the Church of God movement, this goal highlights the importance of the World Forum, World Conference, and International Dialogue on Doctrine. Outside the movement, this goal calls for creative and courageous new relationships on behalf of Christian mission. Let us celebrate the many opportunities before us! Let us celebrate visionary souls who have walked among us as ministers of reconciliation. One was Samuel G. Hines, recently deceased, whose bridge-building ministry was felt from the islands of the Caribbean to the world power center of Washington, DC, to the racially torn nation of South Africa.

6. We should celebrate by *Rejoicing!* We celebrate the God who is, who comes in Jesus, and who forms the church, a new community of the Kingdom of God. This Kingdom community, this Pentecost people is not a place of restrictive law and arrogant creed, not a place of authoritarian priests and mandatory cultic practices. The church is the family of the Spirit, a house of prayer for all the nations (Mark 11:17). It is the "eschatological" community of Christ. This does not mean that the church should be a hotbed of rash speculation about the details of God's future. It does mean that in the church there should be an unbounded and thrilling belief that:

(1) God's future is already here in Jesus Christ (Mark 1:15);
(2) What now is important is preaching the good news to all the nations (Mark 13:10);
(3) What is required is being willing to leave all for the sake of Jesus and the gospel (Mark 10:28–30);
(4) God will be with us in the face of all obstacles, even to the end of the age (Matt. 28:20). Therefore, rejoice!

So, let's celebrate! How? We celebrate best by remembering, reassessing, reaffirming, reuniting, reaching out, and rejoicing in the gospel of Christ, in the reality of the church, and in our movement's heritage and mission responsibility within the church. These things should be done together with all of God's people, in humble recognition of the Kingdom's presence and power. All of this can bring so much joy and hope—if together we will be holy, living in the unity Christ gives, sharing with the church Christ forms, and serving the mission Christ brings.

Section III
Assemblies and Countries

Section III
Assemblies and Countries

155. Development of Regional Assemblies

Editor's note: Although there was an international dimension of the work of the Church of God movement from almost its beginning, formalized international mission structures developed very slowly. In the most recent decades, however, regional assemblies have evolved and become significant. A brief overview of them follows. The regional directors named are employees of the Missionary Board in the United States. National leaders for each country are named in entry 156 below. Typical purposes of these assemblies (fellowships) are: (1) to facilitate effective communication; (2) to promote fellowship and unity; (3) to facilitate cooperative ministry partnerships; and (4) to offer educational opportunities for church leaders.

James Albrecht, Director, Europe

Robert Edwards, Director, Africa

Victor Babb, Director Caribbean-Atlantic

Johnny Snyder, Director Latin America

Michael Kinner, Director Asia

Year Estab.	Regional Organization	Basic Information
1960	**European Ministers' Conference**	
	Countries.......17	
	School...........Fritzlar Bible College (Germany)	
	Publication....*German Gospel Trumpet*	
	Regional Director....James Albrecht	
1962	**Inter-American Conference**	
	Countries.....................19	
	School.........................La Buena Tierra (Mexico)	
	Publication.................*LaTrompeta*	
	Regional Director.......Johnny Snyder	
1980	**Mediterranean Area Fellowship**	
	Countries...........9	
	School...........Mediterranean Bible College (Lebanon)	
	Publication.......*Arabic Gospel Trumpet*	
	Regional Director... James Albrecht	
1981	**Caribbean/Atlantic Assembly**	
	Countries......14	
	School......West Indies Theological College (Trinidad)	
	Publication....*Cross Talk*	
	Regional Director...Victor Babb	
1982	**Asian Church of God Conference**	
	Countries.............19	
	Schools..................Asia Bible College (India)	
	Nichols-Roy Bible College (India)	
	Han Yang Seminary (South Korea)	
	Publication...........*Asian Church of God Magazine*	
	Regional Director...Michael Kinner	
1990	**Executive Committee for Africa**	
	Countries................13	
	School. Kima International School of Theology (Kenya)	
	Publication..............None	
	Regional Director...Robert Edwards	

156. Church of God Movement in the World Today: Countries, Congregations, Believers, National Leaders (1996)

The Church of God Movement in the World Today

Africa

Countries	Congregations	Believers	National Leaders
Cameroon	5	2,170	Augustine Meta
Cote d'Ivoire	2	80	Ambrose Nwaosuagwu
Ghana	11	825	Edward Nkansah
Kenya	531	106,200	Byrum Makokha
Malawai	170	22,000	Baison Joshi
Mozambique	12	600	Stanley Hoffman
Nigeria	27	4,000	Dianabasi Umondak
Rwanda	204	8,027	Esron Twagiramungu
South Africa	34	4,500	Cyril Pillay
Tanzania	79	4,500	Eliazer Mdobi
Uganda	378	19,684	Moses Abasoola
Zaire	655	21,789	Mianitse Kyambali
Zambia	323	26,809	Afeck Lungu
Zimbabwe	80	4,480	Dzingai Guni
Total	**2,521**	**225,664**	

Asia

Countries	Congregations	Believers	National Leaders
Australia	6	190	Len Bradley
Bangladesh	47	3,100	Robin Das Lawrence Chowdhury
China	?	?	?
Guam	2	200	Gary Bistritan
Hong Kong	2	40	Johnny Yiu
India	650	62,000	George Tharakan Asim Das, Borman Roy Sohkhia, N. Rynjah, Sterling Iangrai

Indonesia	2	270	Tabiha Gunawan
Japan	16	465	Hiroshi Fujita
Malaysia	5	200	Michael Leaw
Myanmar	7	700	Matthew Hla Win
Nepal	7	560	Amos Moore
New Zealand	1	25	David Ravell
Philippines	42	3,000	Conrado S. Deluna
Saipan	1	30	John Ravell
Singapore	2	210	Neivelle Tan
South Korea	51	13,000	Lee Kwang Yeon
Sri Lanka	3	100	Shane Mack
Taiwan	4	170	James Lo
Thailand	18	520	Silawech Kanjanamukda
Total	**866**	**84,780**	

Caribbean Atlantic Assembly

Countries	Congregations	Believers	National Leaders
Antigua	5	500	Edmund Greene
Barbados	19	1,250	George Foster
Bermuda	3	900	Vernon Lambe
Caymans	5	625	Allison Ebanks
Curacao	2	60	Frank Drakes
Grenada	4	130	Dave Quashie
Guyana	9	400	Ronda Abrams
Haiti	135	19,500	Phyllis Newby
Jamaica	106	15,000	Wilmer M. Jackson
Nevis	2	110	Ellsworth Morton
St. Kitts	5	330	Joel Morton
St. Thomas	1	35	Neville Williams
St. Vincent	2	85	Hugh Drakes
Trinidad/Tobago	22	1,200	Clinton Providence
Total	**320**	**40,125**	

Latin America

Countries	Congregations	Believers	National Leaders
Argentina	34	2,200	Victor Ruzak
Belize	4	?	Alfonso Ayala
Bolivia	154	12,000	Victor H. Quispe
Brazil	45	2,800	Nelson Junges
Chile	2	40	Nariciso Zamora
Colombia	16	550	Daisy Taylor
Costa Rica	10	208	Sherman Leon Miller
Cuba	23	1,200	Samuel Contino
Dominican Republic	3	190	Gerardo Taron
Ecuador	9	280	Nicolas Perez
El Salvador	112	12,000	Rigoberto Ayala
Guatemala	110	6,000	Isai Calderon
Honduras	4	165	Donny Allen
Mexico	37	1,100	Jose de la Paz Plata
Panama	23	800	Roberto Christi
Paraguay	5	173	Martin Kurrle
Peru	66	3,000	Lenar Guimaraes
Puerto Rico	4	300	Miguel Cotto
Uruguay	3	130	Jesus Acosta
Venezuela	3	330	Carlos Garcia
Total	**667**	**43,466**	

Middle East/Europe

Countries	Congregations	Believers	National Leaders
Bulgaria	7	600	Tantscho Tantschev
Cyprus	0	10	Christos Psilonis
Denmark	4	150	Freddie Mortensen
Egypt	13	1,200	Morgan Ibrahim
France	1	35	Michel Fegali
Germany	35	3,500	Georg Burgin
Great Britian	5	400	Josiah Jones
Greece	1	75	Timothy Michas
Holland	2	150	Adrian Bais
Hungary	2	100	Chava Vigh
Italy	5	400	Franco Santonocito

Lebanon	15	1,300	Fouad Melki
Russia	2	150	Kelley Philips
Serbia	1	15	Obrad Nikolic
Spain	1	50	Artuor Barisich
Switzerland	2	100	Helmut Krenz
Syria	?	?	?
Total	**96**	**8,235**	

North America

Countries	Congregations	Believers
Canada	51	3,500
United States	2,295	221,346
Total	**2,346**	**224,846**

Total Nations, Congregations, and Believers in the Church of God Around the World

Nations	Congregations	Believers
86	**6,816**	**627,116**

A.V.

897 YES

29 NO